Deciphering the Dead Sea Scrolls

For Beryl and Colin

Deciphering the Dead Sea Scrolls

Second Edition

Jonathan G. Campbell

Blackwell
Publishing

350 Main Street, Malden, MA 02148–5018, USA
108 Cowley Road, Oxford OX4 1JF, UK
550 Swanston Street, Carlton, Victoria 3053, Australia
Kurfürstendamm 57, 10707 Berlin, Germany

First edition published 1996 by Fontana Press
Second edition published 2002 by Blackwell Publishers Ltd,
a Blackwell Publishing company

ISBN 0–631–22992–2 (hardback); ISBN 0–631–22993–0 (paperback)

A catalogue record for this title is available from the British Library.

Set in 10.5 pt Janson Text
by SetSystems Ltd, Saffron Walden, Essex
Printed and bound in the United Kingdom
by MPG Books Ltd, Bodmin, Cornwall

For further information on
Blackwell Publishing, visit our website:
http://www.blackwellpublishing.com

On that day the deaf shall hear
the words of a scroll,
and out of their gloom and darkness
the eyes of the blind shall see.

Isaiah 29:18

Contents

Plates

Maps and Figure

Text Acknowledgements

The author and publisher gratefully acknowledge the following for permission to reproduce copyright material.

Source for plan of Khirbet Qumran: Betz, O. and Riesner, R., *Jesus, Qumran and the Vatican* (1994). By permission of SCM Press Ltd.

Vermes, Geza, *The Complete Dead Sea Scrolls in English* (1997). Allen Lane, The Penguin Press. © G. Vermes, 1962, 1965, 1968, 1975, 1995, 1997.

Unless otherwise stated, scriptures herein are from the *New Revised Standard Version Bible* © 1989 by the Division of Christian Education of the National Council of the Churches of Christ in the USA, and are used by permission. All rights reserved.

Other scriptures, where stated, as from:

The Holy Bible, International Version. © 1973, 1978, 1984 by the International Bible Society. Used by permission of Hodder and Stoughton Limited; and

The Revised English Bible, © Oxford University Press and Cambridge University Press, 1989.

Excerpts from *The Mishnah*, translated from the Hebrew with introductory and brief explanatory notes by Herbert Danby (1933). Reprinted by permission of Oxford University Press.

The following are all reprinted by permission of the publishers and the Trustees of the Leob Classical Library:

Dio Cassius, *Roman History*, Leob Classical Library Vol. III, translated by E. Carey. Cambridge Mass.: Harvard University Press (1914).

Josephus, *The Life*, Leob Classical Library Vol. I, translated by H. StJ. Thackery. Cambridge Mass.: Harvard University Press (1926).

Josephus, *The Jewish War*, Leob Classical Library Vol. II, translated by H. StJ. Thackery. Cambridge Mass.: Harvard University Press (1927).

Josephus, *Jewish Antiquities*, Leob Classical Library Vol. VII, translated by R. Marcus. Cambridge Mass.: Harvard University Press (1943).

Josephus, *Jewish Antiquities*, Leob Classical Library Vol. IX, translated by L. H. Feldman. Cambridge Mass.: Harvard University Press (1965).

Pliny the Elder, *Natural History*, Leob Classical Library Vol. II, translated by H. Rackman. Cambridge Mass.: Harvard University Press (1942).

Author's Acknowledgements

To the Second Edition

This expanded and updated edition would not have been possible without a lot of encouragement from Blackwell, especially from Al Bertrand, Angela Cohen, and Tessa Harvey; freelance editor Louise Spencely also contributed much. Furthermore, I owe a huge debt of thanks to three colleagues who read through chapters and generously gave of their time to provide me with invaluable feedback: Dr James Aitken, Prof. George Brooke, and Dr Charlotte Hempel. Equally helpful were two of my undergraduate students, Danielle Bolton and Mat Collins, who likewise made many constructive suggestions.

J.G.C. *October 2001*

To the First Edition

Several friends and colleagues supported me in the production of this book. Among them Mary Betley and Jason Reese deserve special thanks for the way they selflessly worked through early drafts of each chapter and provided me with feedback. I am equally grateful to Geza Vermes and Alison Salvesen, who made numerous constructive observations at a later stage and helped me bring the project to completion. The eagle eye of proofreader Liz Cowen was also much appreciated. Last but not least, I would like to thank Philip Gwyn Jones and Toby Mundy at Harper-Collins, whose patience and enthusiasm were invaluable in reaching our common goal.

J.G.C. *July 1996*

Abbreviations

ABD	D. N. Freedman (ed.), *Anchor Bible Dictionary*, Volumes I–VI, New York (1992)
CDSSE	G. Vermes, *The Complete Dead Sea Scrolls in English*, London (1997)
CHJ III	W. Horbury and others (eds.), *Cambridge History of Judaism*, Volume III, Cambridge (1999)
DJD(J)	Discoveries in the Judaean Desert (of Jordan)
DSS	Dead Sea Scroll(s)
DSSFY, I–II	P. W. Flint, J. C. VanderKam (eds.), *The Dead Sea Scrolls After Fifty Years: A Comprehensive Assessment*, Volumes I–II, Leiden (1998–99)
DSSHC	T. H. Lim and others (eds.), *The Dead Sea Scrolls In their Historical Context*, Edinburgh (2000)
EDB	D. N. Freedman (ed.), *Eerdmans Dictionary of the Bible*, Grand Rapids (2001)
ed(s).	editor(s)
EDSS	L. H. Schiffman, J. C. VanderKam (eds.), *Encyclopedia of the Dead Sea Scrolls*, Volumes I–II, New York (2000)
LXX	Septuagint
MT	Masoretic Text

NRSV   *Holy Bible: New Revised Standard Version with Apocrypha*, New York (1989)

OCB   B. M. Metzger, M. D. Coogan (eds.), *Oxford Companion to the Bible*, Oxford (1993)

REB   *Revised English Bible with Apocrypha*, Oxford/Cambridge (1989)

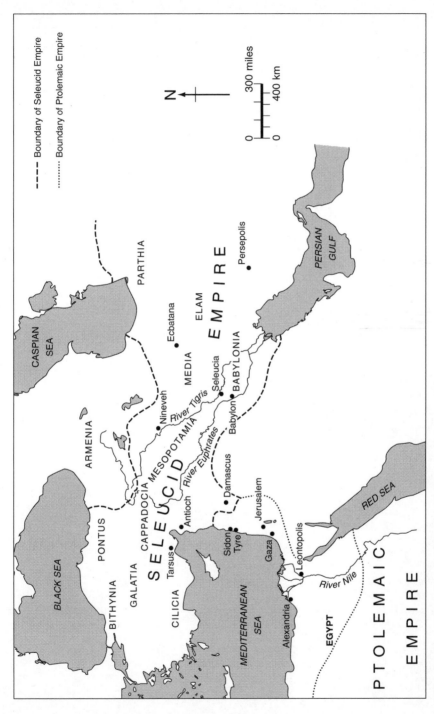

Map 1 *The Ptolomaic and Seleucid Empires in Hellenistic Times*

1

What are the Dead Sea Scrolls?

Setting the Scene

The 'Dead Sea Scrolls' is the name given first and foremost to a unique collection of nearly 900 ancient Jewish manuscripts written in Hebrew, Aramaic, and Greek. Roughly two thousand years old, they were discovered by chance between 1947 and 1956 in eleven caves around a ruined site called Khirbet Qumran on the north-western shore of the Dead Sea.[1] Many important texts were published early on, but it was only after the release of fresh material in 1991 that most ordinary scholars gained unrestricted access to the contents of the whole corpus.

The aim of this book is to explain to the uninitiated the nature and significance of these amazing manuscripts. For over fifty years now, they have had a dramatic effect on the way experts reconstruct religion in ancient Palestine.[2] Cumulatively and subtly, the Dead Sea Scrolls (DSS) from Qumran have gradually transformed scholars' understanding of the text of the Bible, Judaism in the time of Jesus, and the rise of Christianity. In the chapters to follow, therefore, each of these subjects will be looked at in turn, while a further chapter will deal with some of the more outlandish proposals made about the documents over the years. First of all, it will be fruitful to clear the ground by defining more carefully just what the DSS from Khirbet Qumran are.

Discovery of the Century

The DSS from the Qumran area have rightly been described as one of the twentieth century's most important archaeological finds. To begin explaining why, it is best to report how and when the contents of the eleven caves concerned were found.[3] The story has been recounted many times, of course, and it is not always easy to disentangle the facts from legendary accretions. Nevertheless, even though the numerous accounts that exist are difficult to harmonize in every detail, we can get a reasonably accurate overview of what took place from the recollections of several individuals.[4]

In early 1947, three young shepherds from the Ta'amireh Bedouin tribe were in the vicinity of the springs of 'Ein-Feshkha. This site, two miles south of Khirbet Qumran, sits on the narrow coastal plain between the western shore of the Dead Sea and the limestone cliffs marking the edge of the Judaean hills. The three were grazing their flocks on the patches of greenery which here and there break the barren monotony of both the plain and the hills. One evening, while searching for a lost animal, the shepherd known as Jum'a casually threw a stone into one of the hundreds of caves among the surrounding cliffs. An unexpected crashing noise emanated from it and, because it was nearly dark, the young men determined to investigate further the next day. In the morning, Muhammed edh-Dhib was the first to enter the cave and, in one of a number of stone jars, each about two feet high, he found three manuscripts, two of them wrapped in linen cloth. The Bedouin soon brought their unusual booty to the nearest town, Bethlehem, in the hope of a sale. Unsuccessful, they left them with a cobbler-cum-antiquities dealer called Khalil Eskander Shahin, also known as Kando.

We now know that the cave where the scrolls were found – subsequently dubbed Cave 1 to distinguish it from other manuscript caves in the same area – is situated less than a mile north of Khirbet Qumran and some nine miles south of Jericho. Four further scrolls were retrieved from it by the Bedouin and lodged with the same antiquities dealer. Kando, however, was unsure of the age or value of the seven manuscripts in his care. Because they looked to him as though they might be written in the Syriac language, he contacted the Metropolitan Athanasius Yeshue Samuel of St. Mark's Syrian Orthodox Monastery in Jerusalem.[5] In mid-1947, the Metropolitan decided to purchase four of Kando's texts, and these were later identified as a near-complete copy of the biblical book of Isaiah, a previously unknown religious rule book, a similarly distinctive commentary on the biblical book of Habakkuk, and a badly preserved paraphrase of Genesis. Impatient to learn more about the documents, especially how much they might be worth, he investigated several possible avenues of further inquiry.

Eventually, the Metropolitan approached scholars at the American School of Oriental Research in Jerusalem. One of the staff there, John

Trever, took photographs of three of the compositions which, it tran-spired, were written in Hebrew; not long afterwards, the results were published in two volumes.[6] The fourth scroll, containing an Aramaic paraphrase of Genesis, had decomposed and was difficult to unravel.[7] This problem was compounded by the way the document was manufac-tured in ancient times, for all the lengthy Qumran DSS originally consisted of leather or papyrus strips sewn or pasted into a single piece, inscribed in sections or columns, and then rolled up into scroll form. After nearly two millennia, it was not surprising that compositions like the Aramaic Genesis paraphrase had deteriorated or that its internal layers were stuck together.[8]

In the course of 1947, Professor E. L. Sukenik of the Hebrew University in Jerusalem heard rumours of a manuscript discovery. Despite civil unrest over the United Nations resolution to partition Palestine (then under British control) into an Arab state and a Jewish state, he managed to buy the other three scrolls from Kando in Novem-ber and December of that year. The three compositions were all in Hebrew, and they consisted of a collection of hitherto unattested hymns, a dramatic work about an eschatological cosmic battle, and another, less well preserved, copy of Isaiah. Sukenik quickly realized that the scrolls were very old and of momentous significance – he was, after all, an expert in burial inscriptions from the first centuries BCE and CE.[9] So widespread was his reputation that, soon after he had acquired his own documents, an intermediary sought his opinion on the four Cave 1 manuscripts belonging to the Metropolitan. Sukenik was allowed to examine them briefly, risking life and limb by venturing under difficult political circumstances from Jewish Jerusalem to Arab Bethlehem to collect them. But then, much to the professor's disappointment, the Metropolitan unexpectedly opted to submit the four scrolls to the expertise of Trever at the American School of Oriental Research, as observed earlier. As for Sukenik himself, like Trever, he published his material fairly rapidly.[10] And today, these seven substantial Cave 1 manuscripts are in Israeli hands, housed in Jerusalem's specially built Shrine of the Book.[11]

Both the American scholars and Sukenik issued separate press releases in April 1948, describing their documents in brief. So it was that, almost a year after the shepherd had disturbed the jars in Cave 1, the world at large came to hear about the remarkable discoveries that had been made.[12] It took some time for the news to sink in, however. Even experienced scholars were reluctant to believe that ancient documents could have survived in the Judaean desert, for received wisdom held that the conditions were too harsh. Only when further excavations got under

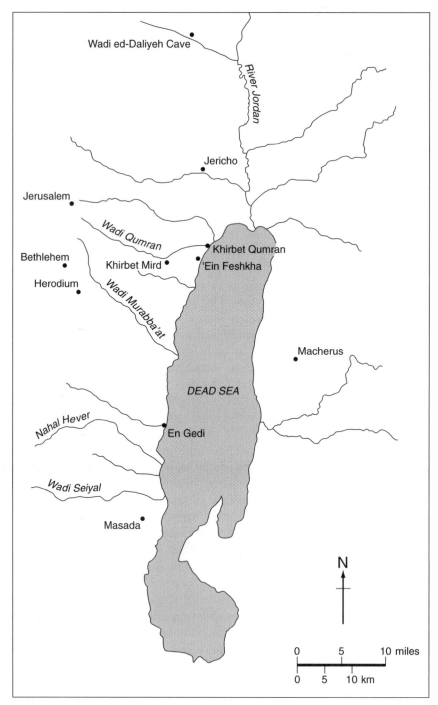

Map 2   *The Dead Sea and Surrounding Area*

way, despite the region's ongoing political tensions, was it possible to demonstrate conclusively just how old the DSS were.

When the British relinquished their mandate on Palestine, David Ben-Gurion immediately declared the establishment of an independent state of Israel on 14 May 1948. In the ensuing military struggle, Israel took possession of the land allotted to it under the earlier partition plan. It also took West Jerusalem, while the state of Jordan annexed East Jerusalem and the West Bank. It was within the latter's boundaries that military officials determined the exact location of Cave 1 in early 1949. Anxious not to lose any DSS to the black market or abroad, the Jordanian Government had authorized the Arab Legion to comb the area, and the site was found by Captain Philippe Lippens of the United Nations Armistice Observer Corps. The soldiers had carried out their laborious task without the aid of the Bedouin who, hoping to find other valuable manuscripts for themselves first, were reluctant at this stage to co-operate with the authorities.

Once its identity had been established, two scholars set about thoroughly excavating Cave 1. They were G. Lankester Harding (director of the Department of Antiquities of Jordan) and Roland de Vaux (director of Jerusalem's famous Dominican college, L'Ecole Biblique et Archéologique Française de Jérusalem). In addition to the documents removed earlier, they retrieved various other artifacts, including pieces of text that had broken off several of the seven large manuscripts, as well as fragments of what were obviously other compositions – including the remains of two appendices to the religious rule purchased earlier by the Metropolitan. All such fragments were published in the first volume of an official series with Oxford University Press: 'Discoveries in the Judaean Desert', or DJD for short.[13] Then, in 1950, the antiquity of the manuscripts and the fragments was dramatically confirmed, when the results of Carbon-14 tests on the linen wrappings from two of the scrolls gave an approximate date of 33 CE. We shall look at carbon dating more closely in Chapter 3, but, even allowing for the two hundred-year margin of error inherent in the process at the time, the ancient origin of Cave 1's literary contents was now beyond doubt.

Surprisingly, in the initial phase of their work, Harding and de Vaux did not link the Cave 1 manuscripts to the nearby old buildings of Khirbet Qumran, perched above the coastal plain on an outcrop from the cliffs overlooking the Dead Sea.[14] In fact, a preliminary survey led them to conclude it was unconnected to the scrolls. A fuller investigation took place in late 1951, however, and the archaeologists came to a different conclusion. The remains of a cylindrical jar like those found in Cave 1 were retrieved from the Qumran site and this important artifactual connection, along with other distinctive pottery items, convinced them that the cave and the ruins were related.

In the ongoing search for new caves and new texts, local Bedouin were at a distinct advantage. Although their interest was financial, their familiarity with the Judaean desert meant they tended to be the first to discover literary deposits, which they would then sell to the archaeologists working under the Jordanian Government's auspices. In this way, the latter was prepared to spend considerable sums acquiring scrolls from the Bedouin and, by preventing their entry into the black market, keep the documents in Jordan under the jurisdiction of the Palestine Archaeology Museum of East Jerusalem. Some of the manuscripts bought from the Bedouin turned out to have no direct connection with either Khirbet Qumran or Cave 1 – such as the finds in caves further south at Wadi Murabba'at and Nahal Hever (described at the end of this chapter). More positively, Cave 2 was discovered in 1952 and, over the next few months, several other sites were located – Caves 3, 4, 5 and 6. Their contents, like those of Cave 1, seemed to be linked with Qumran's ruined buildings. Indeed, Cave 4 is situated right next to Khirbet Qumran and provided particularly rich literary pickings.

In view of the strong link with the caves established by a common pottery style, three further excavations of the ruins took place. During one of them, Caves 7, 8, 9, and 10 were discovered by the archaeologists, who then embarked on a final examination of the Qumran buildings in 1956. On the basis of coins and pottery, as well as distinct layers within the ruins themselves, the excavators concluded that Qumran had undergone two main periods of habitation. In the seventh and eighth centuries BCE, a small town had stood on the site – perhaps the City of Salt mentioned in the Bible at Joshua 15:62. Then, after a break of several centuries, the evidence pointed to a second occupation from some time after 150 BCE until 68 CE. Although the site could have provided up to two hundred people with communal facilities for eating, ritual bathing, and worship, the group's members must have lived elsewhere, probably in tents pitched roundabout or in those surrounding caves which, though bereft of manuscripts, contained various items linking them to the Qumran ruins. Life would certainly have been harsh, for, at 1,300 feet (some 400 metres) below sea level, the Dead Sea region gets very hot and humid and receives under four inches (10 centimetres) of rainfall per annum. However, it was possible to collect runoff water in pools during the rainy season, as the system of channels and cisterns among the buildings testifies, while local springs such as 'Ein-Feshkha – where excavations in 1958 revealed a small satellite settlement connected to Qumran – would have allowed a limited amount of farming. The remains

Plate 1 *Man with Scroll Jar in Cave 4.* © *Estate of John M. Allegro, courtesy of The Allegro Archive (The University of Manchester)*

of pottery kilns and other facilities at Khirbet Qumran, moreover, provide further evidence that a subsistence lifestyle was indeed feasible in this hostile environment. And as hinted already, those using Qumran during this second period presumably busied themselves collecting, copying, composing, and studying the manuscripts found in the surrounding caves almost two millennia later.[15]

The last cave, Cave 11, was discovered by the Bedouin in early 1956. It contained several lengthy texts, including a collection of canonical and non-canonical psalms all ascribed to King David, an Aramaic paraphrase of the biblical book of Job, as well as a copy of Leviticus written in Old Hebrew script.[16] Because the Palestine Archaeology Museum

was experiencing funding problems by this stage, these scrolls were
entrusted for publication to Dutch and American scholars whose institutions bought the documents from the Bedouin. As for the Temple
Scroll, the longest of all the DSS at nearly 27 feet (over 8 metres), it
was not acquired until 1967. As early as 1960, though, rumours were
circulating that it had been hidden by Kando, the antiquities dealer
who had earlier supplied Sukenik and the Metropolitan. The document
was eventually retrieved by the scholar-cum-politician Yigael Yadin
with the help of Israeli military intelligence during the Six-Day War of
1967, when Israel occupied East Jerusalem and the West Bank.[17] By
then, the DSS were becoming symbolic of Israeli identity, providing a
tangible link between the new state and the last time the Jewish people
inhabited their own land as a nation some two thousand years earlier.
The fortress of Masada, which will feature later on, had taken on a
similar status.

Scrolls in Abundance

The results of archaeology and carbon dating soon showed that the
Qumran DSS stemmed from the last two or three centuries BCE and the
first century CE. Certainly, they had lain in the caves undisturbed for
centuries, notwithstanding reports of manuscript finds in the third and
ninth centuries CE.[18] We shall see later that the texts probably belonged
to a religious community with links to the Essenes which flourished at
Qumran for nearly two hundred years. This community apparently
disbanded in the late 60s CE when Roman legions marched past Qumran
on their way to Jerusalem to quash what modern scholars call the First
Revolt of the Jews against Rome.[19] Fortunately for us, its members left
behind a collection of literature which is vast by any standards. It
encompasses both complete manuscripts, like the lengthy Isaiah Scroll
from Cave 1, as well as thousands of minute fragments. Among the
latter, many were recovered from the caves under layers of sand and bat
dung, while Cave 7, for example, had collapsed long before the archaeological excavations. Surprisingly, even such tiny scraps often yield small
amounts of legible text, as in the case of a Cave 1 commentary on the
biblical book of Micah. In between these extremes are many other
manuscripts in varying states of preservation.

  With all these manuscripts, fragments, and caves, it is easy to get
confused. A system of letters and numbers has been devised, therefore,
as a simple way of referring to individual Qumran DSS. Thus, the long
Isaiah scroll just mentioned is usually referred to as lQIsaiah[a]. Here, 1 =

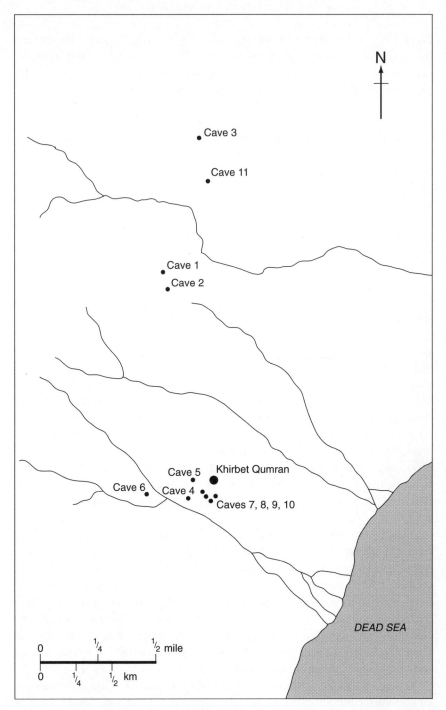

Map 3   *Khirbet Qumran and Caves 1–11*

Cave 1, Q = the site of Qumran, and ᵃ = the particular copy concerned (to distinguish it from lQIsaiahᵇ, the other Isaiah text recovered from the same site). Acronyms of this sort have likewise been apportioned to the other five well-preserved manuscripts of Cave 1:

lQS	Community Rule (S = *serekh*, Hebrew for 'rule')
lQpHabakkuk	Commentary on Habakkuk (p = *pesher*, 'interpretation')
1QHᵃ	Hymns Scroll (H = *hodayot*, 'hymns')
1QM	War Scroll (M = *milhamah*, 'war')
lQapGenesis	Genesis Apocryphon ('ap' stands for apocryphon)[20]

The two messianic appendices to 1QS, removed from Cave 1 by Harding and de Vaux, were naturally dubbed 1QSa and 1QSb. More generally, fragments from Cave 5 and Cave 6 of a work known as the Damascus Document can be referred to as 5QD and 6QD, respectively, while eight Cave 4 copies of the same piece are called 4QDᵃ⁻ʰ. As for 4QAges of Creation A–B, the 'A–B' in such cases represent compositions which, though not identical, contain parallel or overlapping material.

In addition, a numerical system has been constructed in which all but the seven major Cave 1 manuscripts have been given numbers in sequence. According to this scheme, the commentary on Micah noted above may be designated simply as lQ14, while 4QDᵃ⁻ʰ can be dubbed 4Q266–273. However, we shall opt for the lettered system whenever possible, because it normally provides clues for the uninitiated reader as to a document's content. Alternatively, it is sometimes best to employ a work's full name – as in 'Community Rule' or 'Damascus Document' – especially when it was found in more than one cave. Only a few of these titles, it ought to be pointed out, derive from ancient times, most being invented by modern scholars as a handy way of referring to individual texts.[21]

Altogether, almost nine hundred manuscripts were brought to light from the eleven caves. Caves 9 and 10 yielded only one item each. At the opposite extreme, Cave 4 was the richest of all, providing scholars with well over five hundred documents, although some are very scrappy.[22] To keep these numbers in perspective, it should be remembered that they include duplicate copies. The biblical book of Deuteronomy, for instance, was attested in some thirty manuscripts found variously in Caves 1, 2, 4, 5, 6, and 11. Taking such duplication into account, around four hundred distinct compositions have been preserved in all.

To try and make sense of this mass of literature, it is helpful to divide the manuscripts into three broad categories. First, we have writings which were already known before the Qumran DSS were discovered. In such cases, the main contribution of the finds has been to provide specimens much older than anything which had come to light beforehand. By way of illustration, we can turn to 1QIsaiah[a] again, for it predates all complete copies of Isaiah in Hebrew by a thousand years. And nearly all the other scriptural books common to Jews and Christians turned up in the caves as well. To put it more concretely, thanks to the Qumran DSS, we now have specimens of biblical books which were actually being read by Jews when Herod the Great ruled Palestine (37–4 BCE), and when Jesus walked and preached in the Galilean hills (around 27 CE).[23] Alongside these biblical texts were several works from the so-called Apocrypha. This term was coined by the ancient scholar Jerome (*circa* 340–420 CE) to designate a number of books, like Tobit and Ecclesiasticus (or Ben Sira), which Christians in his day regarded as part of the Old Testament, though Jews by then had excluded them from their Bible. Similarly, two fascinating books now called 1 Enoch and Jubilees belong to this first class of Qumran DSS material. Although authoritative for many Jews before 70 CE, they subsequently failed to enter into either the Jewish or mainstream Christian Bible; their text was, however, preserved through the centuries by the Ethiopian church before turning up at Qumran. In fact, 1 Enoch and Jubilees are part of a large body of Jewish texts from the last few centuries BCE and the first few centuries CE which scholars dub the 'Pseudepigrapha'. This term will be explained in the next chapter, when the overall significance of the first category of DSS literature – biblical, apocryphal, and pseudepigraphical works – will be unpacked in more detail.

The second category of Qumran DSS consists of compositions which no one knew about before their chance discovery in the caves around Qumran. Like the first category, though, they were probably widely read in Palestine during the late Second Temple period, either by the Jewish population as a whole or by various sub-sections of it with certain common concerns. Only after 70 CE, when Jews and Christians ceased to preserve them, were they lost to posterity. An example is the interpretative paraphrase of Genesis known as 1QapGenesis which, translating some of the biblical stories about Noah and Abraham into Aramaic, fills gaps in the narrative along the way, often rather imaginatively. Since it refers to none of the distinctive practices and beliefs linked to the Essenes, it was probably in use beyond the confines of the Qumran group, although perhaps mostly among others of a similar religious disposition. In any case, the DSS have revealed a large number of similar writings which, although scholars had previously been unaware of their existence, must likewise have been circulating widely in Palestine during the last two centuries BCE and the first century CE. Included here, for instance, are 4QApocryphon of Moses[a–b] and 4Qpseudo-Ezekiel[a–e] and, as we shall see in the next chapter, many such works were probably treated as scripture by those with access to them in Second Temple times.

By far the greatest sensation was caused by a third category of Qumran DSS, all but one of which were also completely unknown before 1947. The Damascus Document is the exception here, for it was first discovered fifty years earlier in an old Cairo synagogue and dubbed 'CD' (C=Cairo, D=Damascus), before subsequently turning up in a longer edition in the Qumran caves.[24] Still, all the works in this category, including CD, comprise writings which, given their content, must have been composed by the religious group to which those who lived around Qumran were affiliated. As such, they are often referred to as the 'sectarian DSS' and consist of a mixture of legal and poetic texts, as well as pieces of Bible interpretation and narrative. We shall examine some of the most important so-called sectarian documents in Chapter 4. For the moment, it is worth repeating that they almost certainly represent the beliefs and practices of a branch of Essenes – one of several religious parties at the time, alongside the Pharisees, Sadducees, and others. Before 1947, the only substantial information we had about these Essenes was contained in the accounts of two first-century CE Jews, Philo and Josephus, neither of whom were Essenes themselves. Now, to the delight of scholars, the sectarian DSS from Qumran function as a unique window into the world of an actual community with Essene links. In fact, as the only surviving first-hand material from any Jewish group prior to 70 CE, their value is inestimable in all kinds of ways.

The Scrolls and their Times

Just where the value of the Qumran DSS lies will emerge as subsequent chapters unfold. Beforehand, it is a good idea to sketch their general historical background, for all serious scholars now relate the DSS from Caves 1–11 to Palestine during the last two or three centuries BCE and the first century CE. However, it was not always so. Although right from the start Sukenik and Trever thought that the texts were ancient, others disagreed. The main proponent of a medieval date, for instance, was the American scholar Solomon Zeitlin who, right up to his death in 1976, maintained that the Qumran DSS were a forgery.[25] But, in reality, it became increasingly clear that they were ancient. Among the mounting evidence, we have already noted the results of carbon dating, coupled with archaeological study of the Qumran ruins. Later on, we shall see that allusions to people and events contained in some Qumran DSS further corroborate their antiquity.

The three centuries concerned, roughly 250 BCE to 70 CE, are part of what historians call the Second Temple period.[26] This designation covers Jewish history from the rebuilding of the Temple in Jerusalem in the late 500s BCE until its destruction by the Romans in 70 CE. These six centuries, as many readers will realize, partly overlap with the Biblical period, for the Old Testament – also called the Hebrew Bible or Hebrew Scriptures – deals with Israelite and Jewish history up to 400 BCE and beyond.[27] Obviously, such a vast time span is beyond the scope of this introductory study, and we shall focus on the last three hundred years of the Second Temple period in subsequent chapters.[28]

Here, though, it is worth placing the Second Temple period in its broader historical context. Strictly speaking, it began in 515 BCE or shortly thereafter with the rebuilding of the Temple in Jerusalem on the site of the sanctuary that had been constructed in the tenth century under King Solomon.[29] Those responsible for its re-establishment were members of the tribes of Judah and Benjamin who had been given permission in 537 BCE to return to their homeland from exile in Babylon – although it is important to remember many chose to remain behind, while large numbers had never left Palestine in the first place. By this time, of the original twelve tribes of Israel, Judah and tiny Benjamin were the only ones left and, as such, it is not wrong to go on referring to their members as Israelites. More normally, whether in Babylon or in Palestine, they are called Judahites or, better still, 'Jews', while the term 'Judaism' designates their religion.

Unfortunately, the sources for the first half of the Second Temple period are sparse. Nonetheless, on the basis of late Old Testament books and some other writings, it appears that the Jewish community was fairly autonomous. The Persian authorities were content to let it regulate its own affairs, albeit normally under the watchful eye of an approved governor, as long as taxes were duly paid. This arrangement made sense, for, from the imperial viewpoint, the Jews lived in a far-flung and relatively unimportant corner of the Persian empire. Indeed, the small province of Judah or Yehud, as it was called, consisted only of Jerusalem and its immediate environs. As for the Jews themselves, life probably focused on the Temple in Jerusalem, as well as on the High Priest and other officials in charge of both worship and the people on a day-to-day level. At the same time, relevant late biblical books – like Ezra, Nehemiah, Haggai, Zechariah, Malachi – reflect considerable religious and political tensions between factions of this early Jewish community, although it is now difficult to be precise about their nature and extent.

Nevertheless, central to the culture of all Jews was the belief that God, although creator of the whole world, had a special relationship with the Jewish people in view of the covenant or agreement he had made with their ancestors long ago. The terms of that relationship were laid down in the Law of Moses (the biblical books of Genesis, Exodus, Leviticus, Numbers, and Deuteronomy). This Law or Torah, also called the Pentateuch by modern scholars, contained the guidelines for regulating the community, ostensibly in the form of a divine revelation given to Moses centuries earlier on Mount Sinai. A range of other scriptural books also began to circulate during this period broadly in the form in which we would still recognize them today – Joshua, Judges, 1–2 Samuel, 1–2 Kings, Isaiah, Jeremiah, Ezekiel, the Twelve Minor Prophets, and many individual Psalms. Yet, how to interpret this diverse body of scriptural writings increasingly became a matter of contention for Jews during the second half of the Second Temple period, as we shall discover.

With the conquest of Judah by Alexander the Great in 333 BCE, things started to change. Although Greek culture had already made in-roads into Palestine by then, it slowly began to permeate the Jewish community at large. As long as this influence was superficial, touching merely on language or commerce, it remained unproblematic. But Greek religion and philosophical ideas were another matter and, by the second century BCE, those aspects of Greek culture were causing serious strife within Jewish society. Some rejected any religious assimilation at all; others preferred to see Jewish and Greek religious ideas as essentially compatible. But with the outright prohibition of traditional Judaism by the region's main political force, the foreign king Antiochus IV Epiphanes, probably in response to fighting between rival claimants to the High Priesthood in Jerusalem, outright rebellion erupted in 167 BCE. It was led by a certain Mattathias and then by three of his sons, the so-called Maccabee brothers. Under their successors, the Hasmoneans, Judah – or Judaea, as it was called in Greek – expanded as a more-or-less independent Jewish state between 142 and 63 BCE.

Notwithstanding their new-found independence, as well as a concomitant reassertion of traditional identity, the Jews remained divided. Various religious parties came into being from the middle of the second century BCE onwards, including the Pharisees, Sadducees, and Essenes mentioned earlier. Although we shall see in Chapter 5 that it may also make sense to envisage an overarching 'Common Judaism', these groups vied with each other for the attention of the Jewish masses, offering them alternative interpretations of Judaism for the age in which they lived. This complex state of affairs continued after the Romans took control of the area in 63 BCE. In fact, discontent increased under their rule, especially in the first century CE. The Emperor Caligula (37–41 CE) did not help matters when, in search of divine honours, he decreed from Rome in 40 CE that a statue of himself was to be erected within the Jerusalem Temple. The turmoil that would have been sure to accompany such sacrilege was only averted by Caligula's timely death in early 41 CE.[30] The Roman administration on hand in Palestine, however, was little better. The ineptitude of a succession of Roman governors merely aggravated Jewish exasperation, particularly during the 50s and 60s CE. Eventually, armed revolt broke out in 66 CE, but the superior strength of the Roman forces in the region inevitably proved decisive. This First Revolt of the Jews against Rome was quashed in 70 CE and culminated in the destruction of the Jerusalem Temple, bringing the Second Temple period to a close.[31]

The above account is a brief overview of the Second Temple period; we shall have an opportunity to unpack it further in Chapter 3. Hopefully, enough has been said to show that the six centuries concerned had a distinctive history and identity, especially during the last three hundred years. In other words, Judaism in Second Temple times was different both from what preceded and what followed. As implied already, the exile of the sixth century BCE and the destruction of the Temple in 70 CE constituted turning points of momentous historical and religious significance.

Second Temple Judaism should not, therefore, be viewed simply as a continuation of the religion of Israel which had existed before the sixth-century exile to Babylon. To help maintain this distinction, experts usually refer to the latter as the 'religion of Israel' to differentiate it from the 'Judaism' of the Jews after 515 BCE. Although many Jewish and Christian readers of the Bible today would not be familiar with this distinction, there can be no doubt that the exile caused the religious traditions of Israel to undergo substantial transformation. For example, it is almost certain that the Torah did not exist before the exile in the form in which it circulated afterwards – even though Jews from Second Temple times onwards came to believe that it had been revealed *en bloc* to Moses on Mount Sinai. Likewise, it is highly probable that, contrary to the perception of Second Temple Jews, many Israelites before the exile were not strict monotheists; only in the Second Temple period did monotheism emerge clearly as one of Judaism's distinguishing traits.[32]

In a similar way, it would be wrong to assume that Judaism as it developed after 70 CE was a straightforward continuation of what had gone before. In reality, the loss of the Temple and priesthood required Jewish religion to change in important respects. This process culminated in the publication of the Mishnah (200 CE) and, later still, in the compilation of the Babylonian Talmud (*circa* 550 CE). Both writings place obedience to the Torah at the heart of Judaism. Of course, Jews had kept to the Law of Moses before 70 CE, but that had been only one element in their religious culture. Now, the Torah became the very essence of Judaism. For the Jews of the Mishnah and the Talmud, moreover, the Torah did not simply denote the Pentateuch (Genesis, Exodus, Leviticus, Numbers, and Deuteronomy). It also came to include what is dubbed the Oral Torah – additions to the written Law which, it was believed, had also been revealed to Moses and could now be found in the Mishnah and Talmud themselves. This distinctive belief in the Oral Torah became characteristic of Judaism after 70 CE but seems not to have been a feature of Jewish religion in Second Temple times.

Second Temple Judaism, then, was not the same as the religion of Israel before 587 BCE or Judaism as it evolved after 70 CE. The distinctions involved here may at first seem perplexing to modern Jews and Christians, not least because both ancient and modern religious authorities prefer to emphasize elements of continuity. Such elements are real enough – before and after the exile, for example, the Temple was important, while prior to 70 CE and afterwards the Law played a vital role. Nevertheless, only by highlighting discontinuity and change can we appreciate the distinguishing characteristics of Judaism in Second Temple times, especially during the last three hundred years. It is that distinctive context, moreover, within which we shall discover the full significance of the Qumran DSS themselves.

Conspiracy or Complacency?

At the start of this chapter, we noted that it is only in the last ten years that all scholars have been given free access to the whole Qumran DSS collection.[33] At first, this might seem a little incongruous, for we saw that the Cave 1 manuscripts were published in the 1950s, while the contents of the so-called 'minor caves' (Caves 2–3 and Caves 5–10) appeared in 1962.[34] But, in contrast, relatively little of the Cave 4 material was published between the early 1950s and the end of the 1980s. Such a delay seems lax, to say the least. Back in 1977, after nearly twenty-five years of waiting for their appearance, Professor Geza Vermes of Oxford University rightly described the situation as 'the academic scandal *par excellence* of the twentieth century'.[35] Nevertheless, there are no grounds for positing a conspiracy to withhold Cave 4 texts damaging to Judaism or Christianity, as some have alleged. Claims along these lines made over the decades since 1947 are sensationalist nonsense and will be dealt with in our final chapter.

The real causes of the delay are disappointingly mundane and, with hindsight, three stand out. First, there has long been a tradition of 'finders keepers' within the world of archaeology. In other words, it is assumed that, when ancient texts are discovered, they are the property of the excavators concerned until official publication has taken place. This way of thinking explains the reluctance of those entrusted with the Cave 4 documents to share their work with anyone outside the team. Unlike Trever and Sukenik, their insistence on producing definitive studies of every scrap in their care slowed down the process by many years.

Second, in retrospect, the vast amount of material disgorged by Cave 4 was simply too much for the small team put in charge of the thousands of fragments – some of them no bigger than a postage stamp! Back in 1952, Roland de Vaux was made editor-in-chief of all the finds in the Judaean Desert. He was assisted initially by three colleagues from the Ecole Biblique – M. Baillet, P. Benoit and J. T. Milik – who worked with him in the Palestine Archaeology Museum. When the sheer quantity of Cave 4 texts became apparent, de Vaux decided to draw on a wider band of international scholars. In the decades that followed, J. M. Allegro, F. M. Cross, C. H. Hunzinger, P. W. Skehan, and J. Strugnell were each given a portion of manuscripts to work on. But even this enlarged team was not up to the enormity of the task.

A third impediment explains why, inasmuch as most of these academics had other jobs at the same time as working on the DSS. We may imagine that their enthusiasm waned as the years rolled on and, not surprisingly, the first volume of Cave 4 material did not appear until 1968. Even then, it received bad reviews from other scholars for its sloppiness and inaccuracy, and a further nine years elapsed before a second volume was completed.[36]

During the Six-Day War of 1967, Israel seized control of the West Bank and East Jerusalem from Jordan. Automatically, jurisdiction over the Qumran region and over the Palestine Archaeology Museum – renamed the Rockefeller Museum – fell into Israeli hands. Sensitive to any external criticism, however, the Israel Antiquities Authority decided not to interfere with existing arrangements for the publication of the Qumran DSS. As a result, the status quo under de Vaux continued. Even when P. Benoit succeeded him in 1971, he was no more successful in expediting progress.[37] The same applies to John Strugnell, who, taking the reigns in 1987, increased the editorial team to twenty. As Vermes recalls, when he confronted Strugnell at a London conference that same year and asked for the photographic plates of the remaining Cave 4 material, his request was flatly refused.[38]

Things only began to improve significantly in 1990 when the Israel Antiquities Authority accepted Strugnell's resignation after an Israeli newspaper reported that he had made uncomplimentary remarks about Judaism.[39] Strugnell was replaced by Emanuel Tov, Professor of Biblical Studies at Jerusalem's Hebrew University and the first Jewish scholar in charge of the DSS. Although he continued to restrict access, he reallocated the unpublished DSS among a much larger body of scholars – over fifty-five in total. Goaded by ongoing pressure from Herschel Shanks, editor of the widely read *Biblical Archaeology Review*, this alone would probably have speeded up publication to an acceptable rate.

Yet, the situation soon changed beyond all recognition. In 1991, two scholars issued a computer-based reconstruction of seventeen unpublished Cave 4 manuscripts.[40] They had used as their basis a copy of the Preliminary Concordance, a list of key words in the Qumran DSS, issued privately in twenty-five copies under the auspices of the official editorial team in 1988. Then, the Huntington Library of San Marino, California, one of a few institutions with a complete photographic record of DSS for safekeeping, announced it would give scholars working in the field access to them; it was able to do so because, by historical accident, it alone had never signed up to an agreement preventing people from seeing its photographs. At first, the Israel Antiquities Authority opposed this development, but by the autumn of 1991 it was fighting a losing battle. As a result, all restrictions were lifted. Any scholar with a legitimate interest was allowed to view the photographs at Huntington, as well as the duplicate collections stored at the Ancient Biblical Manuscript Center in Claremont, California, in Hebrew Union College, Cincinnati, and in the Oxford Centre for Hebrew and Jewish Studies. In November of the same year, an edition of the photographs was published in book form by Eisenman and Robinson.[41] And there is now a microfiche edition of all the DSS, prepared under the auspices of the Israel Antiquities Authority itself, while a CD-ROM version has also been issued.[42]

As a result of these dramatic changes, publication of those Cave 4 texts which had been kept under lock and key for over forty years has moved apace since 1991.[43] Included among them are important biblical manuscripts, in addition to sectarian works such as the text known as 'Some Precepts of the Law' (Hebrew, *Miqsat Ma'ase ha-Torah*), or 4QMMT[a–f] for short. Most scholars outside the editorial team had hitherto only heard rumours about such documents – although a few had been circulating semi-secretly at conferences or between individuals over the years. In Chapters 3 and 4, we shall return to the impact of these newly released compositions, while Chapter 2 will examine the impact of the Qumran DSS on our knowledge of the Bible.

Competing Discoveries in the Judaean Desert

The basic contours of the corpus of DSS from Khirbet Qumran will hopefully be clear by now. But before moving on, it is worth introducing four other bodies of ancient manuscripts discovered in the same broad vicinity.[44] Indeed, over many centuries the Judaean desert to the west of the Dead Sea was utilized by all kinds of religious zealots and political refugees. Its sparsely populated and inhospitable terrain provided the sort of environment conducive to 'religious experience', while the wilderness helped dissidents requiring anonymity to remain elusive to the authorities. Despite the geographical connection, however, these other collections of literature, significant as they are in their own right, do not link up directly with the DSS we have just described. Yet, as we shall see, there are some important indirect links.

The first to mention is a body of texts, coins, and seals found at a site known as the Abu Shinjeh Cave in the Wadi ed-Daliyeh region, some nine miles north of Jericho.[45] The documents, written in Aramaic and dating from around 375 to 335 BCE, are mostly of a legal nature. They were the property of nobles from the city of Samaria who, recently conquered by Alexander the Great's army, had to flee after unsuccessfully rebelling against their new overlords in 331 BCE. The rebels were pursued and massacred under siege in the cave where their skeletal remains, along with the documents they left behind, were recovered during archaeological excavations in 1963 and 1964.[46] Although fascinating, these writings from Wadi ed-Daliyeh are quite distinct from those found in the caves around Qumran, notwithstanding the fact that some of the material has been published in the DJD series.[47]

A second collection comes from the impressive fortress of Masada, south of Qumran, originally built by the Hasmoneans. It was also home to some rebels of the First Revolt against Rome until 73 CE and, not surprisingly, a number of texts from that occupation were found by excavators during two periods of archaeological activity between 1963 and 1965.[48] Among them were the remains of biblical, apocryphal, and pseudepigraphical books, as well as more mundane works.[49] Among them also was a fragment of a document identical to one found in Caves 4 and 11 at Qumran, known as 'Songs of the Sabbath Sacrifice' (Hebrew, *Shirot 'Olat ha-Shabbat*) – or 4QShirShab[a-h] and 11QShirShab for short. This interesting overlap has led some to propose that, when the Qumran community abandoned its settlement in 68 CE, a proportion joined the Masada rebels, only to be defeated with them in 73 CE. Although possible, this is speculation and depends on identifying the composition concerned as clearly sectarian. Equally feasible is the proposal that Songs of the Sabbath Sacrifice circulated more widely in late Second Temple times and that its presence at both Qumran and Masada was little more than coincidental.

Thirdly, numerous documents in Hebrew, Aramaic, and Greek were discovered in caves around Wadi Murabba'at and Nahal Hever during the same period that the Qumran discoveries were being made and again in the early 1960s.[50] Once more, as is only to be expected, the remains of some biblical books were found.[51] But the most fascinating texts relate to the Second Revolt of the Jews against Rome which took place between 132 and 135 CE. That uprising's leader, Simeon bar Kosba, is actually mentioned by name in several letters.[52] Nevertheless, all the documents from Wadi Murabba'at and Nahal Hever clearly post-date even the youngest manuscripts from the Qumran caves, although some, as in the case of Wadi ed-Daliyeh, have been published in the same official series.[53] Like the Wadi ed-Daliyeh material, moreover, a number of texts can be precisely dated. Accordingly, a comparison of works from the Qumran caves with those from Wadi ed-Daliyeh and from Murabba'at and Nahal Hever has allowed scholars to work out a general picture of the way Jewish handwriting developed between the fourth century BCE and the second century CE. The technical term for this kind of academic research, to be considered more fully in Chapter 3, is palaeography.

Finally, a cache of texts in Greek, Syriac, and Arabic was retrieved from Khirbet Mird, midway between Bethlehem and Qumran, during 1952 and 1953. The location turned out to be a ruined Christian monastery, founded in 492 CE on a site on which a fortress called Hyrcania had been built in the second century BCE. As such, the documents uncovered are all Christian, dating from no earlier than the fifth century CE. They obviously have no connection with the Qumran finds.

All four of these collections of literature from the Dead Sea vicinity can be called DSS – alongside the documents from the Qumran caves – in view of their common geographical origin. However, despite the perplexing link just mentioned between one Qumran composition and one Masada fragment, as well as the useful palaeographical information to be gleaned by comparing the handwriting at Qumran with that from other sites, they do not relate directly to the contents of the eleven caves around Khirbet Qumran, as should be clear by now.

For the sake of convenience, in the chapters to follow, we shall adopt the shorthand 'Qumran DSS' for the manuscripts of Caves 1–11, even though, strictly speaking, no literary texts were recovered from the Khirbet Qumran site itself.[54] Without further ado, therefore, let us turn to the impact of these Qumran DSS on our understanding of the Bible, Apocrypha, and Pseudepigrapha.

2

The Dead Sea Scrolls and the Bible

Which English Bible?

The aim of this chapter is to explain what the Qumran DSS tell us about the state and status of the Bible in the last two or three centuries BCE and the first century CE. As we shall see, the biblical text in circulation was less fixed than modern people are used to, while the 'canon' or official list of books deemed scripture was – if it existed at all – more open-ended than in later times. For many readers, the subject will be a new one and, understandably, a little daunting. A few words on the Bible in the vernacular are in order first, therefore, to lay the ground for what follows.

Most people today encounter the Bible through a translation in their own language, usually a Christian Bible containing the Old Testament and the New Testament. The first major English translations were produced by John Wycliffe (*circa* 1330–84) and William Tyndale (*circa* 1494–1536), two Englishmen whose work was not always to the liking of the church authorities. Tyndale, in fact, was strangled and burnt at the stake in 1536 for producing an unauthorized vernacular rendering of the Bible, hitherto generally available in the Western Church only in its approved Latin version. Nevertheless, by the end of the sixteenth century, the Geneva Bible of 1560 and the Bishop's Bible of 1568 were popular English versions with official sanction. But both were overtaken by another translation, produced under the authority of James VI of Scotland who ascended the English throne as James I in 1603. Among Anglicans and Protestants, this so-called Authorized or King James Version (KJV) of 1611 dominated the English-speaking world for over three centuries, although the Roman Catholic Church produced its own

English Douay-Rheims Bible in 1609–10. By around 1870, however, it had become clear that the KJV, despite its literary beauty, had many defects.

The most serious was its dependence on late and unreliable manuscripts containing words and phrases which were almost certainly never part of the original. The following arrangement of 1 John 5:7–8 in the KJV, for instance, shows clear-cut belief in the doctrine of the Trinity:

> [7]For there are three that bear record *in heaven, the Father, the Word and the Holy Ghost: and these three are one.* [8]*And there are three that bear witness in earth*, the spirit, and the water, and the blood: and these three agree in one.

The KJV's words represented in italics here are absent from early New Testament manuscripts in Greek. They almost certainly constitute an addition to 1 John 5:7–8 from the third or fourth century CE, when church disputes about the Trinity were intense.[1]

In light of this and other examples, the Church of England commissioned a revision of the KJV. It appeared as the Revised Version (RV) of 1885, with a sister translation in the United States of America called the American Standard Version (ASV) in 1901. While the intention was to produce definitive new British and American versions, their publication marked merely the beginning of a long line of English-language Bibles offered to the public in the course of the twentieth century. Several were produced by individuals frustrated with the archaic language of the KJV and RV.[2] After all, both employed an old-fashioned English from which many words had either dropped out of use or changed in meaning by the late nineteenth century. 'Ghost', for example, is employed in its seventeenth-century sense of 'spirit', while 'to prevent' and 'to suffer' regularly mean 'to proceed' and 'to allow', respectively. For modern readers, such shifts in meaning obviously left a lot of room for misunderstanding.

Other twentieth-century translations were put together by panels whose members had to assent to one sort of theological creed or another, thereby calling into question the enterprise's objectivity, at least to a degree.[3] The *New International Version* (NIV), first produced in 1978, probably falls into this category, for, despite its readability and popularity, its text sometimes reflects the translators' theological baggage. Thus, Isaiah 7:14 is rendered as follows:

> Therefore the LORD himself will give you a sign: The virgin will be with child and will give birth to a son, and will call him Immanuel.

Though the Hebrew word *almah* in Isaiah 7:14 clearly means 'young woman', the NIV renders it 'virgin'. This reflects an old Greek translation, which does have 'virgin' (*parthenos*) here, and it has presumably been followed because Matthew 1:23 cites it in association with Mary's miraculous conception of Jesus. But that is not explained to the reader, despite the Preface's assurance that all diversions from the traditional Hebrew text are highlighted in footnotes.[4] Consequently, the translators have engaged in what most experts would consider an unjustifiably 'christianizing' rendering of Isaiah 7:14.[5]

Fortunately, four accurate English renderings of the Bible have appeared in the last decade or two, each a revision of an earlier one. The first to mention is the New Revised Standard Version (NRSV) of 1989. This constituted a revision of the Revised Standard Version (RSV) of 1952 – which in turn derived from the ASV of 1901 – and was sponsored by the National Council of the Churches of Christ in the United States of America. Although the language of the NRSV is modern throughout, the translators chose to follow in the tradition of the KJV, RV/ASV, and RSV. In other words, they tried to be 'as literal as possible and as free as necessary' in their rendering of the Hebrew and Aramaic of the Old Testament and the Greek in the case of the New Testament.[6]

In contrast, the Revised English Bible (REB) is a freer translation. It was published in 1989 by a team of scholars supported by most Christian churches in Britain and Ireland.[7] Following in the footsteps of its predecessor, the New English Bible of 1970, the REB rejects a concern for literalness in favour of an equally accurate but more idiomatic English rendering. Just as fresh in its approach is the New Jerusalem Bible, published in 1985. It is a revision of the Jerusalem Bible of 1966, based on the work of Roman Catholic scholars from the Ecole Biblique in Jerusalem – an institution which featured in the last chapter. Finally, also in 1985, the Jewish Publication Society of America produced *Tanakh: the Holy Scriptures*, having previously issued *The Holy Scriptures* in 1917.[8] In use among English-speaking Jews around the world, the Society's translation obviously does not include the New Testament.

All four of these translations have been produced by competent scholars. Naturally, they target Jewish and Christian readers who have neither the time nor the skills to read the Bible in its original languages. And it should be stressed that each editorial team adopted a strictly historical approach to its task. The purpose, in short, was to offer the public versions accurately translating the underlying Hebrew, Aramaic, or Greek texts in terms which reflect the author's original intentions as far as possible. Such a commitment requires that Old Testament passages, famous among Christians for the way they have been applied to Jesus, should be treated solely in relation to what they meant within ancient Israel centuries earlier. For instance, in contrast to the NIV's approach sketched above, Isaiah 7:14's *almah* should be translated straightforwardly as 'young woman', irrespective of later Christian belief in Mary's virginal conception of Jesus. In sum, although commissioned by explicitly Jewish or Christian institutions, readers can be sure that versions like the NRSV or REB constitute reliable, as well as readable, renderings of the scriptures into English.

Despite their common commitment to accuracy, however, a closer look uncovers noticeable differences between even trustworthy translations such as those just described. For the moment, it is worth explaining two types. The first has already been hinted at and is more apparent than real. At base, it is simply a matter of the style preferred by a given editorial team. The scholars behind NRSV and REB, for example, have chosen to translate the same underlying Hebrew words in Numbers 22:28 somewhat differently:

NRSV	REB
Then the LORD opened the mouth of the donkey, and it said to Balaam, 'What have I done to you, that you have struck me these three times?'	The LORD then made the donkey speak, and she said to Balaam, 'What have I done? This is the third time you have beaten me.'

In this example, the NRSV has a fairly literal, although perfectly understandable, translation, whereas the REB is more upbeat. In neither case is the verse's meaning in dispute.

The second sort of divergence is of greater significance and reflects points where the underlying words are either ambiguous or problematic. In such cases, various translation teams have opted for quite different ways of handling the text. Isaiah 40:9 provides a suitable illustration:

NRSV	REB
Get you up to a high mountain, O Zion, herald of good tidings; lift up your voice with strength, O Jerusalem, herald of good tidings . . .	Climb to a mountaintop, you that bring good news to Zion; raise your voice and shout aloud, you that carry good news to Jerusalem . . .

In this verse, the Hebrew of the second and fourth phrases is unclear, for 'Zion' and then 'Jerusalem' may be either the bringer or the recipient of good news. Hence, the experts behind the NRSV and the REB have plumped for the former and latter, respectively, differing as to the most likely meaning of Isaiah 40:9. Both would doubtless agree, however, that certainty is impossible in such cases.

As a result, modern English Bibles often fall back on footnotes to suggest alternative renderings of such ambiguous passages or to alert the reader to more serious textual problems. This can include appeal to biblical manuscripts among the DSS, but, as we shall see, they often raise as many new problems as they solve.

Biblical Studies and the Dead Sea Scrolls

Some readers may be disconcerted by the examples just given, for, contrary to popular belief, the text of the Bible at many points is not entirely fixed, either in its wording or its meaning.[9] Fortunately, the difficulties involved do not usually affect the basic significance of a given passage. But there are exceptions. And we shall learn that even the list or 'canon' of books contained in the Bible varies from one religious tradition to another – depending on whether a Bible is Jewish, Roman Catholic or Orthodox, or Protestant.

In many other respects too, scholars working in the field of Biblical Studies – historical and literary analysis of the Old and New Testaments – have shown that the Bible is a less black-and-white affair than is often supposed.[10] Turning specifically to the Old Testament, also called the Hebrew Scriptures or Hebrew Bible, much has been learned about ancient Israel and early Judaism up to 400 BCE and beyond.[11] For example, it seems clear that many stories about the people of Israel in, say, Joshua or 1–2 Kings are idealized presentations. The narratives are not so much concerned with objective history as with theological lessons about Israel's relationship with God. What is more, Israelite practice and belief altered over the centuries and, as in our own day, rivalry between 'traditionalists' and 'progressives' was intense at certain times.[12] These and other insights have shown that the religion of the people of the Old Testament was not some monolithic edifice but underwent periods of turmoil and change; as mooted in the last chapter, the exile of the sixth-century BCE was a particularly important watershed.

Due to this kind of academic work on the Bible over the past century, many Old Testament books have been redated. Study of the Pentateuch and Isaiah, for example, has produced a re-evaluation of their age and origin.[13] The results have understandably upset many Jews and Christians, especially around the start of the previous century. By then, tradition had long held that Moses wrote the Pentateuch or Torah sometime in the second half of the second millennium BCE (1500–1000 BCE). Likewise, the great eighth-century BCE prophet Isaiah of Jerusalem was assumed to lie behind all sixty-six chapters of the book bearing his name. From the mid-nineteenth century, however, scholars began to overturn many traditional notions like these. They concluded that the Pentateuch was compiled in the sixth or fifth century BCE from disparate sources. As for the book of Isaiah, only parts of Isaiah 1–39 reflect the ministry of the eighth-century prophet, while Isaiah 40–55 and 56–66 represent the work of anonymous figures working several centuries later.

In fact, a wealth of data supports the thesis that most Old Testament books were composed between around 550 and 300 BCE after a long process of growth.[14] It would be tedious to go into too much detail, but a few illustrations may help. Thus, numerous turns of phrase in the Pentateuch could only have been penned after Moses' time, such as the explanation that 'at that time the Canaanites were in the land' (Genesis 12:6) or mention of a period 'before any king reigned over the Israelites' (Genesis 36:31). The first of these phrases is merely an aside but clearly reflects a situation long after Moses, for the Canaanites are assumed to be no longer resident in Palestine; the second must stem from a time when Israel had already been ruled by its first kings in the tenth century BCE. Similarly, various repetitions or contradictions in the Pentateuch point to a long and complex editorial history rather than authorship by an individual.[15] The divine name, for example, normally translated into English as 'the LORD', is introduced as if for the first time in Exodus 3:13–15, even though Genesis 4:26 assumes it was in use much earlier. In this case, as in many others, two once-independent traditions seem to have been combined by an editor to give us the Pentateuch as we now find it.

With the book of Isaiah, the vocabulary and imagery of chapters 40–55, unlike much of Isaiah 1–39, assume an audience already experiencing the exile of the mid-500s BCE – not life in eighth century BCE Judah when Isaiah of Jerusalem lived. In need of reassurance rather than warning, Isaiah 40–55 promises that restoration is not far away. Indeed, Cyrus king of Persia – who allowed the exiles to return to Judah from 537 BCE onwards – is mentioned by name in Isaiah 44:28 and 45:1–8.[16] Given the force of such observations, the need to re-date Isaiah, as well as the Pentateuch and most other Old Testament books, is today accepted by all serious scholars.

Nevertheless, some early commentators wondered whether the biblical

DSS from Qumran might provide fresh support for traditional datings. It was pointed out, for example, that the community behind the sectarian DSS treated the Pentateuch as a unit derived from Moses. Similarly, the fact that 1QIsaiah^a contains all sixty-six chapters of Isaiah in one long manuscript might suggest that the whole book derived from the eighth-century BCE prophet after all.[17] But there was a fatal flaw in the logic of such arguments. Although much older than anything available before 1947, even the biblical DSS are not sufficiently ancient to provide direct evidence for the state of individual books during the period under dispute (*circa* 550–300 BCE). To do so, they would have to be several centuries older than they are. Returning to our concrete examples, only if 1QIsaiah^a stemmed from around 600 BCE could it reaffirm a traditional date of authorship, proving that all sixty-six chapters existed as a fixed entity before the sixth-century BCE exile. Likewise, it would take copies of the Pentateuch from 600 BCE or, preferably, earlier to reaffirm Mosaic authorship, thereby counteracting modern scholarly theories.

In reality, 1QIsaiah^a was probably copied around 125 BCE, while the oldest Pentateuchal text from Qumran is 4QExodus^f from *circa* 250 BCE. The most such manuscripts demonstrate is that, by the third or second century BCE, Jews had come to associate a sixty-six chapter collection with the eighth-century prophet Isaiah. They had also come to view Exodus, along with the rest of the Torah, as emanating from Moses. Yet, it has never been disputed that nearly all Old Testament compositions were in circulation by 300 BCE and that Jews by then had developed strong traditions about these writings' origins – traditions which have persisted until recent times. It is no great surprise, therefore, to find both factors confirmed by the Qumran DSS, stemming as they do from the last few centuries BCE and the first century CE. But the relevant manu-scripts are not old enough to provide access to the previous stage in the biblical text's development.

Central here is a distinction which will crop up later on, for it is important to distinguish between a given text's original composition date, on the one hand, and the time a particular copy of it was subsequently made. The former is often a rather speculative matter, while palaeogra-phy and carbon dating can allow reasonable accuracy for the latter. Thus, as just observed, the Pentateuch probably came into existence in some-thing like the form in which we still know it during the late 500s or 400s BCE, whereas its oldest Qumran exemplars stem from no earlier than *circa* 250 BCE. A parallel distinction has to be made for non-biblical DSS, including sectarian compositions, as we shall see in Chapters 3 and 4.

In any case, to sum up so far, it makes sense to follow the main conclusions of academic study of the Hebrew Bible. All serious scholars, although disagreeing over points of detail, would conclude that most Old Testament books underwent a long period of growth, originally reaching their final edition between roughly 550 and 300 BCE. This judgement is based on clues gleaned from meticulous study of the text, as we have just glimpsed in relation to the Pentateuch and Isaiah 40–55. The biblical DSS from Qumran do not alter this impression. Nowadays, indeed, many within the synagogue and church accept these sorts of conclusions. Only conservative Jews and Christians, with a prior theological commitment to traditional datings, feel obliged to reject such findings.[18]

The Hebrew Bible Before 1947

Despite the apparently negative conclusion reached above, we should not forget that the Qumran DSS have provided scholars with specimens of biblical books in Hebrew and Aramaic up to one thousand years older than anything previously to hand. This alone renders the DSS among the most significant archaeological discoveries of modern times, for they teach us much about the state and status of the biblical text in the last two or three centuries BCE and the first century CE. To appreciate their contribution, it will be helpful to assess the evidence available before the DSS were found. Essentially, there were three primary versions of the Old Testament text available before 1947: the Masoretic Text, the Septuagint, and the Samaritan Pentateuch.[19] We shall say a few words about each.

The traditional Jewish Bible as transmitted for centuries by the synagogue is usually referred to as the Masoretic Text – or MT for short. The name is linked to the medieval Jewish scholars, known as the 'Masoretes' from the Hebrew *masorah* ('tradition'), who gave it its definitive shape in the eighth to tenth centuries CE. The MT is written in Hebrew, the original language of all books of the Hebrew Bible – except for one verse at Jeremiah 10:11 and a few chapters in Ezra and Daniel which are in Aramaic. Now, when Hebrew and Aramaic operate as living languages, as in biblical times or modern Israel, they are written down solely by means of consonants. This may seem odd to those familiar with English, but it is quite normal for Semitic languages like Hebrew and Aramaic. The MT, therefore, consists essentially of consonants. For medieval Jews, however, Hebrew was a sacred tongue and not in everyday use. Although the biblical text's consonants had been stable for centuries, its lack of vowels laid it open to occasional mispronunciation and misinterpretation. Here, the ingenuity of the Masoretes came in, for they incorporated a secondary system of vowels, placed above and below the main line of consonants, and thereby guaranteed both its pronunciation and interpretation. This improvement meant that vowelless copies of biblical books were discarded. None from that period, unfortunately, has survived, and so the oldest complete Masoretic Bible is the so-called Leningrad Codex of 1008 CE, with Masoretic vowels intact.[20] The first printed edition of the MT was published in Venice in 1524–5 and remains the basis of the modern Jewish Bible.

The second source for the Old Testament text before 1947 was an old Greek translation of the Hebrew Scriptures named the Septuagint or LXX. According to a second-century BCE work called the Letter of Aristeas, the Egyptian king Ptolemy II Philadelphus (283–246 BCE) decreed that a Greek translation of the Jewish Law should be prepared for his library in Alexandria.[21] Seventy-two Jewish scholars were brought to Egypt to fulfill this task, although some parallel accounts envisage only seventy – hence the name Septuagint (or LXX) from the Latin for seventy.[22] According to the Letter of Aristeas, the translators worked with God's miraculous help, thereby guaranteeing the LXX's accuracy and authority. Such details show that the account is partly legendary, but it is likely that a Greek rendering of the Hebrew Scriptures was prepared in Egypt in the last two or three centuries BCE. A sizeable Greek-speaking Jewish community certainly grew up in Alexandria during this time. Moreover, a Greek translation was readily available by the first century CE, for it is regularly quoted by New Testament writers. With the spread of Christianity in the first and second centuries CE, it was the LXX that became the church's Old Testament. As a result, the oldest surviving substantial specimens of the LXX before 1947 were Christian copies from the third and fourth centuries CE.[23] Although that leaves a gap of several hundred years from the original translation, these ancient LXX manuscripts happen to take us further back in time than the oldest copies of the MT which, as observed above, stem from the Middle Ages.

The third source available before 1947 was the Samaritan Pentateuch, preserved over the centuries by the Samaritan community. The Samaritans separated from Judaism at some uncertain point during the Second Temple period, one of their main distinguishing features being a preference for a temple on Mount Gerizim near Shechem, rather than that on Jerusalem's Mount Zion. As its name implies, the Samaritan Pentateuch contains only the five books of the Torah, for the rest of the Old Testament possessed by Jews and Christians is rejected. As for the text of the Samaritan Pentateuch, it is now extant only in medieval copies and is written in what scholars call Old Hebrew or Palaeo-Hebrew.[24] This script was the regular form of Hebrew employed in Israel before the exile and continued in use among the Samaritans afterwards, whereas for most purposes the Second Temple Jewish community replaced Old Hebrew with the precisely equivalent letters of the Aramaic script. So thorough was this replacement that it has remained in force to the present day. In fact, what were originally Aramaic letters are now considered the standard Hebrew script – often called Square Hebrew to distinguish it from Old Hebrew.

Much of the time, these three versions of the Old Testament text say the same thing. Taken as a whole, nonetheless, there are literally thousands of divergences between the MT, the LXX, and Samaritan Pentateuch. The majority are minor. They concern the presence or absence of the definite article ('the'), or variations in the spelling of proper names, or else differences in number. By the time of the flood recounted in Genesis 6–9, for instance, the MT assumes that the world had existed for 1,656 years, while the LXX presupposes 2,242 years.[25]

More substantial disagreements also occur, although scribal carelessness rather than deliberate alteration often seems to have been the cause. Detailed examination can sometimes show what has happened, as a comparison of Genesis 4:8 in the MT and LXX, adapted from the NRSV, makes clear:

MT	LXX
Cain said to his brother Abel.	Cain said to his brother Abel, 'Let us go out to the field.' And when they were in the field, Cain rose up against his brother Abel, and killed him.
And when they were in the field, Cain rose up against his brother Abel, and killed him.	

The LXX here contains a straightforward rendering of the MT and so, presumably, the original translators had a Hebrew text the same as that still in the possession of the synagogue centuries later. Yet, as the parallel arrangement highlights, there is one major discrepancy: the words 'Let us go out to the field' are absent from the MT. Because this phrase is required to complete the sense of 'Cain said to his brother Abel', it must have dropped out accidentally in the course of transmission. Hence, the LXX reflects a better form of Genesis 4:8, based on a more accurate Hebrew version in circulation before the omission took place. Most English Bibles rightly follow the LXX at this point, therefore, rather than the defective MT.

Elsewhere, discrepant readings are not so easy to sort out. Amos 3:9 in the MT, for example, refers to the coastal town of 'Ashdod', while the LXX talks of the vast empire called 'Assyria'. Because 'Ashdod' and

'Assyria' look almost identical in Hebrew, a tired scribe presumably misread one for the other in the course of transmission, although we can no longer tell which way round this mistake took place. Such ambiguity explains why the NRSV has 'Ashdod' at Amos 3:9, while the New Jerusalem Bible prefers 'Assyria'. In this case, whichever option is taken, Amos 3's overall meaning remains unaffected.

In other instances, however, the import of divergences is more significant. The whole book of Jeremiah is a good case in point. In the LXX, it is about one-eighth shorter than the MT and ordered differently. This level of disagreement can hardly be accidental, as Jeremiah 10:3–11, again adapted from the NRSV, illustrates:

> ³For the customs of the peoples are false: a tree from the forest is cut down, and worked with an ax by the hands of an artisan; ⁴people deck it with silver and gold; they fasten it with hammer and nails so that it cannot move. ⁵Their idols are like scarecrows in a cucumber field, and they cannot speak; they have to be carried, for they cannot walk. Do not be afraid of them, for they cannot do evil, nor is it in them to do good. *⁶There is none like you, O LORD; you are great and your name is great in might. ⁷ Who would not fear you, O King of the nations? For that is your due; among all the wise ones of the nations and in all their kingdoms there is no one like you. ⁸They are both stupid and foolish; the instruction given by idols is no better than wood!* ⁹Beaten silver is brought from Tarshish, and gold from Uphaz. They are the work of the artisan and of the hands of the goldsmith; their clothing is blue and purple; they are all the product of skilled workers. *¹⁰But the LORD is the true God; he is the living God and the everlasting King. At his wrath the earth quakes and the nations cannot endure his indignation.* ¹¹Thus shall you say to them: The gods who did not make the heavens and the earth shall perish from the earth and from under the heavens.

In this arrangement, the italicized text appears in the MT but is missing from the LXX. Faced with such a glaring disparity, an obvious question is which version is correct? The likeliest candidate might seem to be the MT, for the original language of Jeremiah was undoubtedly Hebrew. But why should the LXX be so different? Were the translators incompetent? Did they arbitrarily decide to omit several verses? Or, is it possible that the Hebrew being translated, though subsequently lost, was different from the MT preserved by the synagogue?

Before the discovery of the Qumran DSS in 1947, scholars had little to go on to answer such questions, for the precise origins of the MT, LXX, and Samaritan Pentateuch were lost in the mists of time. Normally they preferred the MT. After all, the books of the Hebrew Bible had originally been written in Hebrew or Aramaic, and Jewish scribes were generally renowned for their accuracy. Yet, mistakes had crept in, as always happens when a text is reproduced from generation to generation by hand and, in such cases, it made sense to appeal to the LXX or the Samaritan Pentateuch. The LXX, in particular, often helped, as we saw in relation to Genesis 4:8. As for the Samaritan Pentateuch, it has usually been treated with more caution, for some of its distinctive readings seemed like deliberate changes reflecting the ideological split between Samaritans and Jews.[26]

This approach to the relative merits of the MT, LXX, and Samaritan Pentateuch still acts as the point of departure for most Old Testament translations. There are two main reasons. First, since the time of the Protestant Reformation, Christians have increasingly come to the theological view that the Hebrew best represents their sacred text of the Old Testament and that, in any case, it is most likely to contain the original. Second, some such guiding principle is attractive to scholars engaged in the practicalities of translation, for any concrete edition of the Bible requires a starting point. Both factors mean that all four English versions commended earlier take the MT as their base for Jeremiah. Quite sensibly, on the other hand, when it comes to individual difficulties, such as that in Genesis 4:8, it is not unusual for the LXX to be followed.

Nevertheless, recent work suggests that the priority accorded to the MT can no longer be sustained. When the biblical DSS are added to the MT–LXX–Samaritan Pentateuch equation, they further accentuate the complexity of an already complex situation. We shall now explain why.

Biblical Manuscripts from Qumran

The Qumran caves yielded copies of Old Testament books much older than scholars had ever dreamt was possible. Approximately 220 manuscripts recovered from the caves are biblical works and, although some found in Caves 4 and 7 are in Greek translation, most are written in the original Hebrew or Aramaic.[27] The great majority are in Square Hebrew but some are penned in Old Hebrew. The sheer number of relevant documents, however, as well as the scrappy nature of many, makes grasping the biblical DSS's significance no easy task. So, first of all, it is worth gaining an overview of the manuscripts.

Given the Torah's centrality in Judaism, it is not surprising that books from the Pentateuch predominate, as seen from the following table:[28]

Biblical Book	No. of Copies	Biblical Book	No. of Copies
Genesis	20	Psalms	37
Exodus	17	Proverbs	2
Leviticus	14	Job	4
Numbers	8	Song of Songs	4
Deuteronomy	30	Ruth	4
Joshua	2	Lamentations	4
Judges	3	Ecclesiastes	2
1–2 Samuel	4	Esther	0
1–2 Kings	3	Daniel	8
Isaiah	21	Ezra	1
Jeremiah	6	Nehemiah	0
Ezekiel	6	1–2 Chronicles	1
Twelve Minor Prophets	8		

Genesis, Deuteronomy, Isaiah, and Psalms stand out as of prime significance and, as it happens, three of these (Deuteronomy, Isaiah, Psalms) are the most frequently cited in the sectarian DSS from Qumran. But, although the above figures suffice as a general guide, we should resist reading too much into them in view of the impact the Judaean desert's harsh conditions can have on written documents. Some of the badly damaged biblical manuscripts, for instance, might in fact be other compositions in which only scriptural citations have survived. That Nehemiah is missing may similarly imply merely that the Qumran copies had disintegrated by the time the DSS were found between 1947 and 1956, especially since small portions of the related works of Ezra and 1–2 Chronicles were recovered. However, the absence of Esther may be more intentional. This is because the Jewish festival known as Purim, prominent in Esther, had no place in the special calendar followed by the community behind the Qumran DSS. Notwithstanding the existence of the fragmentary 4QprotoEsther, therefore, Esther's absence from the Qumran caves was probably more deliberate than accidental.[29]

What, then, do the Qumran DSS teach us about the state of the biblical text in the last three hundred years of the Second Temple period? More particularly, do they have any bearing on the reliability of the MT, LXX, and Samaritan Pentateuch? There are two essential points to be gleaned from the manuscripts. Let us look at each, before considering some general lessons to be learned in their wake.[30]

The first seems reassuring, at least initially, because the biblical DSS confirm that the MT is an ancient tradition carefully preserved by Jewish

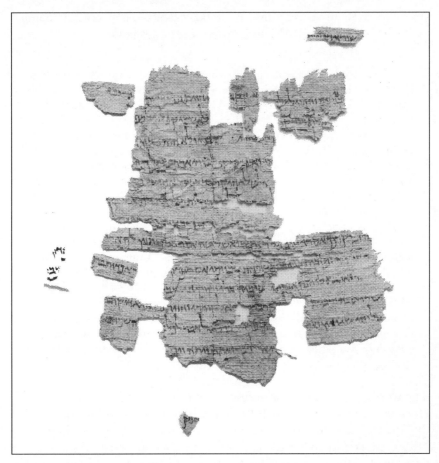

Plate 2   *4QTobitᵃ in Aramaic on papyrus* © *Estate of John M. Allegro, courtesy of the Allegro Archive (The University of Manchester)*

scribes over the centuries. 1QIsaiahᵃ acts as a good illustration, for it is close to medieval copies of the same book. Of course, there are discrepancies – as is only to be expected when over one thousand years of copying by hand separate two specimen documents. The well-known threefold acclamation of Isaiah 6:3 ('Holy, holy, holy is the LORD God almighty'), for example, takes a twofold form in 1QIsaiahᵃ ('Holy, holy . . .'). Elsewhere, the Qumran copy has a superior reading, as in Isaiah 49:25. The MT of this verse contains the awkward 'captives of a righteous person'. 1QIsaiahᵃ, however, reads 'captives of a tyrant' and, because this fits the surrounding context better, it has been adopted by the NRSV.

Occasionally, the biblical DSS from Qumran furnish us with more striking cases of correction. A good example concerns 1 Samuel 10:26–11:4. In the NRSV, this passage reads as follows:

> ²⁶Saul also went to his home at Gibeah, and with him went warriors whose hearts God had touched. ²⁷But some worthless fellows said, 'How can this man save us?' They despised him and brought him no present. But he held his peace.
>
> *Now Nahash, king of the Ammonites, had been grievously oppressing the Gadites and the Reubenites. He would gouge out the right eye of each of them and would not grant Israel a deliverer. No one was left of the Israelites across the Jordan whose right eye Nahash, king of the Ammonites, had not gouged out. But there were seven thousand men who had escaped from the Ammonites and had entered Jabesh-Gilead.*
>
> *About a month later,* ¹Nahash the Ammonite went up and besieged Jabesh-Gilead; and all the men of Jabesh said to Nahash, 'Make a treaty with us and we will serve you.' ²But Nahash the Ammonite said to them, 'On this condition I will make a treaty with you, namely that I gouge out everyone's right eye, and thus put disgrace upon all Israel.' ³The elders of Jabesh said to him, 'Give us seven days' respite that we may send messengers through all the territory of Israel. Then, if there is no one to save us, we will give ourselves up to you.' ⁴When the messengers came to Gibeah of Saul, they reported the matter in the hearing of the people; and all the people wept aloud.

The words in italics here are present neither in the MT nor in the LXX. However, they are found in 4QSamuelᵃ. Because the extra words improve the story's flow by contextualizing Nahash's eye-gouging threat, the NRSV editors included them in their translation. That was a sensible decision, for the fact that 'But he held his peace' and 'About a month later' look very similar in Hebrew almost certainly caused a scribe's eye to pass over the intervening words accidentally at an early stage of transmission. Such a slip explains why the words are absent from the MT and LXX, while Josephus, writing in the first century CE, mirrors the details they contain in his own account of ancient Israel.[31]

Overall, nevertheless, the evidence presented so far might be taken to confirm the MT's priority. But there is another side to the coin, for our second principal deduction is that other forms of the scriptural text circulated during the Second Temple period alongside the MT. More precisely, diverse editions of biblical books were recovered from the Qumran caves. 1QIsaiahᵃ, for instance, is not so near the MT when set alongside 1QIsaiahᵇ, which is even closer. And, while many other scriptural DSS almost replicate the MT, some variously reflect the text of the LXX or the Samaritan Pentateuch. 5QDeuteronomy, in fact, contains wording paralleled by all three. Still others exhibit new readings unknown before the discovery of the DSS.

The implications of this kind of divergence can be highlighted by returning to Jeremiah, for we earlier noted that the MT and LXX represent substantially different editions. When the remains of five copies of Jeremiah turned up in Cave 4, the assumption was that either the longer (MT) or shorter (LXX) version would be shown to have priority. As it happens, the bearing of 4QJeremiah[a-e] on the issue is not quite what was expected. On the one hand, most Cave 4 Jeremiah manuscripts are close to the MT, confirming its antiquity. However, 4QJeremiah[b] and 4QJeremiah[d], though fragmentary, contain the remains of a Hebrew version of the shorter LXX text. Their existence proves that, in the case of Jeremiah at least, the Second Temple translators of the LXX were neither incompetent nor deliberately altered the text; they simply utilized an alternative Hebrew edition circulating alongside a longer one. Although one of these could ultimately prove to be earlier or more original, it may never be possible to be sure whether this was so or, if it was, which one had priority. And the evidence is mounting that multiple editions existed for many other scriptural works or, at least, some of their constituent parts.[32]

Taken together, these two main features of the biblical DSS from Qumran have in recent decades led to a gradual transformation of the way scholars view the Old Testament text. Not only does the MT tradition go back to Second Temple times, but so do the traditions reflected in the LXX. Indeed, all but a handful of the Samaritan Pentateuch's distinctive readings now seem to be merely general variations, devoid of specifically Samaritan influence inasmuch as they have been found in manuscripts that did not belong to Samaritan people. Clearly, therefore, many biblical books existed in more than one version during the last two or three centuries BCE and the first century CE. Such diverse editions lay side by side in the Qumran caves and, since there is nothing specifically sectarian about the variations, the same situation presumably prevailed outside the community as well.[33]

Put this way, the evidence of the Qumran DSS challenges what most biblical scholars have assumed for over 100 years. It used to be thought that the divergences between the MT, LXX, and Samaritan Pentateuch would be greatly diminished if sufficiently ancient manuscripts could be found, for it was believed that an original text had once existed for most, if not all, biblical books. The original's purity was corrupted over the centuries as errors and deliberate changes crept in, leading eventually to the multiplicity evident in the MT, LXX, and Samaritan Pentateuch. Faced with this situation, the pre-1947 scholar's task was to recover the original text as far as possible. But the biblical DSS undermine these assumptions. With direct access to manuscripts of such antiquity, the reality was probably quite the opposite in Second Temple times, for the diversity reflected in the DSS is greater than ever. To simplify matters after 70 CE, the synagogue and the church independently chose editions of every biblical book in the form of the MT and LXX, respectively. Indeed, remains of the second-century CE biblical books retrieved from Nahal Hever and Murraba'at are more consistently close to the MT than the Qumran documents, reflecting just such a later selection among Jews.[34] The Samaritan community presumably made similar decisions, although we do not know when.

In light of the above discussion, it is worth considering the implications of the biblical DSS from Qumran in one final respect. The oldest scriptural manuscript dates to around 250 BCE and, as cautioned earlier, we should be wary of extrapolating from such material anything about the biblical text in the previous period. But it is difficult to imagine that the diversity evident in the Qumran documents stemmed from a more homogeneous tradition in the immediately preceding era. In fact, since most Old Testament writings began to take shape in something like the forms in which we would still recognize them between *circa* 550 and 300 BCE, it seems likely that from the start they existed in diverse versions. The discovery of multiple editions at a single location inhabited by a distinctive Second Temple religious group makes it difficult to maintain earlier hypotheses that geographical or sectarian factors were responsible for the differences.[35]

If this general picture is accurate, it may be wise to give up the whole idea of the original text of the Hebrew Scriptures in favour of more fluid traditions. In that case, for example, lQIsaiah[a] and lQIsaiah[b] are individual written manifestations of a broad and shifting Isaiah tradition. The same would apply to the editions of Jeremiah evidenced in 4QJeremiah[a–e], for they reflect a tradition in a state of flux well into the Second Temple period. In short, and inasmuch as the biblical DSS from Qumran reveal a textual variety unimaginable before 1947, scholars are ceasing to speak of the original text of a given Old Testament book. Although some manifestations may be older than others, such an original, in many cases, may never have existed.

Apocrypha and Pseudepigrapha from Qumran

The biblical books just surveyed make up the Hebrew Scriptures or Hebrew Bible of the synagogue. More commonly, of course, they are referred to as the Old Testament – although originally this was a solely Christian designation assuming the existence of a New Testament. The limits of what were included in the Jewish Bible were fixed around 100 CE or shortly thereafter. The decisions taken have remained in force ever since, and the Jewish Publication Society's *Tanakh: the Holy Scriptures* illustrates the standard three-fold arrangement into the Torah (Law), Nevi'im (Prophets), and Ketuvim (Writings):

Torah	*Nevi'im*	*Ketuvim*
Genesis	Joshua	Psalms
Exodus	Judges	Proverbs
Leviticus	1–2 Samuel	Job
Numbers	1–2 Kings	Song of Songs
Deuteronomy	Isaiah	Ruth
	Jeremiah	Lamentations
	Ezekiel	Ecclesiastes
	Twelve Minor Prophets	Esther
	(Hosea, Joel, Amos,	Daniel
	Obadiah, Jonah, Micah,	Ezra
	Nahum, Habakkuk,	Nehemiah
	Zephaniah, Haggai,	1–2 Chronicles
	Zechariah, Malachi)	

Before 70 CE, however, there were probably no fixed lists of authoritative books. As we shall discover in the next section, it is better to picture instead an amorphous pool of scriptural works with the Torah at its centre. The early Christians naturally inherited this state of affairs in the mid-first century CE, and it was not until well after the destruction of the Temple that they too defined more carefully those books which were to be considered biblical. But Jews and Christians had parted company by then, and the various Christian churches included in their Old Testament a number of works which Jews had discarded.

Some of these books were originally composed in Greek, although many first circulated in Hebrew or Aramaic. But it was in Greek that they were appropriated by the church, as with the remainder of the Old Testament. Thus, only in LXX manuscripts have most of these extra works survived intact to the present day. Allowing for some fluctuation between different Catholic and Orthodox churches, a total of sixteen additional compositions have featured in this way within their Old Testament canon:

Tobit	1 Maccabees
Judith	2 Maccabees
Additions to Esther	1 Esdras
Wisdom of Solomon	Prayer of Manasseh
Ecclesiasticus (or Ben Sira)[36]	Psalm 151
Baruch	3 Maccabees
Epistlce or Letter of Jeremiah	2 Esdras
Additions to Daniel	4 Maccabees

Nowadays, these works are usually referred to as the Apocrypha, a term first coined by the ancient Christian scholar Jerome in a pejorative sense.[37] Working in around 400 CE, he was of the opinion that Christians ought to have admitted into their Old Testament only books contained in the Jewish scriptures. He sought to persuade his co-religionists that they should discard the extra writings listed above, just as the Jews had done in *circa* 100 CE. As it turned out, the church authorities of the day rejected Jerome's recommendation. At the time of the Reformation, however, Protestants took his advice on board, believing that the synagogue's shorter Hebrew Scriptures would have been the Old Testament circulating in Jesus' day. Although they were probably mistaken in this belief, as we shall learn in the next section, it has been common practice since the Reformation for Protestant and Anglican Bibles to relegate the books of the Apocrypha to a separate appendix or to omit them altogether. Roman Catholic and Orthodox Bibles, on the other hand, continue to incorporate these works within the main body of the Old Testament, normally referring to them as writings deemed 'Deuterocanonical'.[38]

These historical developments explain the third major difference between English Bibles mentioned in passing at the start of this chapter, for there are essentially three biblical canons: the Jewish, the Roman Catholic or Orthodox, and the Protestant.[39] Again, such variety might surprise those who have always assumed the Bible to be a fixed entity, but, as has hopefully been made clear, the reasons behind it are relatively straightforward.

Returning to the DSS from Qumran, the remains of four works from the Apocrypha were found among the manuscripts. They were copies of Tobit in Hebrew and Aramaic (4QTobit[a–e]), two portions of Ben Sira in Hebrew (2QSira and part of 11QPsalms[a]), a Hebrew version of Psalm 151 (also in 11QPsalms[a]), and a Greek papyrus fragment of the Letter of Jeremiah (7QLXXEpJeremiah). Although the first three had survived intact in the LXX's Greek translation, their presence at Qumran showed that they had circulated during the Second Temple period in an original Semitic language.[40] In relation to Tobit, however, the propensity of the Qumran DSS to baffle, as well as to inform, shines out once again. Whereas scholars had long speculated over whether the LXX of Tobit was made from a Hebrew or Aramaic original, the DSS yielded both Hebrew and Aramaic editions lying side by side in Cave 4. Rather like lQIsaiah[a–b] or like 4QJeremiah[a–e], therefore, it is likely that these alternative Hebrew and Aramaic versions constitute particular manifestations of a fluid Tobit tradition current in late Second Temple times.

There is a final corpus of literature that needs to be considered in this chapter. Scholars usually call it the 'Pseudepigrapha' and it includes a large body of religious works from the last few centuries BCE and first few centuries CE.[41] The writings concerned are Jewish in origin, though some have subsequently either had Christian additions incorporated or undergone a more thoroughgoing Christian metamorphosis. With two significant exceptions, none entered into the Jewish or Christian Bible. Nevertheless, many were preserved through the ages in exotic languages in some parts of the Christian church.

The name Pseudepigrapha itself is simply a convenient term first employed by eighteenth-century scholars. It means literally 'false ascriptions' and reflects the pseudonymous nature of the compositions concerned. In other words, although ascribed to one of ancient Israel's heroes like Abraham, Moses, or Ezra, they were penned anonymously by Jews – and subsequently adapted by Christians – during the last few centuries BCE or the first few centuries CE.[42] Given their number, we cannot list all the Pseudepigrapha here, but included among the principal texts are 1 Enoch, Jubilees, Testaments of the Twelve Patriarchs, Assumption of Moses, Psalms of Solomon, Ascension of Isaiah, and 2 Baruch.[43] Of these, 1 Enoch and Jubilees entered the Old Testament of the Ethiopian Church.

Apart from several damaged copies of texts relating to the Testaments of the Twelve Patriarchs, the main contribution of the Qumran caves to our understanding of the Pseudepigrapha concerns Jubilees and Enochic traditions. Before 1947, they had survived only in translations of translations passed on by the church. More precisely, the complete text of both had been preserved in an Ethiopic rendering of a Greek translation of the lost Hebrew or Aramaic originals. Thanks to the Qumran DSS, we now have access to parts of each work in its original language – 1 Enoch in Aramaic (4QEnoch[a–f]) and Jubilees in Hebrew (lQJubilees[a–b], 2QJubilees, 4QJubilees[a–h], 11QJubilees).[44] Judging by the number of copies, both were popular with the group behind the Qumran DSS. And, because they contain nothing narrowly sectarian, they were doubtless just as popular among other sections of the late Second Temple Jewish community.

The second category of DSS, defined in Chapter 1 as previously unknown but non-sectarian texts, can be thought of as comparable to these Pseudepigrapha. Despite being unfamiliar to modern scholars before 1947, they too were probably circulating beyond the confines of the religious sect at Qumran in Second Temple times. In fact, their chief distinguishing characteristic seems to be that, unlike books from the Bible, Apocrypha, and Pseudepigrapha, they were lost after 70 CE. As with lQapGenesis, 4QApocryphon of Moses[a–b], and 4Qpseudo-Ezekiel[a–e], historians simply did not know of their existence until 1947.[45] Alongside writings of this type which we have already met in passing, scraps of other works similar to the Pseudepigrapha abound among the DSS – featuring ancient heroes such as Noah, Jacob, Joseph, Joshua, Moses, David, Jeremiah, Ezekiel, and Daniel.

The extent of such material has only begun to be fully appreciated with the release of Cave 4 texts in 1991. Speculation about prominent biblical heroes, as well as more obscure characters like Qahat (Moses' grandfather) in 4QTestament of Qahat and Amram (Moses' father) in 4QVisions of Amram[a–f], was evidently popular both with those who owned the Qumran DSS and a lot of their Jewish contemporaries.[46] Many of these anonymously penned works were presumably treated as scripture by those in ancient times who accepted their authorial claims. Some of them, furthermore, may have acted as sources for several late books now considered part of the Hebrew Bible. For instance, similarities between 4QprotoEsther and Esther, such as a common setting in the Persian court, suggest that the author of the latter may have drawn on the former. Or again, parallels in phraseology concerning Antiochus IV Epiphanes' activities before his persecution of Judaea's Jews in 167 BCE suggest 4QHistorical Text A was a source for the book of Daniel several years later.[47]

Boundaries of the Qumran Canon

The subject of this chapter so far has been complicated. If the information on the Hebrew Scriptures available before 1947 seemed complex enough, then the situation after the discovery of the Qumran DSS might be described as chaotic! Yet, this impression reflects the nature of the evidence itself. Judging by the plethora of Qumran witnesses, the biblical text in the last few centuries of the Second Temple period was in a state of flux, for multiple editions of biblical works were in circulation.

Sometimes the divergences between editions were minor, as in lQIsaiah[a–b], but in other cases they were considerable, as 4QJeremiah[a–e] demonstrate. In response to this overwhelming diversity, Jews and Christians after 70 CE took it upon themselves to simplify matters: the synagogue opted for a particular edition of each biblical book which, when taken together, eventually came to be called the MT; the Christian community likewise chose specific Greek translations of every scriptural work and these are now collectively known as the LXX. The Samaritans must have made similar decisions about their Pentateuch, as learned above, although we do not know when.

As also seen in the last section, moves were further made after 70 CE to limit exactly what books should be included in the Bible, although once again Jewish and Christian leaders decided differently. That is why, taking developments during the Reformation into account as well, there are three major canons of scripture amongst Jews and Christians to this day. It is also why, notwithstanding this variation, most people are used to viewing the contents of the Bible as a fixed entity in the form of one of these canonical collections. In contrast, a more open-ended corpus of books was in use among Jews in Second Temple times, although the Torah was doubtless at its centre.

It may surprise readers, therefore, to learn that this conclusion is not shared by all scholars. In fact, since the start of serious academic study of the Bible, a different viewpoint has become the norm. It assumes that the traditional Jewish tripartite division of the Hebrew Bible – into the Law, Prophets, and Writings – originated in the Second Temple period. According to this reconstruction, not only does the Pentateuch as a fixed authority stem from the sixth or fifth century BCE, but the Prophets as a defined collection was in existence by the second century BCE. A third body of writings, headed by the Psalms, was all but complete by the first century CE, its precise contents finally settled by the Jewish community at around 100 CE. The evidence adduced to support this synthesis seems compelling at first. For example, the prologue to Ecclesiasticus, the Greek rendering of Ben Sira translated in the 130s BCE, speaks of 'the Law itself, the Prophecies, and the rest of the books . . .', while the late first-century CE reference in Luke 24:44 to the 'Law of Moses, the prophets and the psalms' might point in the same direction.[48]

Nevertheless, an alternative is preferable, holding that the three-fold division of the Jewish Bible was an innovation from after the Temple's destruction. As already hinted, there were in reality no fixed boundaries outside the Pentateuch beforehand.[49] In Second Temple times, the scriptures consisted of the Torah, God's principal revelation to the people of Israel and their descendants, the Jews, supplemented by an open-ended pool of other works referred to loosely as the 'Prophets'. In support of this alternative reconstruction, 'the law and the prophets' is the more usual way of referring to scripture in Second Temple literature, especially in the Apocrypha and New Testament.[50] The apparent third element in Luke 24:44 and elsewhere, in that case, merely reflects an isolated secondary sub-division for a particular purpose. Indeed, the recently released 4QMMT[a-f] supports this view, for, while mentioning three elements (the 'Book of Moses', the prophetic books, and 'David') at one point, it elsewhere seems to prefer a two-fold reference to Moses and the prophets (the '[Book] of Moses' and 'Boo[ks of the Prophet]s').[51]

In this sort of usage, a prophet was any pious hero from the period up to the return from exile (up to, say, *circa* 400 BCE) whose words might be construed as coming from God. Accordingly, a prophetic book was any work believed to have been written by one of a long line of holy people – from Enoch and Abraham through David and Solomon to Isaiah, Jeremiah, and Ezra. With the main exceptions of Ecclesiasticus (or Ben Sira) and 1–4 Maccabees, self-consciously and explicitly second or first century BCE in origin, therefore, most of the Apocrypha and much of the Pseudepigrapha would have been treated as prophetic scripture by Second Temple Jews. Even Psalms collections could be reckoned as prophetic from this perspective, for, associated with King David, their contents were thought to speak afresh to each new generation, even if not set in the narrowly prophetic genre of Isaiah or Habakkuk. This explains why Acts 2:30, citing Psalm 16, describes David, its presumed author, as a prophet. It also doubtless explains why Psalms manuscripts were so popular at Qumran.[52]

Unfortunately, nowhere do the Qumran DSS overtly address the issue of a canon, for no catalogue has come to light listing the works viewed as authoritative scripture. But this lack of definition itself indirectly confirms the thesis outlined above, namely, that such canonical decisions had not yet been made. Two further details likewise support it. First, given the multiple Cave 4 copies of Jubilees, as well as numerous texts related to the later 1 Enoch, it is difficult to avoid concluding that these compositions were treated as scripture. Both types of literature claim to be connected with two of Israel's holiest men of old, Enoch and Moses, respectively. Assuming these ancient links were accepted by those utiliz-ing the Qumran DSS collection, such documents would have been as worthy as Isaiah, Psalms, or even the Pentateuch.[53]

Second, some sectarian Qumran DSS quote words from books rejected by Jews and by most Christians after 70 CE. The clearest examples are in the sectarian work known as the Damascus Document. In CD 16:3–4, for instance, we find the following reference to Jubilees:

As for the exact determination of their times to which Israel turns a blind eye, behold it is strictly defined in the *Book of the Divisions of the Times into their Jubilees and Weeks.*

These words show that Jubilees was an authoritative text, presumably because its association with Moses was accepted by the writer.[54] Both 4QText with Citation of Jubilees and 4QApocryphon of Jeremiah B, although fragmentary, seem to contain similar citations from Jubilees, while 4QpApocalypse of Weeks could be a commentary or *pesher* on part of the Enochic corpus known as the Apocalypse of Weeks (1 Enoch 93:1–10; 91:11–17). A parallel case occurs in the New Testament, for Jude 14–15 cites 1 Enoch 1:9 as though it had scriptural status.

In sum, we have learned in this chapter that the DSS from Qumran reveal a situation prevailing in Second Temple times which was doubly different to what most modern readers of the Bible would expect. On the one hand, the manuscripts show that the actual words on the page, as it were, of particular biblical books were not fixed. To repeat an earlier observation, divergent editions of biblical texts existed in the last two centuries BCE and the first century CE. Remarkably, some were found lying side by side in the Qumran caves.

The second surprise is that there was no list or 'canon' of books which constituted a definitive Bible with fixed boundaries agreed by all Second Temple Jews. Only the Torah may have been thought of in these terms, for it contained the very blueprint of Judaism. Alongside it circulated an open-ended scriptural collection which incorporated all or most books of the Old Testament subsequently shared by Jews and Christians. But it also encompassed a lot more besides, including most books from the later collections known as the Apocrypha and Pseudepigrapha – as well as similar works from our second DSS category lost after 70 CE but rediscovered in the Qumran caves between 1947 and 1956.

In the following chapters, we shall continue to speak of certain compositions as 'biblical', 'apocryphal', or 'pseudepigraphal', since these categories are familiar to people today. However, in light of the above discussion, such usage is merely for the sake of convenience. From a historical perspective, the distinctions represented by these terms only developed after 70 CE, while a more fluid situation *vis-à-vis* scripture prevailed in the late Second Temple period itself.

3

The Dead Sea Scrolls and the Essenes

Dating the Qumran Dead Sea Scrolls

At the start of this book, the DSS from the caves around Khirbet Qumran were defined as important Jewish texts from the last three centuries of the Second Temple period. Such an assertion rests on the findings of carbon dating, palaeography, and archaeology, as well as on references to historical characters in some non-biblical manuscripts. Before considering the Essene identification of the corpus in the second half of this chapter, it is worth spelling out in more detail what these various means of inquiry have revealed and, in addition, the broad contours of Second Temple history in Palestine.

Let us start with carbon dating or, more precisely, radiocarbon dating.[1] It measures the radioactive isotope of carbon, known as carbon-14, which is present in all plant and animal life but deteriorates at a predictable rate after death. Back in 1950, radiocarbon tests on some linen wrappings attached to a decomposing Cave 1 manuscript gave a date of 33 CE – albeit within a 200-year margin of error – and thereby confirmed the documents' antiquity.[2] More recent analysis has taken place through Accelerator Mass Spectrometry, or AMS for short. This technique measures the level of carbon-14 more accurately, so that tests in 1991 on a selection of Qumran writings included these results:[3]

Text	Palaeographical Date	AMS result
1QIsaiah[a]	125–100 BCE	335–327 or 202–107 BCE
4QSamuel[c]	100–75 BCE	192–63 BCE
11QTemple[a]	*circa* 1 BCE/CE	97 BCE–1 CE
1QapGenesis	*circa* 1 BCE/CE	73 BCE–14 CE
1QH[a]	50 BCE–70 CE	21 BCE–61 CE

Even AMS provides no more than an approximate time span within which a given document was probably copied.[4] And in a few cases, as the table indicates in relation to 1QIsaiah[a], the analysis can produce more than one range of possible dates. Nevertheless, the figures demonstrate that the Qumran DSS stem from the second half of the Second Temple period. Further AMS tests published in 1995 confirmed that judgement, as have the most recent refinements in the light of an improved calibration of the results.[5] In particular, it has been shown beyond reasonable doubt that 1QpHabakkuk, one of the most important sectarian manuscripts, comes from the first century BCE.[6]

Long before these AMS tests, those working in the field of palaeography – analysis of ancient handwriting – had come to the same broad conclusion. Although there was little material of a similar age with which to compare the DSS, scholars in the late 1940s and early 1950s surmised that the Qumran documents were penned between *circa* 200 BCE and 70 CE. As evidence, similarities and differences were observed in relation to writing on Egyptian papyri, as well as that on funerary inscriptions from Palestine and on the so-called Nash Papyrus.[7]

Then, as learned in Chapter 1, in the 1950s and 1960s, documents were unearthed at Wadi ed-Daliyeh, Masada, Murabba'at, and Nahal Hever.[8] Some of the latter writings, unlike those from Qumran, consisted of letters explicitly dated by their ancient authors. These internal dates mirrored those suggested independently by palaeographers, thereby confirming the overall accuracy of palaeographical analysis; both have since been confirmed by more recent carbon dating.[9] This important match between the ancient dates and modern palaeography, furthermore, provided the palaeographical framework necessary for characterizing the handwriting of the Qumran compositions. To be more precise, the writing style of the Qumran material slots neatly between the fourth-century BCE handwriting of the Wadi ed-Daliyeh texts, on the one hand, and the second-century CE Murabba'at and Nahal Hever documents, on the other.

In light of such palaeographical study, every Qumran manuscript can be roughly classified in one of three ways: archaic (*circa* 275–150 BCE), Hasmonean (*circa* 150–30 BCE), and Herodian (*circa* 30 BCE–70 CE). Most of the Qumran DSS are either late Hasmonean or Herodian. And this threefold classification can be further sub-divided, depending on whether a particular author's script is formal, semi-formal, semi-cursive, or cursive.[10]

The perimeters set by carbon dating and palaeography were confirmed by archaeology, for artifactual links between Caves 1–11 and Khirbet Qumran encouraged five seasons of excavation, headed by

Roland de Vaux, at the ruined site between 1951 and 1956. In addition, archaeological work was undertaken at the nearby settlement of 'Ein-Feshkha in 1958. Despite gaps in the evidence, as well as re-assessment of de Vaux's efforts in recent years, these locations yielded clear general results.[11]

De Vaux showed that Khirbet Qumran had been settled during ancient Israelite times but was destroyed towards the end of the seventh century BCE. It was then reoccupied, along with 'Ein-Feshkha, by a Jewish religious group during the second half of the Second Temple period, before being overtaken by Roman soldiers for several years from 68 CE. Moreover, detailed examination of what archaeologists call the material culture – building and cemetery remains, pottery and coins – allowed this Second Temple phase of habitation to be further subdivided. We shall consider this in relation to Qumran, before turning briefly to Feshkha.

In what was labelled Period Ia, the initial resettlement at Khirbet Qumran occurred in the second half of the second century BCE, when buildings were restored and new rooms added. According to de Vaux, this reoccupation probably took place in the reign of the Hasmonean ruler John Hyrcanus (134–104 BCE) but might have been earlier under Simon Maccabee's rule (143–134 BCE) or even that of Jonathan Maccabee (152–143 BCE).[12] During Period Ib which followed, the site was expanded to include a tower, dining facilities, an assembly room, and a complex water system. These features suggest that Qumran provided communal facilities for up to two hundred people, though surrounding caves and tents served as living quarters and limited excavations at the adjacent cemetery show it is likely most of the inhabitants were male. On the basis of coins found in the relevant layer of the ruins, Period Ib stretched from *circa* 100 BCE until the reign of Herod the Great (37–4 BCE). De Vaux surmised that the buildings were then abandoned for a generation after an earthquake, the resultant fire causing considerable destruction. Certainly, Josephus tells us that a tremour struck Judaea in 31 BCE, and its impact explains well the structural damage still evident at Qumran.[13] In any case, other coin finds were taken to show that Period II began from the start of the first century CE. Associated with it are the famous table and inkwells de Vaux reckoned to be part of a 'scriptorium' – a room for copying or composing manuscripts.[14]

Period III commenced with the arrival of Roman forces in the vicinity. It is known from elsewhere that the Tenth Legion captured Jericho in 68 CE and, in light of Roman coins left behind, Qumran was doubtless overrun too in the military campaign to quash the First Revolt. As for the Romans, they remained for several years whilst crushing pockets of resistance that persisted in the desert, most notably that at Masada which held out until 73 CE.

Turning to 'Ein-Feshkha, the archaeological work of de Vaux and others suggests it was occupied from *circa* 100 BCE to 68 CE, correlating to Periods Ib and II at Qumran. Pottery and coin finds, more particularly, strongly suggest that Feshkha was utilized by the same group inhabiting Khirbet Qumran.[15] The former was a satellite of the latter, in other words, supplying some of its agricultural and industrial needs. Indeed, Feshkha's natural springs would have supported limited crops and livestock, while what remain of its installations witness some kind of manufacturing activity, although exactly what is unclear.[16]

The main contours of de Vaux's archaeological reconstruction of the Second Temple settlements at Khirbet Qumran and 'Ein-Feshkha still hold good. However, several aspects require amendment in light of recent re-evaluation.[17] Two such alterations are worth mentioning. First, de Vaux's date for the start of Period Ia may be too early, for the oldest Maccabean–Hasmonean coins retrieved from the site, belonging to the reign of John Hyrcanus (134–104 BCE), are few in number and demonstrate merely that it was occupied some time after their minting. Second, it is not clear that Khirbet Qumran was abandoned in the aftermath of the 31 BCE earthquake. It is just as likely that repairs were carried out immediately and life carried on as before. On the other hand, a hoard of silver coins, all minted before 8 BCE and never retrieved by those who hid them, suggests a crisis hit the area some two decades later. Although certainty is impossible, therefore, Khirbet Qumran may have come under attack during the disturbances which Josephus tells us took place in the wake of Herod the Great's death in 4 BCE.[18]

Despite such uncertainties, the degree of correlation between the three separate means of inquiry just described – carbon dating, palaeography, archaeology – is remarkable. It shows that Khirbet Qumran was occupied from towards the end of the second century BCE until 68 CE, while its satellite centre at 'Ein-Feshkha was utilized from *circa* 100 BCE to 68 CE. That some biblical, apocryphal, and pseudepigraphal manuscripts from Caves 1–11 are more ancient can easily be explained by the likelihood that those who first settled Khirbet Qumran brought with them scriptural documents already in their possession.

The cumulative force of all this evidence is bolstered by a final feature, for a few Qumran DSS in our second and third categories actually name historical personages. Some instances have been in the public domain for decades. Thus, 4QpNahum 1:1–3 refers to two Greek kings of Syria who are almost certainly Demetrius III Eukairos (94–88 BCE) and Antiochus IV Epiphanes (174–164 BCE):[19]

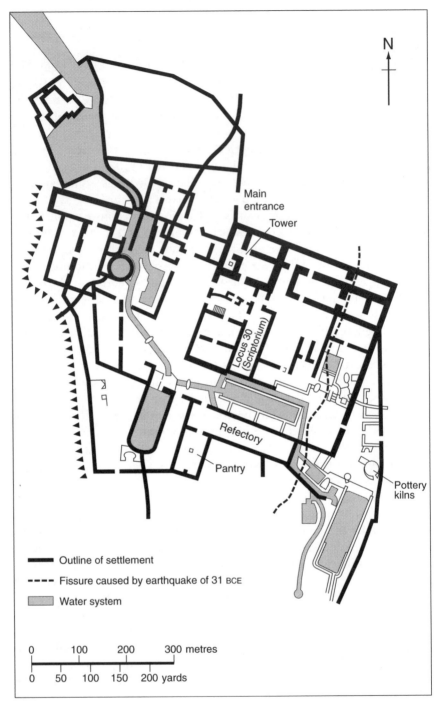

N

Main
entrance

Tower

Locus 30
(Scriptorium)

Refectory

Pantry

Pottery
kilns

Outline of settlement

Fissure caused by earthquake of 31 BCE

Water system

0   100   200   300 metres

0   50   100   150   200 yards

Figure 1   *Plan of Khirbet Qumran*

Whither the lion goes, there is the lion's cub, [with none to disturb it] (ii, 11b).

[Interpreted, this concerns Deme]trius king of Greece who sought, on the counsel of those who seek smooth things, to enter Jerusalem. [But God did not permit the city to be delivered] into the hands of the kings of Greece, from the time of Antiochus until the coming of the rulers of the Kittim.

Other documents mentioning late Second Temple individuals have become available more recently. Hence, the badly damaged 4QCalendrical Document C, released in 1991, refers to 'Salome' and 'Aemilius'. The former is the Jewish queen who ruled Judaea between 76 and 67 BCE, and the latter, known more fully as Aemilius Scaurus, was Syria's first Roman governor between 65 and 62 BCE.

Combined with the results of carbon dating, palaeography, and archaeology, these references leave no doubt that the context for understanding the Qumran DSS is that of the last two or three hundred years of the Second Temple period. Accordingly, let us now turn to these centuries in more detail, so that we can then proceed to the identity of the religious group behind the Qumran DSS.

Understanding the Second Temple Period

The Second Temple period covers roughly six centuries of Jewish history from the return of the Babylonian exiles in the 500s BCE to the destruction of the Jerusalem Temple in 70 CE. Aside from the Qumran DSS, a variety of literary sources allows us to reconstruct the period's history in broad outline: late biblical books, the Apocrypha and Pseudepigrapha, the New Testament, and the works of two first-century CE Jewish writers, Philo and Josephus, who are counted among the classical authors of the ancient world. We shall say a little more about some of this literature, all of it available before the Qumran DSS were discovered, in Chapter 5.

For now, it is worth noting that most of the material relates only to the last three hundred years of Second Temple times. Because the vast majority of DSS from Khirbet Qumran similarly slot neatly between *circa* 250 BCE and 70 CE, it makes sense for us to concentrate on the second half of the Second Temple period in the following synopsis.[20] Of all the relevant literature, Daniel, 1–2 Maccabees, and the writings of Josephus are most useful in gaining a historical overview, while other compositions provide important supplementary insights.

As remarked in Chapter 1, the conquest of Judaea by Alexander the Great had long-lasting repercussions for the Jews and Judaism.[21] After his death in 323 BCE, two opposing kingdoms emerged out of his vast empire in the geographical region of greatest interest to us: the Ptolemaic kingdom in Egypt, and the Seleucid kingdom, including what is now Lebanon and Syria.[22] The small province of Judaea continued under Egyptian control for most of the third century BCE, but the Seleucids wrested it from the Ptolemies in 200 BCE. The sensibilities of both governments, as well as of Alexander the Great before them, can be described as Greek or 'Hellenistic'. Put another way, they were much influenced by Hellenism – an appropriation of the language, customs, and ideas of ancient Greece, adapted somewhat for the later times in which they themselves lived. By the second century, accordingly, a number of Greek cities or *poleis* (singular, *polis*) had been established on the Mediterranean coast (Gaza, Ascalon, Joppa, Dor, and Ptolemais) and inland (Philadelphia, Scythopolis, and Samaria). The inhabitants of these largely independent city-states, headed by a legislative council, were left to organize themselves according to a semi-democratic structure. They were also encouraged to adopt Greek language and social customs – and to make room for Greek deities in their religious systems.

Such developments inevitably had a slow Hellenizing impact on the nearby indigenous people, including those living in Judaea. As long as this influence was confined to matters of language and commerce, it was unproblematic. But religious and philosophical issues were more controversial and, from around 200 BCE, serious divisions over how to respond to these aspects of Greek culture emerged among Jews.[23] In Ben Sira 41:8, for instance, the early second-century author complains that some of his fellow Jews had 'forsaken the law of the Most High God'. A similar concern in the book of Jubilees, written soon afterwards, is evident in its exhortations to keep the Sabbath and observe the rite of circumcision, implying that some were neglecting these traditions.[24]

Tensions came to a head during the reign of the Seleucid monarch Antiochus IV Epiphanes (175–164 BCE). Short of funds in the imperial treasury, he accepted a bribe in 175 BCE from a certain Jesus, whose brother was High Priest in Jerusalem. In return, this Jesus, who preferred the Greek name Jason, was given the High Priesthood in place of his brother. Jason then set about turning Jerusalem into a *polis*, establishing institutions for inculcating Jewish youth with Greek intellectual and sporting ideals. Many were offended by these developments, as 1 Maccabees 1:11–15 makes clear:

[11]In those days certain renegades came out from Israel and misled many, saying, 'Let us go and make a covenant with the Gentiles around us, for

since we separated from them many disasters have come upon us.' [12]This proposal pleased them, [13]and some of the people eagerly went to the king, who authorized them to observe the ordinances of the Gentiles. [14]So they built a gymnasium in Jerusalem, according to Gentile custom, [15]and removed the marks of circumcision, and abandoned the holy covenant. They joined with the Gentiles and sold themselves to do evil.

This passage shows there was a strong Hellenizing faction within Jerusalem in the early to mid-second century BCE. In the eyes of traditionalists, however, its desire to absorb Hellenistic values and customs was a threat to Judaism's distinctiveness. Nevertheless, the High Priest's position was purchased again in 172 BCE by another Greek enthusiast called Menelaus. And the changes introduced included nude participation in athletics – thereby flouting the biblical taboo against nakedness and causing some Jewish embarrassment over circumcision, viewed by Greeks as a crude practice.

Then, events took a turn for the worse. Not only did Antiochus IV Epiphanes raid the Jerusalem Temple's funds, but in 167 BCE he set about eradicating Judaism altogether. Such religious persecution was unheard of in the ancient world and scholars disagree as to its causes and precise nature. Our best guess is that Antiochus IV was quashing rival supporters of Jason and Menelaus, rather than opposing Judaism itself; he may also have felt the need to reassert his authority after a recent military withdrawal from Egypt forced on him by the Romans.[25] In any case, Antiochus banned Jewish customs on pain of death. Worse still, pagan sacrifice was introduced into the Temple, which was rededicated to the Greek god Olympian Zeus. This sacrilege probably lies behind the reference to the 'abomination that makes desolate' in Daniel 11:31. Under these difficult circumstances, many Jews simply acquiesced (1 Maccabees 2:23), while others hoped for divine intervention (Daniel 7–12). Yet others embarked on a course of violent resistance to Antiochus IV's measures. They were led by a priest from Modein called Mattathias and his five sons – most notably Judah (or Judas), Jonathan, and Simon. Judah gained the nickname 'Maccabee', of uncertain meaning, and so the brothers are often referred to collectively as 'the Maccabees'.

These Maccabees, aided by the obscure Hasideans or 'pious ones' mentioned in 1 Maccabees 2:42, slowly undermined the Seleucid army through guerrilla warfare. As the Seleucids sent reinforcements, their armies were outwitted, ambushed, and defeated by Maccabean supporters, who were then able to confiscate their opponents' weaponry. In 164 BCE, Judah Maccabee succeeded in his main aim of restoring proper

Jewish worship to the Jerusalem Temple.[26] Then, with the accession of
Antiochus V Eupator to the Seleucid throne, the oppressive measures of
his predecessor were rescinded and, as life returned to normal, the
impetus behind the Maccabean campaign faded. A peace deal was struck
between Antiochus V and Judaea's Jews, marginalizing the Maccabees,
who withdrew to the small town of Michmash.

Some years later, however, two rival claimants to the Seleucid throne
tried to court Maccabean military support. Jonathan Maccabee eventually
threw his lot in with Demetrius I Soter in return for the High Priesthood. His appointment in 152 BCE must have earned him many enemies,
for neither Jonathan nor his brothers belonged to the priestly family
descended from Zadok – prominent in the days of King David and King
Solomon – which held the exclusive right to supply High Priests. But
since no one was powerful enough to challenge him, Jonathan's rule
continued until he was captured through trickery by a foreign general
and executed in 143 BCE. Thereupon, his brother, Simon, took over and,
with the weakening of the Seleucid empire, he all but declared the small
province of Judaea an independent state in 142 BCE, expelling in the
process the garrison of Seleucid troops which had remained in Jerusalem
until then. Against this background, 1 Maccabees 14:4,12 glorifies
Simon's achievements:

> [4]The land had rest all the days of Simon.
>> He sought the good of his nation;
> his rule was pleasing to them,
>> as was the honour shown him, all his days . . .
> [12]All the people sat under their own vines and fig trees,
>> and there was none to make them afraid.

Writing propaganda for the Maccabees' successors in around 100 BCE,
the author deliberately echoes the glorious days of King Solomon in his
final sentence.[27]

Simon was succeeded by his son and subsequent offspring. Like
Jonathan and Simon Maccabee, they combined the role of High Priest
with that of secular ruler; they are collectively known as the Hasmo-
neans.[28] The first three Hasmoneans were skillful in military matters:
John Hyrcanus I (134–104 BCE), Aristobulus I (104–103 BCE), and
Alexander Jannaeus (103–76 BCE). Between them, they added to the
Jewish state Samaria, Idumaea, Peraea, Galilee, the *poleis* on the Mediter-
ranean coast, as well as territory to the north-east of the Sea of Galilee.[29]
As part of the process, some of the non-Jewish population was expelled
or converted. So thorough was this policy that the Idumaeans, converted

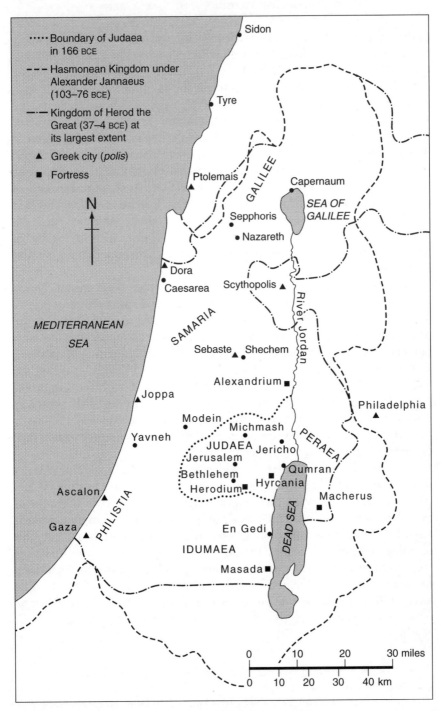

Legend:

····· Boundary of Judaea in 166 BCE

--- Hasmonean Kingdom under Alexander Jannaeus (103–76 BCE)

—·— Kingdom of Herod the Great (37–4 BCE) at its largest extent

▲ Greek city (*polis*)

■ Fortress

N

Sidon

Tyre

Ptolemais ▲

GALILEE

Capernaum

SEA OF GALILEE

Sepphoris

Nazareth

Dora ▲

Caesarea

Scythopolis ▲

River Jordan

MEDITERRANEAN SEA

SAMARIA

Sebaste ▲ Shechem

Alexandrium ■

Joppa ▲

Philadelphia ▲

Modein

Michmash

PERAEA

Yavneh

JUDAEA Jericho

Jerusalem

Bethlehem

Qumran

Herodium ■ Hyrcania ■

Macherus ■

Ascalon ▲

PHILISTIA

En Gedi

DEAD SEA

Gaza ▲

IDUMAEA

Masada ■

0   10   20   30 miles

0   10   20   30   40 km

Map 4   *The Hasmonean and Herodian Kingdoms*

under Hyrcanus I, and the non-Jewish inhabitants of Galilee, forcibly circumcised by Aristobulus I, remained Jewish even after the Hasmonean state fell to Rome in 63 BCE.[30]

Such religious zeal helped consolidate the Hasmonean kingdom. And, in contrast to Antiochus IV Epiphanes' efforts to eradicate Judaism, the Hasmoneans managed to forge a workable Jewish–Greek synthesis. Many practical aspects of public and private life under the Hasmonean dynasty were influenced by Hellenism, therefore. Coins, for example, show the traditional Hebrew name of the High Priest on one side, while the reverse bears his Greek secular title. Again, the remains of the recently excavated Hasmonean palace at Jericho combine the best of Hellenistic artistry with the provision of ritual baths, so that the High Priest could maintain ritual purity in line with the Law of Moses.[31] Among the wider populace, burial customs exhibit a similar fusion of cultures.[32]

However, it should not be supposed that everyone was content. Nor is it coincidental that Josephus first mentions three distinct religious parties – the Sadducees, Pharisees, and Essenes – in his accounts of the Maccabees and Hasmoneans. Indeed, while the Sadducees seem to have been largely supportive of the Hasmonean dynasty, Jonathan Maccabee's scandalous assumption of the High Priesthood in 152 BCE – ousting the 'sons of Zadok' in the process – has often been thought an important factor leading to the formation of the Essenes, as we shall presently discover. The position of the Pharisees on specific issues is less easily determined, but Josephus informs us that ordinary people often supported their interpretation of Jewish law.[33]

Josephus also tells us that the wider populace was capable of making its feelings known in a more dramatic fashion from time to time. When Alexander Jannaeus was officiating as High Priest one year at the Feast of Tabernacles, for example, crowds of pilgrims in the Temple gave vent to their disaffection by pelting him with ceremonial fruit![34] As his standing plummeted further among the common people, the Pharisees were implicated in a plot to unseat him by calling on the Seleucid king mentioned earlier, Demetrius III Eukairos, in *circa* 88 BCE. The attempted coup failed, and Jannaeus had eight hundred of his Pharisaic opponents crucified.[35] This cruel act is alluded to in 4QpNahum 1:6–7, as follows:

> *[And chokes prey for its lionesses; and it fills] its caves [with prey] and its dens with victims* (ii, 12a–b).
> Interpreted, this concerns the furious young lion [who executes revenge] on those who seek smooth things and hangs men alive . . .

In this passage, which, as seen in the last section, is preceded by mention of '[Deme]trius king of Greece', the 'furious young lion' is certainly Jannaeus. Because we know from Josephus that his victims were linked to the Pharisees, 'those who seek smooth things' must describe Pharisaic opponents thought to engage in lax or 'smooth' interpretations of the Law. 4QpNahum 2:2 also goes on to dub the Pharisees 'Ephraim', while the corresponding term of abuse, 'Manasseh', seems to be a nickname for the Sadducees.[36]

After Jannaeus' death in 76 BCE, his wife, Salome Alexandra, became queen; the High Priesthood, open only to males, went to their son Hyrcanus II. On the advice of her late husband, Salome allied herself with the Pharisees, and we are encouraged by much later sources to view her reign as a golden age.[37] Whether that was true or not, things certainly deteriorated with her death in 67 BCE. Aristobulus II, younger brother of Hyrcanus II, seized the High Priesthood and set himself up as king. Naturally, this was not to the liking of Hyrcanus II, and the two rivals became locked in confrontation. To break the stalemate, both sides petitioned Rome for help, aware that the powerful general Pompey was in the region. Their competing requests enabled this Roman military leader to take control of Jerusalem in 63 BCE, thereby rendering the Jewish state a political puppet of Rome up to the end of the Second Temple period and beyond. After the removal from Jewish jurisdiction of the Greek cities on the Mediterranean coast, Aristobulus II was deposed and Hyrcanus II left in charge.

Some time later, one of Hyrcanus II's advisers, an Idumaean convert called Antipater, was made overseer of Judaea. Thanks to his influence within the weak Hyrcanus II's court, his sons Phasael and Herod also achieved prominent administrative positions.[38] Even after Antipater's assassination in 42 BCE, Phasael and Herod seemed destined for success, despite opposition among Jerusalem's aristocracy, because of their late father's good relations with Rome. But then, with the sudden invasion of Judaea from the east by the Parthians in 40 BCE, the situation changed dramatically. The Parthians, Rome's main rival in the region, set up Antigonus, son of Aristobulus II, as High Priest and king in Jerusalem. Herod fled to Rome, where he was declared King of Judaea by the Senate.[39] Returning with an army, he recaptured Jerusalem from the Parthians in 37 BCE and thereby brought Hasmonean rule to an end. With Roman backing, he subsequently reigned for more than thirty years over a territory similar in size to the Hasmonean kingdom at its greatest.

Usually, of course, the latter figure is referred to as Herod the Great.[40] His rule was a mixture of opposites, coupling prosperity and an extensive building programme with domestic strife and political intrigue. To offset his image as the son of a converted Idumaean and therefore a kind of impostor, Herod presented himself within Judaea as a pious adherent of Jewish practice and belief. Most notably, he embarked on a massive expansion of the Jerusalem Temple to court the favour of the Jews. But he lavished substantial sums on pagan temples and other Hellenistic institutions in towns which were predominantly non-Jewish in order to win Gentile loyalty. He spent a vast amount constructing the city port of Caesarea, for example, as a tribute to Emperor Augustus Caesar. To guard against insurrection, he also strengthened or built from scratch various impressive fortresses – such as those at Masada, Herodium, Alexandrium, Hyrcania, and Macherus. Indeed, as Herod became increasingly paranoid about plots against him towards the end of his reign, he ordered the execution or assassination of many of his own family, including his sons and one of his wives.

After his own death in 4 BCE, Herod's kingdom was divided among his three remaining sons.[41] Herod Antipas took control of Galilee and Peraea, while Philip ruled the territory to the north-east of the Sea of Galilee; Judaea and Samaria were given to Herod Archelaus. Due to incompetence, however, Archelaus was relieved of his post by the Romans in 6 CE. His inheritance was turned into a Roman province under the rule of a series of prefects – the most famous being Pontius Pilate who was in office when Jesus was executed.[42] Between 41 and 44 CE, Herod the Great's grandson, Agrippa I, was appointed king over all of what had been his grandfather's territory. But after his untimely death, the whole region came under direct Roman rule, this time under officials called procurators.

In large measure, the ignoble behaviour of the procurators paved the way for the First Revolt of the Jews against Rome. More particularly, it began in 66 CE when Procurator Gessius Florus (64–66 CE) took money from the Temple for alleged unpaid taxes. This sort of incident had happened before, of course, but sensitivities were high after a recent dispute between Caesarea's Jewish and Greek inhabitants in which the procurator had sided with the majority non-Jewish population. When, therefore, following his raid on the Temple, some among the Jerusalem crowds mockingly made a collection for 'poor' Florus, only to be butchered in the streets by his soldiers, Jewish anger boiled over, plunging the country into rebellion. Despite initial success, Roman military might quashed the Revolt, helped by internal divisions on the Jewish side. Jerusalem and its Temple were destroyed, bringing the Second Temple period to a close in 70 CE. Whilst some one thousand rebels held out in the desert fortress of Masada, they committed mass suicide in 73 CE rather than admit defeat.[43]

The subjugation of the rebels in 70 CE, coupled with the failure of a Second Revolt against Rome in 135 CE, precipitated one of Judaism's most important turning points. With the loss of the Temple and priesthood, Jewish religion slowly turned its attention almost exclusively on the Torah. Thus was born what historians call Rabbinic Judaism, finding classic expression in the Mishnah (*circa* 200 CE) and, eventually, in the Babylonian Talmud (*circa* 550 CE), although other forms of Judaism doubtless persisted into the third century CE and beyond. Rabbinic Judaism itself underwent further elaboration in medieval times by famous rabbis like Rashi and Maimonides. We shall have an opportunity to return to the Rabbinic period briefly in Chapter 5.

The Essenes and the Qumran Scrolls

The history of the late Second Temple period, as just outlined, supplies the framework necessary for making sense of the Qumran DSS, given their likely dates of origin on the basis of carbon dating, palaeography, and archaeology. More concretely, while most of the writings in our first category (biblical, apocryphal, and pseudepigraphal works) and second category (previously unknown yet non-sectarian compositions) defined in Chapter 1 will have been in widespread use, the third class of sectarian texts will presumably have been the preserve of a particular segment of the Jewish population in Palestine during the centuries concerned.[44] The latter is often referred to by scholars as the 'Qumran Community' or 'Qumran Sect', even though its earliest history may have been centred elsewhere and although, in any case, the movement of which it was a part almost certainly existed in other places too.

At first sight, various groups and individuals suggest themselves as having potential links with the Qumran DSS, including well-known religious parties like the Pharisees, Sadducees, and Essenes, as well as prominent individuals among the Maccabean, Hasmonean, and Herodian dynasties. Indeed, scholarly attempts to equate the Qumran Community with various Second Temple movements have abounded over the past fifty years. Most have concluded that the group is to be linked with the Essenes described by several ancient authors whose writings were available before 1947. In what follows, therefore, we shall outline in brief these previously-known sources so that, when we view their obvious parallels with the sectarian manuscripts, we will be able to see why the majority of scholars have opted for an Essene connection.

Prior to the discovery of the Qumran DSS, historians drew most of their information on the Essenes from Philo and Josephus, whom we mentioned earlier.[45] Josephus also furnishes us with details of other Second Temple groupings, especially the Pharisees and Sadducees. In one passage, he makes a rare general characterization of what he deems the three major religious parties:[46]

> As for the Pharisees, they say that certain events are the work of Fate, but not all ... The sect of the Essenes, however, declares that Fate is mistress of all things, and that nothing befalls men unless it be in accordance with her decree. But the Sadducees do away with Fate, holding ... that all things lie within our own power ...

Notwithstanding the language of Fate, well-suited to his Graeco-Roman readers, there is no reason to doubt Josephus' basic point here: the Essenes believed everything to be foreordained by God, the Sadducees held the opposite view, and the Pharisees took up a midway position. Other Essene traits mentioned by the Classical Sources include an interest in angels, an emphasis on 'holy books', a concern for secrecy, and belief in an immortal soul.[47] Chronologically, moreover, Josephus places the Essenes – including several named individuals – between the mid-second century BCE and the first century CE.[48]

Turning to specific details, a combination of Philo and Josephus' evidence on the Essenes provides us with a range of defining characteristics which can be summarized under eight headings:[49] (1) the name 'Essene' itself; (2) the location of the Essenes; (3) their entry procedures; (4) community organization; (5) common property; (6) celibacy and marriage; (7) the daily work of the Essenes; and (8) their ritual practices. We shall consider each in turn:

(1) Certainty on the meaning of the title 'Essene' (Greek, *essenos* and *essaios*) is impossible, but it is worth noting that Philo links it with the Greek for 'pious' (*hosios*). Although a Semitic origin is more likely, Philo might inadvertently point in the right direction, for 'Essene' may relate to the Aramaic *hassaya*, equivalent to Hebrew *hasidim*, meaning 'pious ones'.[50] Less likely, since healing plays only a minor part in the Classical Sources' descriptions, it could derive from the Aramaic *'assaya*, 'healers'.[51] A more hopeful alternative is to link 'Essene' with the Hebrew *'osim*, 'doers', as in the phrase 'doers of the Law' in 1QpHabakkuk 7:11.[52]

(2) The location of the Essenes is an important factor, for both Philo and Josephus state that over 4,000 lived in numerous Palestinian cities. Although Philo elsewhere presents a variation on this by claiming they favoured smaller towns, the basic picture is clear: groups of Essenes were located in different places throughout Judaea.

(3) Josephus describes in some detail the movement's three-year

admission process. During the initial phase, a prospective member was to adopt Essene practices yet remain outside the group at large; in the second and third years, the candidate partook of its ritual baths but could not attend common meals. Finally, at the end of three years, full membership was acquired upon swearing 'awesome oaths'.[53]

(4) Turning to internal organization, the Essenes formed a strictly hierarchical body, according to Josephus. Disobedience towards superiors, as well as breaches of community rules, was handled by a hundred-strong court, with expulsion as punishment for the most serious offenses. In this regard, for instance, both classical authors indicate that the Essenes kept the Sabbath strictly, whilst, rather more idiosyncratically, Josephus tells us of an unusual taboo in that they were 'careful not to spit into the midst of the company or to the right'.[54]

(5) The Classical Sources testify that the Essenes organized themselves along communitarian lines, pooling resources of food and clothing. Thus, Josephus describes how a new member's goods were absorbed into a common fund:[55]

> Riches they despise, and their community of goods is truly admirable . . . They have a law that new members on admission to the sect shall confiscate their property to the order . . .

(6) Both authors similarly concur that the Essenes comprised celibate males, although Josephus adds that one branch of the movement did marry.[56] Those who remained unattached, we are further told, adopted children and trained them in the Essene way of life.[57]

(7) As for work, Philo and Josephus inform us that the Essenes engaged in agriculture and crafts, with their daily routine punctuated by regular prayer, shared meals, and purification rites.

(8) Lastly, indeed, both writers stress the group's emphasis on ritual purity, as explained by Josephus in relation to communal food:[58]

> . . . they . . . bathe their bodies in cold water. After this purification, they assemble in a private apartment which none of the uninitiated is permitted to enter; pure now themselves, they repair to the refectory, as to some sacred shrine . . . Before meat the priest says a grace, and none may partake until after the prayer.

As this excerpt shows, the Essenes offered prayers before and after meals, while observing in a distinctive manner the purity rules common to all Jews. Here, it is also appropriate to mention their peculiar toilet practices, for Josephus tells us that Essenes would retire to an isolated place to relieve themselves, digging a hole in the ground with a special hatchet.[59]

Before considering the relationship of the accounts in Philo and Josephus to the Qumran DSS, we have to mention a third Classical Source available before 1947 from a non-Jew, the Roman geographer Pliny the Elder (23–79 CE). Although presented in idealized terms for his Latin readers, his short notice from the *Natural History* is worth citing:[60]

> On the west side of the Dead Sea . . . is the solitary tribe of the Essenes, which is remarkable beyond all the other tribes in the whole world, as it has no women and has renounced all sexual desire, has no money, and has only palm trees for company. Day by day the throng of refugees is recruited to an equal number by numerous accessions of persons tired of life and driven thither by the waves of fortune to adopt their manners. Thus through thousands of ages . . . a race in which no one is born lives on for ever: so prolific for their advantage is other men's weariness of life!
>
> Lying below the Essenes was formerly the town of Engedi, second only to Jerusalem in the fertility of its land and in its groves of palm-trees, but now like Jerusalem a heap of ashes. Next comes Masada, a fortress on a rock, itself also not far from the Dead Sea.

Not only does this passage echo the celibacy and communitarianism described by Philo and Josephus, but it also directs us to an Essene (Latin, *essenos*) settlement on the western shore of the Dead Sea near 'Ein-Gedi. This location, most have concluded, must surely be Khirbet Qumran.[61]

Indeed, the sectarian DSS from the caves surrounding Qumran reflect a group remarkably close to Philo and Josephus' Essenes. Even though, as we shall see presently, the 1980s saw radical reformulations of this Qumran-Essene link, and while the release of fresh texts in 1991 has complicated matters in other respects, the parallels noted by scholars in the 1950s and 1960s remain overwhelming. Certainly, by the 1970s, the majority of experts had concluded that the Essenes of the Classical Sources and the Qumran Sect were to be more or less equated, for general similarities and detailed overlaps pointed clearly in that direction.

Thus, parallel to Josephus' description cited above, a belief in the predetermined nature of all things comes across from a range of sectarian DSS. lQS 3:15–16 provides a good example:[62]

> From the God of knowledge comes all that is and shall be. Before ever they existed He established their whole design, and when, as ordained for them, they come into being, it is in accord with His glorious design that they accomplish their task without change.

Similarly, a general focus on angelic beings is present in a variety of documents (e.g. 1QS 3:20; 1QH^a 11:22–23; 1QM 1:16), whilst the very existence of the Qumran collection testifies to an interest in books, the true significance of which was to be kept secret from outsiders (e.g. 1QS 5:11; 1QpHabakkuk 7:4–5). Furthermore, belief in 'everlasting life' is a feature of the non-biblical DSS (e.g. 1QS 4:6–8; 1QH^a 9:19–23), even though it remains unclear whether the soul's immortality, bodily resurrection, or some combination of both, was envisaged.[63] At a general level, then, it is clear that the Qumran Sect shared various features with the Essenes of the Classical Sources. The chronological framework provided by archaeology, carbon dating, and palaeography, moreover, roughly matches that within which Josephus places the Essenes in his accounts of Second Temple history in Palestine.

Beyond such generalities, a series of more direct overlaps can be seen. To illustrate, we shall draw on the eight headings listed earlier:

(1) The title 'Essene', however, is problematic, inasmuch as it occurs nowhere among the Qumran DSS. The simplest explanation is probably that the word was coined by outsiders as a nickname, as may have happened to 'Pharisees' and 'Christians' too.[64] If so, although the appellation remained in use by non-Essenes until Josephus' day, the Essenes themselves preferred other epithets – such as 'doers of the law', 'house of Judah', 'men of the law', 'sons of light' – prominent in various sectarian texts. In fact, we saw above that one possibility is that the name Essene itself derives from 'doers' (Hebrew, *'osim*) in the first of these self-designations.[65]

(2) The question of location is more straightforward, for the geographical position of Khirbet Qumran, on the one hand, and Pliny's description of an Essene settlement near 'Ein-Gedi, on the other, is unlikely to be coincidental. Presumably, Qumran was one of the more important Essene settlements scattered throughout Judaea according to Philo and Josephus. It may possibly also have been the movement's headquarters, at least for some of its history.

(3) The procedures in 1QS 6:13–23 for new entrants are remarkably close to what is found in the Classical Sources. Thus, we read of the swearing of an oath and an initial phase outside the group, followed by two years further initiation inside, with limited access to food and drink prior to full membership.

(4) The community's organization recommended in works like 1QS and CD reflects a hierarchical grouping with an emphasis on obedience, as well as on punishment – or even expulsion – for breaches of conduct. Indeed, paralleling the Classical Sources, a strict observance of the Sabbath comes across, while a further example brings us back to Jose-

Plate 3   *Inside the 'Scrollery' in the Palestine Archaeology Museum.* © *Estate of John M. Allegro, courtesy of The Allegro Archive (The University of Manchester)*

phus' mention of the sect's rule against spitting. The same prohibition is found in 1QS 7:13, and its appearance in a sectarian Qumran work seems too specific – not to say odd! – to be coincidental.

(5) 1QS envisages a common pool of resources, with the transfer of a new member's property to the community and its subsequent absorption upon full membership.[66] For this and other features of the Qumran Community, 1QS 6:18–2:3 is illuminating:

> And if it be his destiny, according to the judgement of the Priests and the multitude of the men of their Covenant, to enter the company of the Community, his property and earnings shall be handed over to the Bursar of the Congregation who shall register it to his account and shall not

spend it for the Congregation ... But when the second year has passed, he shall be examined, and if it be his destiny, according to the judgement of the Congregation, to enter the Community, then he shall be inscribed among his brethren in the order of his rank for the Law, and for justice, and for the pure Meal; his property shall be merged and he shall offer his counsel and judgement to the Community.

This excerpt stresses the centrality of the group's hierarchy, according to which each member was graded every year in line with his spiritual standing; the priests and, as we learn elsewhere, the sons of Zadok seem to have held an elevated position within this hierarchical structure, at least during some phases of the community's history. And, of course, the passage expresses the group's commitment to communal ownership and a common pure meal, both of which are described in the Classical Sources.

(6) Another characteristic of 1QS is the apparent celibacy of the community it envisages, for this central work contains no mention of women. Such a feature seems to parallel the statements of Philo, Josephus, and Pliny on the Essenes' unmarried status. Moreover, that CD 7:6–9 speaks of those who do take wives and have children, together with the fact that the Qumran cemetery probably contained a few female skeletons, is reminiscent of Josephus' additional statement that some Essenes did marry.

(7) Regarding work, archaeology at Khirbet Qumran and 'Ein-Fesh-kha has shown that a subsistence lifestyle – producing crops, livestock, and pottery – was adopted by those utilizing these sites, once more matching the Classical Sources' picture.

(8) As for ritual practice, archaeological excavations also revealed a complex network of channels and cisterns at Qumran.[67] Some were doubtless employed for regular water storage, but steps down into and up from the water make it clear that others were built for the full immersion of ritual purification. In this context, we should lastly mention the fragmentary 4QLegal Text C which, released in 1991, may reflect the distinctive Essene toilet practices described by Josephus.[68]

All in all, these parallels are ample demonstration of clear overlaps between the Qumran Community and the Essenes of Philo, Josephus, and Pliny. As well as general connections, we have observed many detailed parallels between the Classical Sources and 1QS in particular. Since 1QS, in turn, is close in vocabulary and ideology to other Qumran documents, especially CD, most scholars by the 1970s concluded that the contents of Caves 1–11 represented an Essene library. This has remained the dominant view, notwithstanding the fact that the 1980s saw several new challenges to it, while important new Cave 4 texts were released in 1991. Although we shall return to these two complicating factors, an Essene origin for the Qumran DSS remains a thesis which, for the reasons already outlined, still holds sway.

However, various contradictions also exist. Some of these can be found within the manuscripts themselves, others in the classical accounts, while the two bodies of literature together exhibit further contradictions. The first two types of discrepancy are not especially difficult and can be explained by two factors: development of Essene belief and practice over time, on the one hand, and diversity within the group at any given point in time, on the other. Put another way, not only can we assume that the Essene movement evolved in organization and outlook during its exist-ence, both at Qumran and elsewhere, but different segments of its membership at any one time probably adopted somewhat variant relig-ious practices and theological emphases.

These considerations can explain the fact that, for example, both the Classical Sources and the sectarian DSS seem to assume the existence of both celibate and married members. They could also account for appar-ent discrepancies in the rules governing the community's life, such as that between a fully communal pooling of resources and the retention of some possessions by individuals.[69]

More problematic are outright contradictions. For instance, the Classi-cal Sources contain no mention of the calendrical and purity issues prominent in a variety of sectarian DSS, nor of individuals like the Teacher of Righteousness and Wicked Priest who will feature promi-nently in our discussion below. Again, while Philo states that the Essenes outlawed war and slavery, both appear in sectarian texts like 1QM, detailing the final battle between good and evil, and CD, including rules on keeping slaves.[70] Such contradictory information might suggest that the two bodies of literature are not describing the same or closely related groups after all.

Yet, that would not necessarily follow. Not only can the notion of development through time, as well as diversity at any given point in time, explain some of these discrepancies, but a third factor is relevant: the contrasting perspectives of the two sets of evidence. In other words, Philo and Josephus only had superficial knowledge of the Essenes, for, even if we accept Josephus' claim to have tried out the sect in his youth, neither he nor Philo was ever a fully-fledged member.[71] While the generality of their descriptions are reliable, the sectarian DSS are prob-ably more trustworthy when omissions or contradictions emerge. The absence of the Teacher of Righteousness and Wicked Priest from the Classical Sources, for example, is not so surprising when considered from this perspective. Similarly, 1QS's probationary period, where the oath is taken at the outset, is more likely to be accurate than Josephus' simpler divergent account, in which an oath is the culmination of the admission process.

A fourth and final factor explaining apparent contradictions is the intended audience. While most sectarian DSS were clearly directed at initiates, the writings of Philo, Josephus, and Pliny were aimed at a mixed Jewish–Gentile non-Essene audience. Understandably, the three classical authors tailor-made what they wrote for their readership. That much is evident when Josephus presents the Essenes as analogous to the Pythagoreans, just as the Pharisees are likened to the Stoics.[72] Both comparisons should, of course, be taken with a pinch of salt, and it may well be that the outright Essene rejection of war and slavery according to Philo constitutes a similar idealization. The ethos of the Qumran DSS themselves, in contrast, is more uncompromisingly Jewish. The documents also contain an exhortatory passion which, while lacking in the Classical Sources, is to be expected of a zealous religious community.

In sum, the evidence reviewed in this section has rendered overwhelming the case for identifying the group behind the Qumran DSS as some kind of Essene community. Over the past 50 years, the majority of experts have come to the same conclusion, albeit with disagreements as to how this Essene link is to be more closely defined. We shall investigate some of these differences presently, as well as issues raised by the fresh manuscript releases of 1991. Meanwhile, it is worth considering several alternative hypotheses put forward in the early years of DSS research, only to be rejected by most scholars.

What about Sadducees, Pharisees, Zealots?

It should be clear by now that a good case can be made for attributing an Essene identity to the community utilizing Khirbet Qumran. However this is to be further defined, the strength of the evidence adduced lies in its cumulative force. Nevertheless, during the 1950s and 1960s other identifications were proposed, based on apparent links between the Qumran DSS and what is known of the Sadducees, Pharisees, and 'Zealots'. We shall comment on these three alternative theories.[73]

First, let us consider the Sadducees. The only explicit information we possess about the Sadducees comes from three sources penned by non-Sadducees – the New Testament, Josephus, and Rabbinic literature written after 70 CE. Still, all three provide intermittent information which suggests that the Sadducees were closely connected to Jerusalem's leading aristocratic and priestly families in the last two hundred years of the Second Temple period. The name itself probably derives from Zadok (Hebrew, *Tsaddoq*), the priest from the days of King David and King Solomon whose line, as we have seen, was supposed to supply High Priests; the word is also similar to the Hebrew for 'righteous' (*tsaddiq*). In any case, the Sadducees were wealthy and influential and, understandably, their favour was courted by all Second Temple leaders of Judaea from the Hasmoneans to the Roman procurators.[74] Only Salome Alexandra, in the first half of the first century BCE, seems definitely to have allied herself with the Pharisees in view of their popularity.[75]

Even this briefest of outlines makes it clear that genuine links exist between the Sadducees and the Qumran Community. Most noticeable is the emphasis placed by both on the priesthood, especially the Zadokite line, for the 'sons of Zadok' are prominent in several Qumran writings. As we shall see in Chapter 7, there are also real parallels when it comes to interpretation of the Pentateuch's laws. But there the similarities end. The Sadducees come across as part of a rich ruling elite, centred on Jerusalem and its Temple, and relatively content with the status quo. As for the Qumran Sect, a tone of dissatisfaction permeates writings like 1QS, 1QpHabakkuk, and CD, as will be discovered in more detail in the next chapter. In contrast to the Sadducees, moreover, 11QT[a] and 1QM have an expectation that the present order, especially the Temple and its priesthood, will soon be swept away and replaced by a system in line with God's will.[76] More specifically still, other compositions betray a belief in angels (Songs of the Sabbath Sacrifice) and an afterlife (1QS, 1QH[a]). Since Josephus informs us that the Sadducees rejected both, any attempt to identify the Qumran Community as straightforwardly Sadducean must fail.[77]

Might it be possible to argue instead that the Pharisees lie behind the Qumran manuscripts? To piece together a picture of the Pharisees, we are again dependent on the New Testament, Josephus, and Rabbinic literature after 70 CE.[78] Each of these is problematic in one way or another, and so the origins and nature of the Pharisees are hotly debated. Nevertheless, it seems safe to say that the Pharisees were predominantly lay Jews who, in varying degrees, sought to organize their lives as though they were priests subject to Temple purity rules.[79] Consequently, they were fastidious when it came to applying the Torah's commands about diet and purity; this, in turn, resulted both in their reputation as experts in scriptural interpretation and in a body of Pharisaic 'regulations' handed down within the group.[80] As remarked earlier, the Pharisees seem to have been highly regarded by ordinary people, though they only numbered about six thousand even by the first century CE.[81] They may also have formed fellowships, entry into which was permitted after a trial period. As for the name Pharisee, probably derived from the Hebrew verb *parash* ('to separate'), it may originally have been applied by outsiders as a nickname because of the Pharisaic tendency to segregate for the purposes of ritual purity.

There are obvious similarities between the Pharisees and the group behind the sectarian DSS.[82] Each was concerned with ritual purity and biblical interpretation. Likewise, before full membership was permitted, the Pharisees may well have had a training period not dissimilar to that which pertained among the Essenes. Such parallels, however, are outweighed by differences. Despite a common zeal for purity, the Qumran Community's concern stemmed from the special place allotted to the priesthood – including, at least some of the time, the 'sons of Zadok' – in its midst, while the Pharisees were essentially lay. The latter's separation, moreover, was not as strict as that envisaged by the Qumran manuscripts, nor is there any sign that it extended to keeping its teachings secret. Notwithstanding some real general overlaps, therefore, it is unlikely that those responsible for the sectarian DSS were Pharisees. On the contrary, we concluded earlier that the insulting nicknames 'Ephraim' and 'Manasseh' in 4QpNahum and 4QpPsalms[a] probably refer to the Pharisees and Sadducees, respectively, as external opponents.[83]

Another group of Second Temple Jews has been put forward as a third candidate for the community at Qumran – 'the Zealots'.[84] Unfortunately, gleaning objective data about them from Josephus, our major source, is problematic. Josephus makes plain his loathing for the Zealots and others of a similar mindset, blaming them almost entirely for the disaster of the First Revolt against Rome. Given his own involvement in that Revolt, his representation should not be taken at face value. It is possible, nevertheless, to build up a general picture. Accordingly, rather than 'Zealot' which is utilized by Josephus in relation to one particular group of rebels, we might best employ the label 'revolutionary nationalists' as an umbrella term denoting a variety of individuals and their followers, all of whom were united by their zeal for an independent Jewish state. This revolutionary outlook can be traced back to the transformation of Judaea and Samaria into a Roman province in 6 CE, when Archelaus, Herod the Great's son, was deposed as ruler and replaced by a series of Roman prefects. That development necessitated a census, a foreign imposition which, according to Josephus, outraged one Judas the Galilean and a Pharisee called Zadok.[85] Although disturbances at the time were put down, members of Judas' family remained prominent in the following decades in a loose coalition of revolutionary nationalists – including the sicarii, men armed with a dagger or *sica*, active in Judaea during the 60s CE – who sought freedom from Rome under the jurisdiction of God alone.

At first sight, several features suggest the Qumran Sect was part of the revolutionary nationalist phenomenon.[86] 1QM's expectation of a final cosmic battle, with the Romans as the arch-enemy, points in this direction, as does the presence of a copy of the Songs of the Sabbath Sacrifice at Masada, a definite outpost of the sicarii. But other explanations for the latter overlaps are preferable, as noted in Chapter 1. It is possible, for example, that some Qumran members fled to Masada in desperation as Roman armies loomed on the horizon in 68 CE, taking a handful of documents with them; alternatively, Songs of the Sabbath Sacrifice may not be strictly sectarian and hence more widely available in late Second Temple Palestine than scholars have hitherto assumed.[87] A more significant circumstance further militates against a direct association between Qumran and revolutionary nationalists. Although the latter arose in the first century CE, the Qumran site had by then been in use for about one hundred years. It is this factor, coupled with allusions in the sectarian documents to people and events in the first and second centuries BCE, which makes it difficult to give credence to the notion that the Qumran Community was principally a revolutionary nationalist community.

The above outline has shown why alternative proposals for the identity of the Qumran Sect, as put forward in the 1950s and 1960s, were judged unlikely to be correct. Nothing has come to light since then which undermines that judgement, not even among previously unpublished Cave 4 texts released in 1991. Nonetheless, we shall see in Chapter 7 that their weaknesses have not prevented renewed efforts to resurrect some of these theories. Schiffman, for instance, has revived a Sadducean hypothesis, while Eisenman has tried to forge a link between the Qumran DSS and early Christian revolutionary nationalists. But for now, it is worth reaffirming that, given both general and specific connections between the sectarian DSS from Qumran and the accounts of Philo, Josephus, and Pliny, some form of Essene hypothesis seems inescapable.

The Qumran–Essene Hypothesis

Indeed, by fitting most of the pieces of the jigsaw, as it were, into a broad coherent whole, the Essene theory in its various manifestations has remained the dominant explanation for the Qumran DSS collection for some fifty years. We have seen that, while other theories put forward in the 1950s and 1960s could conjure up alternative linkages between items of data, they were unable to account for the totality of the evidence and were further undermined by serious contradictions. Most scholars, therefore, have felt they had two essential choices: either to conclude the Qumran Community was closely linked to the Essenes of Philo, Josephus, and Pliny, or else to propose that it constituted a previously unknown group remarkably similar to the Essenes of the Classical Sources in all but name!

Consequently, on the basis of the Classical Sources combined with the main sectarian DSS then available (1QS, 1QSa, 1QSb, 1QpHabakkuk, 1QM, 1QH[a], 4QpNahum, and CD), a consensus in the shape of what we may call the 'Qumran–Essene Hypothesis' established itself in the first two decades of Qumran research, gaining almost universal assent by the 1970s.[88] According to this thesis, the Essenes of the Classical Sources and the group behind the Qumran DSS were to be equated. Although adherents of this Qumran–Essene Hypothesis have disagreed on many points of detail, the main contours of its classic expression run as follows:[89]

When Jonathan Maccabee scandalously assumed the High Priesthood in 152 BCE, the Essenes broke away from a previously-existing movement called the 'Hasidaeans' or 'Hasidim', a shadowy body that had hitherto supported the Maccabee brothers according to 1 Maccabees 2:42.[90] Thereafter, they dubbed Jonathan Maccabee the 'Wicked Priest' (Hebrew, *kohen ha-rashaʿ*), a play on 'High Priest' (*kohen ha-rosh*), and his fall from grace is recounted in the interpretation of Habakkuk 2:5–6 in 1QpHabakkuk 8:8–12, as follows:

> *Moreover, the arrogant man seizes wealth without halting . . . All the nations are gathered to him . . . Will they not . . . taunt him . . . saying, 'Woe to him who amasses that which is not his! How long will he load himself up with pledges?'* (ii, 5–6)
> Interpreted, this concerns the Wicked Priest who was called by the name of truth when he first arose. But when he ruled over Israel his heart became proud, and he forsook God and betrayed the precepts for the sake of riches.

Under their founder, the Teacher of Righteousness, these Essenes formed their own religious sect in the mid-second century BCE and absconded to Khirbet Qumran, where they flourished for some two hundred years.[91] Adhering to a distinctive interpretation of the Torah and of recent events in Palestine, including their own origins, they believed their community to be the sole repository of divine truth for the age in which they lived. With their leaders, the priestly sons of

Zadok, the sectarians lived a celibate and communal life according to the rules of 1QS 5–9, shunning the Jerusalem Temple and awaiting God's dramatic intervention in history as the decisive climax to the final battle between good and evil, as envisaged in 1QM and probably also in 1QSa and 1QSb. They not only studied the scriptures but wrote sectarian compositions, including 1QpHabakkuk and 1QH^a, revealing something of their history and spirituality. Less strict Essenes lived in Judaean towns and, following the variant rules of CD 9–16, were allowed to marry and have limited dealings with the Temple and outsiders, looking to Qumran as a kind of headquarters.

Non-Essene Jews, in contrast, were held in contempt for their ignorance of the sect's teachings and resultant legal and moral bankruptcy, although 1QSa suggests they would have a chance to mend their ways during the final eschatological battle. More particularly, the Qumran Community's enemies included the Hasmonean establishment in Jerusalem, as well as the Sadducees (nicknamed 'Manasseh' in 4QpNahum 3:9), representing the errant Temple authorities, and the Pharisees (dubbed 'Ephraim' and 'Seekers of Smooth Things' in 4QpNahum 2:2), comprising those Hasidim who rejected the Teacher of Righteousness in favour of Jonathan Maccabee. With the Roman advance against the First Revolt, the Qumran site was overrun around 68 CE, just before which the sectarians ensured all their texts were secreted in the surrounding caves. But the Essene movement failed to survive this disaster, although no evidence survived as to what exactly happened to the secondary settlements elsewhere.

The main contours of this Qumran–Essene Hypothesis, as just summarized, still hold good in the eyes of most experts. However, it is important to realize that several aspects of the theory have been challenged in the course of the past twenty-five years. Such challenges are of two main types. First, during the 1970s and 1980s, several scholars proposed that those at Qumran should not be equated with the Essenes proper, as defined by the Classical Sources, but rather seen as a splinter faction which had seceded from that parent Essene movement. Second, the release in 1991 of unpublished Cave 4 texts has taken Qumran research into an exciting fresh phase. In the remainder of this chapter, therefore, we shall consider both these developments in a little more detail.

Questioning the Qumran–Essene Hypothesis

We have just learned that, by the 1970s, the Qumran–Essene Hypothesis was firmly established in the minds of most experts. Nonetheless, over the past two or three decades, some have cast doubt on this synthesis.

Indeed, it is worth saying more about the partially-related proposals associated with Jerome Murphy-O'Connor and Philip R. Davies, on the one hand, and the architects of the Groningen Hypothesis (A. S. van der Woude and F. García Martínez), on the other. These scholars have argued in different ways that the Qumran Sect should be seen as a splinter faction which broke away from a broad Essene movement. Schism, in other words, rather than development over time, explains many disparities between the Qumran manuscripts and the writings of Philo, Josephus, and Pliny. Particularly significant are three portions of CD (CD 1:3f; 3:12ff; 6:2ff) which seem to describe the formation of the Essenes as a faithful remnant after the Babylonian exile in the sixth century BCE. Of these, CD 1:3–13, is the most clear-cut:[92]

> [3]For when they were unfaithful and forsook Him, He hid His face from Israel and His Sanctuary [4]and delivered them up to the sword. But remembering the Covenant of the forefathers, He left a remnant [5]to Israel and did not deliver it up to be destroyed. And in the age of wrath, three hundred [6]and ninety years after He had given them into the hand of King Nebuchadnezzar of Babylon, [7]He visited them, and He caused a plant root to spring from Israel and Aaron to inherit [8]His Land and to prosper on the good things of His earth. And they perceived their iniquity and recognized that [9-10]they were guilty men, yet for twenty years they were like blind men groping for the way.
>
> And God observed their deeds, that they sought Him with a whole heart, [11]and He raised for them a Teacher of Righteousness to guide them in the way of His heart. And he made known [12]to the latter generations that which God had done to the latter generation, the congregation of traitors, [13]to those who departed from the way.

This excerpt, coupled with other factors, led Murphy-O'Connor and Davies, as well as van der Woude and García Martínez, to re-consider the neat identification of the Qumran Community with the Essenes of the Classical Sources. After all, it appears to focus initially on a historical scenario long before the arrival of the second-century BCE Teacher of Righteousness. In what follows, therefore, we shall outline their reformulations. It should be noted that Murphy-O'Connor and Davies worked independently in the 1970s and 1980s but came to similar conclusions. García Martínez and van der Woude of Groningen University collaborated during the late 1980s in formulating their so-called 'Groningen Hypothesis' of Qumran origins.

In a series of articles during the 1970s and 1980s, Murphy-O'Connor argued that the Essenes were Babylonian Jews who returned to Palestine in the wake of the Maccabean military success in the 160s BCE.[93] Appealing to CD's three passages listed above, as well as detailed analysis of 1QS, he maintained that the 'Essene Missionary Document' (CD 2:14–6:1) of these returning exiles was not well received by Judaea's inhabitants and, with the Teacher of Righteousness' emergence, the movement split: the majority of Essenes remained scattered throughout Judaean towns, whereas the Teacher of Righteousness and his followers settled at Khirbet Qumran. The former are described by the Classical Sources, but the latter flourished as a separate, though historically and theologically related, Qumranic faction.

Drawing on Murphy-O'Connor, Davies has maintained that the Essenes constituted a Palestinian movement which, whatever the historical veracity, believed it originated in sixth-century BCE Babylon.[94] By the second century BCE, its adherents expected the arrival of one who would 'teach righteousness at the end of days' (CD 6:11). When a person appeared who fulfilled this expectation in the eyes of many (CD 1:11), schism resulted. The parent group rejected the Teacher of Righteousness who, as the archaeology suggests, moved to Khirbet Qumran with his disciples towards the end of the second century BCE. There, they flourished for over 150 years, composing 1QS, 1QpHabakkuk, and the final edition of CD. However, critical analysis suggests that CD – along with 11QT[a], parts of 1 Enoch, and Jubilees – originally reflected the Essene parent group.[95] This distinction, maintains Davies, best explains divergences between the Classical accounts and the sectarian DSS.

The Groningen Hypothesis of van der Woude and García Martínez has placed Essenism's beginnings in Palestine during the late third or early second century BCE.[96] Against Murphy-O'Connor and Davies, they believe CD's theme of a Babylonian origin was intended metaphorically, while they cite 'apocalyptic' circles as the movement's originators.[97] On the basis of CD and portions of 1 Enoch, these scholars have further concluded that, contrary to the Qumran–Essene Hypothesis, nothing marked out the mid-second century BCE as particularly important for Essene origins. Rather, calendrical and purity disputes over several decades led a splinter faction under the Teacher of Righteousness to settle at Khirbet Qumran during the rule of John Hyrcanus (135–104 BCE), as the archaeology requires. The Wicked Priest of 1QpHabakkuk 8–12 indirectly bears this out, for he represents, not Jonathan Maccabee alone, but six Jerusalem rulers over the course of some one hundred years: Judah Maccabee, the High Priest Alcimus, Jonathan Maccabee, Simon Maccabee, John Hyrcanus, and Alexander Jannaeus.

Although most have not followed Murphy-O'Connor and Davies or the architects of the Groningen Hypothesis in detail, their work is important because it highlights shortcomings in earlier formulations of the Qumran–Essene Hypothesis. The latter often neglected, for instance, to treat Khirbet Qumran's archaeological evidence with due rigour, conveniently pushing back the settlement to around 152 BCE to tie in with Jonathan Maccabee's usurpation of the High Priesthood. Similarly, its supporters tended to posit uncritically the existence of a party of the 'Hasidaeans' or 'Hasidim' on the flimsy basis of 1 Maccabees 2:42 and 7:13.[98] Or again, neither CD's exilic claims, nor its links with other compositions containing a similar ideology but lacking sectarian terminology, have been treated sufficiently seriously.

The work of these scholars is also significant for another reason. Although their theories were thought at the time to be direct challenges to the scholarly consensus, they seem with hindsight to be revisions of the Qumran–Essene Hypothesis. In important respects, therefore, they have laid the ground for a more general re-evaluation of that hypothesis in the wake of the 1991 releases. To the latter, we shall now turn.

The 1991 Releases[99]

Earlier, we noted that the publication of the Qumran DSS was not as smooth as it might have been.[100] While the contents of Caves 1–3 and 5–10 were published by the end of the 1960s and much of Cave 11 was available by the mid-1980s, a large proportion of Cave 4 writings remained unpublished by the early 1990s.

With many manuscripts still under lock and key, those which had entered the public domain seemed to divide easily into works known from the later Hebrew Bible, Apocrypha, and Pseudepigrapha, on the one hand, and previously unfamiliar documents, on the other. The natural assumption was that the latter were sectarian.[101] During the first few decades of Qumran research, therefore, it was thought that virtually all the DSS could be ascribed to the first (biblical, apocryphal, pseudepigraphal) or third (sectarian) categories defined back in Chapter 1.[102] The seven manuscripts initially recovered from Cave 1, for example, consisted of two copies of Isaiah (1QIsaiah[a–b]) and five works assumed to be sectarian (1QS, 1QpHabakkuk, 1QM, 1QH[a], and 1QapGenesis). Alongside this neat division went the unconscious assumption that the limited amount of non-scriptural yet non-sectarian material could be more or less ignored, since it seemed merely to comprise works linked to long-known biblical texts (e.g. 4QPrayer of Nabonidus is related to Daniel). As long as the full gamut of Qumran DSS remained unavailable, such a presumption appeared eminently reasonable.

However, the situation changed dramatically in 1991 when outstanding Cave 4 texts entered the public domain. At first, scholars wishing to see them had to visit one of several centres – in San Marino, Claremont, Cincinnati, and Oxford – where photographs were stored for safety. But a collection of the images was soon published, followed by microfiche editions and, most recently, a CD-ROM version.[103] Over the last decade, furthermore, Oxford University Press has proceeded apace with the official publication of Cave 4 texts in its 'Discoveries in the Judaean Desert' series.[104]

Included among the new documents are biblical works, such as 4QSamuel[a–c], and additional sectarian writings, like Some Precepts of the Law (4QMMT[a–f]). Moreover, an extensive body of texts belonging to our second category, neither clearly scriptural nor obviously sectarian, has become available, such as 4Qpseudo-Moses[a–e] and 4Qpseudo-Ezekiel[a–e] or 4QLegal Texts A–C and 4QCalendrical Documents A–H.[105] With these new compositions, however, have arisen new questions. Three stand out.

Firstly, the neat distinction between the Hebrew Bible, Apocrypha, and Pseudepigrapha, on the one side, and the sectarian manuscripts, on the other, has become problematic with the large amount of fresh material in our second category. This development was partially foreseen by Murphy-O'Connor and Davies and by the authors of the Groningen Hypothesis, whose theories sought to explain overlaps in thought between sectarian texts (e.g. CD in its final form) and less clear-cut writings (e.g. 11QT[a], 1 Enoch).[106] But what to make of this non-scriptural yet non-sectarian material has taken on greater significance since 1991. Its sheer quantity, in fact, lay behind Chapter 1's threefold – rather than twofold – description of Qumran DSS.

Secondly, as the full range of manuscripts has been studied over the last decade, even the boundaries between these three categories have become blurred. What exactly was held to be scripture by the Qumran Sect now seems less straightforward than before 1991, for instance. This is because, in the eyes of the community, many texts without sectarian terminology in our second category of DSS may, in fact, have been indistinguishable from the works of the first. After all, we saw in Chapter 2 that Second Temple Jews treated as scripture any document linked with an ancient hero. Those at Qumran, therefore, must have considered much of the Apocrypha and Pseudepigrapha as authoritatively as, say, Deuteronomy and Jeremiah.[107] And since many recently published texts in our second category are similarly linked to past heroes, they would probably have viewed them as scripture too.

What is sectarian has likewise become more difficult to determine because of these new documents in our second category. More particularly, many of the latter overlap ideologically with sectarian texts of the third category but do not contain the latter's distinctive vocabulary. The recently available 4QCalendrical Documents A–H and the long-known 4QLuminaries[a–c] share a common calendrical interest, for example, but only 4QLuminaries[a–c] seems to have stemmed directly from the Qumran Community. This phenomenon has encouraged scholars to revisit long-published works, like 11QT[a–c] or Songs of the Sabbath Sacrifice, questioning their sectarian status.

A third difficulty concerns several documents which, though clearly still to be deemed sectarian, now exist in variant editions. This applies especially to the Community Rule. Known for decades in its Cave 1 version (1QS), it has been available since 1991 in ten Cave 4 copies (4QS[a–j]), some of which contain important divergent readings.

These and others issues will be taken up in Chapter 4, as we attempt to define more precisely the nature of the Qumran DSS corpus and the community behind it.

4

An Essene Community at Qumran

Survey of the Qumran Scrolls[1]

At the end of the last chapter, we saw that the full gamut of Qumran DSS is now available, although we also learned that important new questions have arisen since the 1991 releases. Consequently, a survey of the documents from our second category (previously unknown non-sectarian texts) and third category (previously unknown sectarian works) now seems in order.[2] Space will not allow us to describe even a majority of the 650 or so manuscripts concerned. Moreover, because there is considerable ideological overlap between some works in our second and third categories, as observed above, it is difficult to view sectarian writings in isolation. The following will consider together all substantial manuscripts of these second and third categories, therefore, across several genres. We may then be able to judge whether the Qumran–Essene Hypothesis remains viable in the wake of the fresh 1991 materials, before proceeding to comment further on the corpus' broad historical and theological context.

There are various fruitful ways of arranging generically the writings in our second and third categories. Vermes, for instance, has recently proposed eight genres.[3] For the sake of convenience, we shall adopt this schema, albeit with one modification: we will not ascribe any works to an 'apocalyptic' genre because of widespread confusion over the terms 'apocalypse' and 'apocalyptic'. Fortunately, it is not difficult to suggest alternative designations for the texts in question.[4] And we shall return to the subject of 'apocalyptic' in the next chapter.

Meanwhile, it is important to realize that many documents could be placed in more than one generic class, depending on the features highlighted. The arrangement to follow, then, is not prescriptive but merely an aid to appreciating the collection's diversity. To that end, the seven genres employed are: (1) Rules; (2) Hymns and Poems; (3) Calendars, Liturgies, Prayers; (4) Wisdom Literature; (5) Scriptural Interpretation; (6) New Pseudepigrapha; and (7) Miscellaneous Compositions.

I Rules

What scholars call 'rules' incorporate documents which seem to have regulated the life of the community behind the Qumran DSS. Although the title 'rule' (Hebrew, *serekh*) appears in only three (the Community Rule, Damascus Document, and War Scroll), it is useful to bring together twenty-two works in all. Many either refer to the group's peculiar origins or else reflect a more general partisan outlook. The latter is evident in a special terminology that can help determine which compositions from other genres are sectarian. Whilst this task has become less easy since 1991, relevant terms include 'Wicked Priest' (Hebrew, *kohen ha-rasha*), 'Teacher of Righteousness' (*moreh ha-tsedeq*), 'Scoffer', 'sons of Zadok' (*bene tsadok*), 'messiah of Aaron', 'messiah of Israel', 'Overseer' (*mevaqqer*), 'Master', 'community' (*yahad*), 'council', 'congregation' (*'edah*), 'the Many' (*ha-rabbim*), 'end of days', 'hidden things' (*nistarot*), and 'interpretation' (*pesher*). Several rules lack such vocabulary but, despite presumably originating outside the Qumran Community or its immediate forebears, remained influential.

The first two documents to mention, however, though not containing the usual language, are best deemed sectarian. Thus, the badly damaged 4QMidrash on the Book of Moses (Hebrew, *Midrash Sefer Moshe*), or 4QMSM for short, appears reminiscent of other rules – including 4QMMT[a-f], the Community Rule, and Damascus Document.[5] Carbon dating and palaeography strongly suggest this manuscript, released in 1991 but only just published, must have been copied before the mid-second century BCE. If so, 4QMSM was originally composed in the first half of the second century BCE and belongs to the community's initial phase.[6] Like several other works, it is written in a cryptic script normally thought to be a sign of sectarian origin, safeguarding secret teachings against unauthorized reading.

The second work is Some Precepts of the Law (*Miqsat Ma'ase ha-Torah*), or 4QMMT[a-f]. It too officially entered the public domain in 1991 and, for the most part, discusses ritual purity matters relating to the Temple and priesthood. More particularly, the document seeks to convince an external leader (addressed as 'you') of the legal positions advocated by the author's community ('we'), in opposition to a third party ('they'). Part of 4QMMT[e–f] illustrates this well:[7]

> We have (indeed) sent you [3]some of the precepts of the Torah according to our decision, for your welfare and the welfare of your people. For we have seen (that) [4]you have wisdom and knowledge of the Torah. Consider all these things and ask Him that He strengthen [5]your will and remove from you the plans of evil and the device of Belial [6]so that you may rejoice at the end of time . . .

The official editors have characterized 4QMMT[a–f] as a letter from the Teacher of Righteousness to the Wicked Priest during the second century BCE.[8] It certainly seems safe to say that 'we' stands for a partisan grouping, while, given the comparison with King David, 'you' represents the Maccabean or early Hasmonean authorities. 4QMMT[a–f] may even be the 'law' referred to in 4QpPsalms[a], to which we shall return below.

The next composition is the Community Rule, discovered in Cave 1 in 1947 (1QS) and then found in Caves 4 and 5 (4QS[a–j], 5QS). Although, palaeographically speaking, 1QS was copied in the early first century BCE, the likely date of 4QS[a] suggests that at least part of this work stemmed from the sect's formative period in the second century BCE. Its central core (1QS 5–9) lists regulations for new members and their property, and there are numerous disciplinary rules, as 1QS 7:17–19 demonstrates:

> Whoever has gone about slandering his companion shall be excluded from the pure Meal of the Congregation for one year and shall do penance. But whoever has slandered the Congregation shall be expelled from among them and shall return no more.

Preceding the regulatory core stands a liturgical section and spiritual instruction (1QS 1–4), while after it come guidance and a hymn for the Master, one of the community's leaders (1QS 9–11). Each of these sections is present in at least one Cave 4 copy, although important differences exist. 4QS[d] begins at the equivalent of 1QS 5:1, for example. Most interestingly, 4QS[b,d] replace appeal to the 'sons of Zadok' in 1QS 5:2, 9 with shorter references to the whole congregation (Hebrew, *ha-rabbim*, 'the Many') as the sect's final authority. The following arrangement makes this clear:

1QS 5:1–3	*4QS[d] 1:2–3*
They shall separate from the	And they shall separate from the

congregation of the men of injustice and shall unite, with respect to the Law and possessions, under the authority of the sons of Zadok, the Priests who keep the Covenant, and of the multitude of the men of the Community who hold fast to the Covenant. Every decision concerning doctrine, property, and justice shall be determined by them.	congregation of the men of injustice and shall unite with respect to doctrine and property, and they shall be under the authority of the Congregation
	concerning all matters of doctrine and property.

This divergence may show that the community was democratic at first but was subsequently dominated by a Zadokite elite. Because 1QS is older than either 4QS^b or 4QS^d, however, the opposite is more likely.

Another important composition is the Damascus Document. First discovered in 1896 in two divergent copies from an old Cairo synagogue and dubbed 'CD' (C=Cairo, D=Damascus), a longer edition subsequently turned up in three Qumran caves.[9] No one knows how the work found its way to Egypt, but scholars had to depend on the medieval Cairo text until 4QD^{a-h} became available in 1991.[10] Like CD, 4QD^{a-h} contain exhortatory material and a body of laws. The former presents its own group as the true Israel, founded soon after the Babylonian exile, with access to 'hidden things' (Hebrew, *nistarot*) unknown to others (CD 3:14).[11] More specifically, several cryptic names also appear in association with the second century BCE ('Teacher of Righteousness', 'Scoffer', and 'Spouter of Lies') and the place-name 'Damascus' features in CD 6:5 and elsewhere. The Teacher of Righteousness is doubtless the founding figure known from 1QpHabakkuk, while the Scoffer and Spouter of Lies are widely held to denote an individual who deserted the movement with a following of his own.[12]

The laws in CD and 4QD^{a-h} are similar to those of the Community Rule, but there are notable differences. It is widely held that, while the latter regulated celibate males living around Khirbet Qumran, the Damascus Document was intended for satellite communities or 'camps' elsewhere. If correct, this means that the Qumran Essenes lived without wives according to the strict rules of 1QS and 4QS^{a-j}, shunning outsiders and the Jerusalem Temple. Essenes elsewhere, in contrast, married and had children, countenancing minimal contact with outsiders and the Temple.

Several fragmentary texts relate to the kind of legal material present in the Community Rule and Damascus Document.[13] 4QMiscellaneous

Rules, alongside its own prescriptions, contains similar regulations, including a version of the Penal Code found in divergent forms within each. As for 4QRebukes, it lists individuals breaking sectarian law and subject to discipline. In contrast, 4QWords of the Sage to Sons of the Dawn exhorts those who are not yet full members – 'sons of the dawn' rather than 'sons of light' – to persevere in the community's teachings.[14] Like 4QMSM, it is written in cryptic script.[15]

Four compositions among the rules deal with matters eschatological. The longest is the War Scroll in the form of 1QM, also extant in six damaged Cave 4 copies (4QM[a–f]). It pictures a forty-year battle as the end of time approaches, during which its community restores pure Temple worship. The whole world is then conquered by the forces of good, followed by celebrations and praises. Similar themes occur in the related Book of War (4QBook of War, 11QBook of War), possibly the missing end of the War Scroll, but in neither is it spelled out exactly what happens next. Still, it is clear that, while weapons and soldiers feature, the forty-year battle is as much spiritual as military. Only God's intervention wins the day and, according to 1QM 7:1–3, it matters little that the middle-aged do the fighting, while the young carry the baggage:

> The men of the army shall be from forty to fifty years old ... The despoilers of the slain, the plunderers of booty, the cleansers of the land, the keepers of the baggage, and those who furnish the provisions shall be from twenty-five to thirty years old.

Because the War Scroll in places borrows imagery from Roman military practice, it was composed in its final edition after the Roman conquest of Palestine in 63 BCE.

Another eschatological text is the Rule of the Congregation (1QSa), a composition which, with the recent publication of nine second-century BCE Cave 4 copies dubbed 4QSE[a–i], is the oldest surviving rule.[16] Concerned with Jews joining the community in the last days, it gives instructions for their education.[17] 1QSa 2: 11–17 also describes an eschatological banquet attended by two anointed figures:

> When God engenders the (Priest-)Messiah, he shall come with them [at] the head of the whole congregation of Israel with all [his brethren, the sons] of Aaron the Priests ... and they shall sit [before him, each man] in the order of his dignity. And then [the Mess]iah of Israel shall [come], and the chiefs of the [clans of Israel] shall sit before him, [each] in the order of his dignity ...

The messianic characters featured here are present in the Community Rule and Damascus Document too, although the word translated 'engendered' in this passage is disputed.[18]

The last eschatological text is the Rule of the Blessings or 1QSb which, with 1QSa, was originally appended to lQS. It contains benedictions to be uttered by one of the community's leaders, the Master, during the messianic age, addressing the sect's different elements in turn: ordinary members, the Messiah of Aaron, sons of Zadok, and Messiah of Israel. 1QSb 3:22–3 communicates the document's flavour:

> Words of blessing. The M[aster shall bless] the sons of Zadok the Priests, whom God has chosen to confirm His Covenant for [ever, and to inquire] into all His precepts in the midst of His people . . .

Next, we must consider seven rules lacking sectarian terminology. Among them are three known as Purities A–C (4Q274, 276–7, 278), detailing purification rules to remove ritual uncleanness acquired through skin disease, bodily fluxes, or contact with a corpse.[19] Purities A 1:4–6 reads:

> A woman with a seven-day issue of blood shall not touch a man with a flux, . . . nor anything he has lain or sat on. But if she has touched (them), she shall wash her garments and bathe, and afterwards she may eat.

Purification here is by immersion and the washing of clothes, whereas other impurities require sprinkling with special water prepared using the Red Cow's ashes, as stipulated in Numbers 19:17–19.

More general laws are evidenced in Legal Texts A–C (4Q251, 264a, 472a).[20] Although none appears to contain sectarian vocabulary, the badly damaged Legal Text C may reflect the Essene toilet practices recounted by Josephus, for it speaks about 'excrement' and a 'vessel' (i.e. hatchet).[21] This document, therefore, highlights the difficulty in determining the sectarian status of works which seem to straddle our second and third categories, especially when they are damaged.

Indeed, our final rule, the lengthy Temple Scroll (11QT[a]), now existing in additional fragmentary copies (11QT[b–c], 4QT), replicates this problem.[22] Harmonizing Pentateuchal laws about the wilderness Tabernacle and reapplying them to the Jerusalem Temple and its worship, it is, nonetheless, more than a mere compendium of biblical law. Most remarkably, the composition is set in the first person, as the following illustrates:[23]

Deuteronomy 17:14–16 (NRSV)	*11QT[a] 56:12–18*
[14]When you have come into	[12]When you have come into
the land that the LORD your God	the land that I am
is giving you, and have taken	giving you, and have taken
possession of it and settled	possession of it and settled
in it, and you say, 'I will	[13]in it, and you say, 'I will
set a king over me, like all	set a king over me, like all
the nations that are around	the nations that are around
me,' [15]you may indeed set	me,' [14]you may indeed set
over you a king whom the LORD	over you a king whom I
your God will choose. One of	will choose. One of
your own community you may	your own community you may
set as king over you; you are not	set as king over you; [15]you shall
permitted to put a foreigner over	not put a foreigner over
you, who is not of your own	you, who is not of your own
community. [16]Even so, he must	community. Even so, he must
not acquire many horses for	not acquire [16]many horses for
himself, or return the people	himself, or return the people
to Egypt in order to	to Egypt *for war* in order [17]to
acquire more horses,	acquire *for himself* more horses,
	and silver and gold,
since the LORD has said to you,	since I have said to you,
'You must never return	'You must never [18]return
that way again.'	that way again.'

In 11QT[a] 56:12–18, Deuteronomy 17:14–20 is repeated almost exactly, but God speaks authoritatively in the first person. By way of interpretation, 11QT[a] has added several words, including 'for war', as indicated in italics. Since Israelite heroes, like King Solomon, were known to have traded with Egypt, and because many Second Temple Jews settled there, this supplement shows the author believed it was only a return to Egypt for military action that was forbidden.

Less clear-cut is the status of the Temple Scroll. Since 11QT[a]'s publication in 1977, it has often been assumed to be sectarian because of legal overlaps with the Damascus Document.[24] But despite such parallels, the Temple Scroll lacks community terminology. The conviction that it stems from the Qumran Sect directly has weakened over the last decade, therefore. And once more, the difficulty of determining sectarian and non-sectarian boundaries is evident, justifying our inclusion of writings from both the second and third categories of DSS throughout this generic survey.

II Hymns and Poems

A second genre of some eleven documents contains hymns and poems akin to the Psalms. Their devotional nature communicates aspects of the spirituality of those behind the Qumran DSS absent from other compositions. Around half are probably sectarian, and we shall consider them first.

The Hymns Scroll, chiefly in the form of 1QH[a] but supplemented by 1QH[b], comprises twenty-four or so poems thanking God for his salvation and the special knowledge that goes with it. A further six copies (4QH[a–f]) are now available from Cave 4.[25] The poems themselves constitute individual thanksgiving hymns, rather than communal songs. While most could have been used by any community member, some reflect a rejected teacher's anguish.[26] 1QH[a] 18:14–16, belonging to the former, is representative:

> Blessed art Thou, O Lord, God of mercy [and abundant] grace, for Thou hast made known [Thy wisdom to me that I should recount] Thy marvellous deeds, keeping silence neither by day nor [by night]!

Next comes 11QApocryphal Psalms C, a badly damaged manuscript containing four songs against demons – including Psalm 91 – ascribed to King David. Mention of 'Belial' or Satan, as well as contrasts between 'darkness' and 'light', suggests the collection was sectarian. In that case, the situation envisaged is one of a sick community member in need of exorcism to expel an illness' demonic cause. This text's contents may be the same as the 'four songs to make music on behalf of those stricken (by evil spirits)' listed in 11QApocryphal Psalms A, a non-sectarian manuscript to be considered below.

4QApocryphal Lamentations A–B comprise two works inspired by the biblical book of Lamentations. The imagery employed, therefore, is that of the Babylonian destruction of the Temple and exile of the people of Judah, although 4QApocryphal Lamentations B appears to employ such language in connection with recent Jewish enemies. Consequently, we may tentatively conclude that at least 4QApocryphal Lamentations B is sectarian.

Designed for communal worship are multiple copies of the Songs of the Sabbath Sacrifice (*Shirot 'Olat ha-Shabbat*), known as 4QShirShab[a–h] and 11QShirShab.[27] Widely held to be sectarian until recently, these songs may actually have been circulating widely, as suggested by the fact that a copy was recovered from Masada.[28] In any case, focusing on the heavenly Temple and divine throne, they purport to reproduce the celestial worship of the first thirteen Sabbaths of the year, as 4QShirShab 20, ii, 21–22 shows:

> For the Mas[ter. Song of the holocaust of] the twelfth [S]abbath [on the twenty-first of the third month.]
> [Praise the God of . . . w]onder, and exalt Him . . . The [cheru]bim prostrate themselves before Him and bless. As they rise, a whispered divine voice [is heard], and there is a roar of praise.

'Holocaust' is a term for sacrifice and the 'cherubim' are supernatural creatures, while the general imagery reflects Ezekiel 1 and 10. Those using these songs apparently believed that, in so doing, they could participate in heavenly worship according to the divine calendar. We shall return to matters calendrical presently.

Several other poetic documents are also likely to have originated outside the Qumran Sect, although certainty may never be reached. Thus, 11QApocryphal Psalms A and 4QApocryphal Psalms B are over-lapping but distinct Hebrew collections of Psalms 1–150, coupled with Psalms 151–154 (hitherto known from the Septuagint and Syriac Bible) and three psalm-like pieces unknown before 1947.[29] The former manu-script contains what is probably a sectarian interpolation ascribing the document's contents to King David, although it is made clear they represent only a fraction of his repertoire! Thus, 11QApocryphal Psalms A 27:4–11 reads:

> [David] wrote 3,600 psalms and 364 songs to sing before the altar for the daily perpetual sacrifice, for all the days of the year; and 52 songs for the Sabbath offerings; and 30 songs for the New Moons, for Feast-days and for the Day of Atonement.
> In all, the songs which he uttered were 446, and 4 songs to make music on behalf of those stricken (by evil spirits).
> In all, they were 4,050.
> All these he uttered through prophecy which was given him from before the Most High.

As seen above, the songs for exorcism here may be the four pieces in 11QApocryphal Psalms C.

4QNon-canonical Psalms A–B comprise two related manuscripts of previously unknown psalm-like pieces ascribed to ancient figures, such as the contrite 'Prayer of Manasseh, King of Judah, when the King of Assyria gaoled him'. The language of these damaged compositions is close to the biblical Psalms.

Lastly, 4QApocryphal Psalm and Prayer contains a further copy of Psalm 154, alongside a poem in praise of 'King Jonathan':

Holy City for King Jonathan and for all the congregation of Thy people Israel, who are in the four corners of heaven. May the peace of them all be on Thy kingdom! May Thy name be blessed.

Only released in 1991, scholars are divided as to whether this figure is Jonathan Maccabee or Alexander Jannaeus (whose Hebrew name was Jonathan). Whichever ultimately proves correct, lack of community terminology suggests this poem originated outside the Qumran Sect.

III Calendars, Liturgies, Prayers

This genre covers almost thirty calendars, liturgies, and prayers.[30] Some are clearly sectarian, others probably came from outside our community, and yet others are difficult to characterize. We shall begin with four documents that have long been in the public domain and are normally deemed sectarian.

1QLiturgical Prayers first appeared in 1955, while 4QLuminaries[a-c], 4QDaily Prayers, and 4QFestival Prayers[a-c] were published in 1982.[31] More specifically, 4QLuminaries[a-c] constitute prayers for the week. The title derives from the word written on the back of one manuscript, where 'Luminaries' probably denotes regular prayer-times marked by the appearance of the relevant heavenly bodies.[32] Although the Sabbath petition is focused exclusively on divine praise, each weekday prayer consists of a historical reminiscence and goes on to request divine help, as 4QLuminaries[a] 6:11–15 demonstrates:

Look on [our affliction] and trouble and distress, and deliver Thy people Israel [from all] the lands, near and far, [to which Thou hast banished them], every man who is inscribed in the Book of Life.

4QDaily Prayers also constitute petitions for weekdays and Sabbaths, sharing some phraseology with 4QLuminaries[a-c]. 1QLiturgical Prayers and 4QFestival Prayers[a-c], on the other hand, deal exclusively with worship for the religious year's major festivals.

Also long-known by scholars, at least in part, are 4QCurses and 4QBlessings[a-e].[33] The former curses Melchiresha ('King of Wickedness'), a synonym for Satan or Belial, while the contents of the latter are divided between similar maledictions and contrasting praise for God. 4QBlessings[a] 2:4–5 is a representative sample:

> Cursed be the Wicke[d One in all . . .] of his dominions, and may all the sons of Belial be damned in all the works of their service until their annihilation [for ever, Amen, amen.]

These writings, echoing language in the Community Rule and War Scroll, are sectarian.[34]

Three ritual texts available since 1991 may also come from the Qumran Community. Thus, 4QPurification Liturgy and 4QRitual Purifications A–B tackle ritual uncleanness. The highly fragmentary 4QRitual of Marriage, on the other hand, despite its name, touches on matters more mundane, including husbands and wives and children.

Next come three important calendrical documents. The first one, penned in the cryptic script normally thought to intimate a sectarian provenance, is 4QPhases of the Moon. It records the moon's phases in fourteen stages, as 4QPhases of the Moon 2:2–4 makes clear:

> [On the f]ifth (day) of it (the month), [tw]elve (fourteenths of the moon's surface) are covered and thus it [enters the day. On the sixth (day) of it] thir[teen] (fourteenths of its surface) are covered and thus it enters the day.

The importance of heavenly bodies, and by implication the calendar, for the Qumran Sect is evident here. As such, the work ties in to other calendrical pieces, although they tend to lack partisan features, whether a cryptic script or special vocabulary.

Indeed, only recently available in full, copies of 4QCalendrical Documents A–H correlate three important things: a dominant solar calendar of 364 days per year, a secondary lunar calendar of 354 days, and the twenty-four priestly courses assigned duty in the Temple week-by-week. The end result does not make for exciting reading. But 4QCalendrical Document C, as observed earlier, mentions in passing Shelamzion (Salome Alexandra) and Aemilius Scaurus (the first Roman governor of Syria) of the first century BCE.[35]

4QCalendrical Signs lists the occurrence of a 'sign' every three years and names the relevant priestly course serving in the Temple. The 'sign' is probably the addition to the secondary lunar cycle of an extra 30-day month every three years ($3 \times 354 + 30 = 1092$ days) to ensure its length equals that of three solar years ($3 \times 364 = 1092$ days).

A related calendrical interest informs works like 4QHoroscope and Physiognomy and 4QZodiology, although initially these documents seem a little odd. The latter, a badly worn text released in 1991, tracks the moon through the signs of the Zodiac, predicting marvels and disasters on the basis of thunder on a given day. As for 4QHoroscope and Physiognomy, in the public domain for some time, it correlates a person's physical and spiritual characteristics with the position of the planets at birth.[36] 4QPhysiognomy 2:5–6 reads:

> ... his thighs are long and lean, and his toes are thin and long. He is of the second Column. His spirit consists of six (parts) in the House of Light and three in the Pit of Darkness. And this is his birthday on which he (is to be/was?) born: in the foot of the Bull.

The 'foot of the Bull' probably refers to the sun's location within the constellation Taurus, and the amount of good (light) and evil (darkness) in the case cited constitutes a moderately good man.

Clearly, all these calendrical works were central to the identity and practice of the Qumran Community, although, apart from 4QPhases of the Moon's cryptic alphabet, there is nothing narrowly sectarian about them. Some were probably inherited from the community's forebears or else used by like-minded contemporaries outside. Once more, therefore, we see the difficulty in delineating precisely sectarian and non-sectarian boundaries.

Lastly, we should mention two short general liturgical texts. 4QOrder of Service lists songs to be uttered day and night throughout the year, and 4QLiturgical Work A praises God for religious festivals. Neither evinces partisan traits, although the latter again reflects the special calendar utilized by the Qumran Sect.

IV Wisdom Literature

We shall consider twelve wisdom compositions here, of which eight or nine may have originated within the Qumran Community.[37] Most were released in 1991.

The first, however, Mysteries, was long in the public domain in the form of 1QMysteries, before being supplemented by the fragmentary 4QMysteries[a–c]. Concerned with the struggle between good and evil, it looks to the 'mystery to come' (Hebrew, *raz nihyeh*), which, as 1QMysteries 1:2–4 makes clear, is unknown to outsiders:

> They know not the mystery to come, nor do they understand the things of the past. They know not that which shall befall them, nor do they save their soul from the mystery to come.

The 'mystery to come', also featured in Instruction A, appears to denote the community's teaching about the nature of the cosmos and its eschatological climax. This mystery's content, therefore, was probably to be found in texts like Instruction A and Mysteries themselves.

As for Instruction A, known before 1991 as 1QInstruction A and then supplemented by 4QInstruction A[a–e], it contains terminological links with the Community Rule, Damascus Document, and Hymns Scroll. It speaks of the 'mystery to come', as noted, but also covers traditional wisdom subjects (e.g. the righteous and wicked, business ethics, family relations). The more fragmentary 4QInstruction B appears broadly similar.[38]

4QSongs of the Sage[a–b] is an interesting collection combining sapiential poems in praise of God with incantations against demons. Mention of the 'Master' and 'community' (*yahad*) renders it sectarian in origin.

4QBless, my Soul[a–e] takes its title from the first line of the first fragment, echoing Psalms 103 and 104. The work proceeds to praise God for his faithfulness in language akin to both the Hymns Scroll and Commentary on Psalms. These similarities mean the text could be sectarian.

Mention must now be made of three compositions lacking any clear sign of a community origin. 4QBeatitudes contrasts the lots of the righteous and the wicked, opening with five statements as to who is 'blessed'. 4QBeatitudes 2 2:1–2 is illustrative:

> [Blessed is] . . . with a pure heart
> and does not slander with his tongue.
> Blessed are those who hold to her (Wisdom's) precepts
> and do not hold to the ways of iniquity.

Psalm 1:1 is called to mind here, and there is a general similarity to Jesus' beatitudes in Matthew 5:3–11 and Luke 6:20–23.

Finally, 4QWiles of the Wicked Woman echoes the book of Proverbs, taking up the motif of Lady Folly and her attractions, while 4QSapiential Work comprises a series of instructions in which the Torah features as the personification of Wisdom.

V Scriptural Interpretation

Although writings from other genres sporadically interpret scripture, the twenty-six or so texts described here do so more deliberately.[39] Even among such documents, however, there is variety, for we find Commentaries or Pesharim on a single scriptural book, thematic commentaries drawing on a range of works, and others paraphrasing biblical stories. While most are sectarian, a significant minority were probably inherited from elsewhere. The role of the former, particularly the Pesharim, was to lend weight to the sect's status and teachings.

The best preserved interpretation of a particular book is the Pesher or Commentary on Habakkuk (lQpHabakkuk). Its thirteen columns comment verse by verse on Habakkuk 1–2, frequently employing the Hebrew term *pesher*, 'interpretation' or 'commentary'. Prominent is the Teacher of Righteousness, presumably the founder of the group behind the document, as lQpHabakkuk 7:3–5, citing Habakkuk 2:2, expresses:

> *That he who reads may read it speedily:* interpreted this concerns the Teacher of Righteousness, to whom God made known all the mysteries of the words of His servants the Prophets.

The writer, unlike modern scholars, was not primarily concerned with Habakkuk's original meaning but with its significance for his own day. In lQpHabakkuk 2:10–15, for example, the sixth-century BCE Chaldeans (or Babylonians) of Habakkuk 1:6 are equated with the Kittim or Romans of the first century BCE. Several other historical players in late Second Temple times are likewise mentioned cryptically, notably the Teacher of Righteousness, Wicked Priest, and Liar, each of whom we have encountered before. 1QpHabakkuk can help in reconstructing the origins of the Qumran Community, therefore, especially when combined with the Damascus Document and 4QMMT[a–f].

Also helpful in this regard are less well preserved Commentaries on Isaiah (4QpIsaiah[a–e]), Hosea (4QpHosea[a–b]), Micah (lQpMicah, 4Qp-Micah), Zephaniah (1QpZephaniah, 4QpZephaniah), and Psalms (1QpPsalms, 4QpPsalms[a–b]). The latter speaks of the Wicked Priest and Teacher of Righteousness and, citing Psalm 37:32–33 at 4QpPsalms[a] 4:5–5, apparently reflects some kind of communication between them:

> *The wicked watches out for the righteous and seeks to slay him* . . . (32–3).
>
> Interpreted, this concerns the Wicked [Priest] who [watched the Teacher of Righteousness] that he might put him to death [because of the ordinance] and the law which he sent to him.

It is possible that the 'law' here denotes a version of 4QMMT[a–f] sent to the Maccabean or early Hasmonean authorities. In any case, turning to 4QpNahum, we learned earlier that it refers to Antiochus IV and Demetrius III in connection with the history of early first-century BCE

Judaea.[40] The damaged 4QpApocalypse of Weeks may be a similar *pesher* on the so-called Apocalypse of Weeks (1 Enoch 93:1–10; 91:11–17).

Among texts released in 1991, 4QGenesis Commentaries A–D match the chronology of the Flood (Genesis 6–9) with the community's special 364-day calendar. By stressing the Davidic nature of the biblical kings, moreover, Jacob's blessing of Judah (Genesis 49:10) seems to be interpreted as criticism of the Hasmonean dynasty.

4QAges of Creation A–B is witnessed by two overlapping manuscripts which probably represent similar – but not identical – works.[41] 4QAges of Creation A fragment 1, lines 1–3, opens with:

> Interpretation concerning the ages made by God, all the ages for the accomplishment [of all the events, past] and future.

The employment of the Hebrew *pesher* ('interpretation') is reminiscent of the Pesharim, but, rather than focusing on one scriptural book, 4QAges of Creation A–B divides biblical history into a series of 'ages', contrasting the respective fates of the wicked and the pious.

Other sectarian works of scriptural interpretation, such as 4QFlorilegium and 4QTestimonia, focus on a selection of passages, also, though less frequently, employing the word *pesher*. 4QFlorilegium 1:14–16 illustrates this approach:

> Explanation of *How blessed is the man who does not walk in the counsel of the wicked (Ps. i,l)*. Interpreted, this saying [concerns] those who turn aside from the way [of the people] as it is written in the book of Isaiah the Prophet concerning the last days, *It came to pass that [the Lord turned me aside . . . from walking in the way of] this people* (Isa. viii, 11).

4QFlorilegium culls verses from several scriptural books to bolster its argument, reapplying general statements about the righteous to sectarians, while the wicked are assumed analogous to outsiders. 4QTestimonia, more specifically, relates passages from Exodus, Numbers, and Deuteronomy to a future prophetic figure, as well as to messianic characters named the messiahs of Aaron and Israel. The latter two also feature in the Damascus Document, Community Rule, and Rule of the Congregation, as observed already.

4QCatenae A–B contain 'chains' (Latin, *catenae*) of citations from the Psalms and elsewhere, interspersed with comments employing sectarian phraseology. Indeed, 'end of days' appears six times and infuses the material with an eschatological edge, for the community will ultimately be vindicated and God's enemies defeated. Among the latter are the

Plate 4   *4QTestimonia.* © *Estate of John M. Allegro, courtesy of The Allegro Archive (The University of Manchester)*

'seekers of smooth things' encountered elsewhere. Thus, 4QCatena A fragments 10–11, lines 11–13 state:

> [As for that which] he said, *Lest the enemy say,* [*I have prevailed over him*] (Ps. xiii, 15) . . . They are the congregation of the seekers of smooth things . . .

Steudel has linked 4QCatenae A–B with three other texts, including 4QFlorilegium, claiming that they constitute five copies of an eschatological work.[42] But, without concrete manuscript overlaps, her theory remains speculative.

11QMelchizedek is another piece employing the word *pesher* and drawing on a scriptural selection. The work centres on the mysterious figure from Genesis 14, Melchizedek, whose name means 'King of Righteousness'. Understood as the counterpart of the evil Melchiresha in 4QCurses, this Melchizedek is also equated with the Prince of Light and archangel Michael. Combining laws about the 'year of release' in Leviticus 25:13 and Deuteronomy 15:2 with Isaiah 61:1–2's promise to free captives, 11QMelchizedek 2:6–10 depicts the eschatological finale of a history divided into fifty-year periods or 'jubilees':

> And the Day of Atonement is the e[nd of the] tenth [ju]bilee, when all the Sons of [Light] and the men of the lot of Mel[chi]zedek will be atoned for . . . For this is the moment of the Year of Grace for Melchizedek. [And h]e will, by his strength, judge the holy ones of God, executing judgement as it is written concerning him in the Songs of David, who said, ELOHIM *has taken his place in the divine council; in the midst of the gods he holds judgement* (Psalms lxxxii, 1).

Community members will be forgiven their sins by Melchizedek on the eschatological Day of Atonement. Melchizedek, however, despite having scriptural wording with God (Hebrew, *'elohim*) as its subject applied to him, acts merely as a divine agent; he is not himself equated with God.

Focused more thoroughly on law, 4QOrdinances[a–c] reinterpret legal material in the Torah in a sectarian manner. For example, 4QOrdinances[a] 2:6–7 understands the Temple tax (see Exodus 30:11–16 and Nehemiah 10:32) to be payable once in a lifetime, whereas we know other Jews contributed to it every year:

> Concerning . . . the money of valuation that a man gives as ransom for his life, it shall be half [a shekel . . .] He shall give it only once in his life.

When fully intact, 4QReworked Pentateuch[a–e], or 4QRP[a–e] for short, may have been the longest of all the manuscripts recovered from Caves 1–11. What remains constitutes a rearranged and supplemented Torah. The most notable adaptation is the lengthened Song of Miriam found at the equivalent of Exodus 15:21. Widely held to be non-sectarian, 4QRP[a–e] nevertheless reflects the special calendar adopted by the community.

Not dissimilar are the targums on Leviticus (4QtgLeviticus) and Job (4QtgJob and 11QtgJob), works translating in a fairly literal manner the portions of the biblical text concerned into Aramaic.[43] However, 11QtgJob's ending is more distinctive, as the following arrangement shows:

Job 42:10 (NRSV)	*11QtgJob 38:3–4*
And the LORD restored the fortunes of Job when he had prayed for his friends;	And God returned to Job with mercy
and the LORD gave Job twice as much as he had before.	and doubled all that he had owned.

The shorter Aramaic rendering here departs from the Hebrew text. However, because divergent editions of biblical books existed in Second Temple times, we cannot be sure whether 11QtgJob's wording results from the translator's license or a different underlying original. Either way, the Qumran targums are not sectarian in origin.

More consistently expansive in its approach is one of the first seven manuscripts retrieved from Cave 1, 1QapGenesis, an Aramaic expansion of Genesis in twenty-two columns which covers the periods of Noah and Abraham in what survives. The author included an account of Noah's birth, for his father was concerned that his mother, Bathenosh, may have conceived through an adulterous angelic liaison. 1QapGenesis 2:1–2 purports to supply the thoughts of Lamech, Noah's father, on the matter:

> Behold, I thought then within my heart that conception was (due) to the Watchers and the Holy Ones ... and to the Giants ... and my heart was troubled within me because of this child.

While 1QapGenesis is unlikely to be sectarian, the theme of illicit sexual intercourse between angels and humans is prominent in 1 Enoch and Jubilees, as we shall see in the next chapter.

4QBiblical Chronology is a fragmentary account of history from earliest times to the period of the Judges. Rather like 1QapGenesis, this non-sectarian piece has drawn on interpretative traditions found in Jubilees and 1 Enoch, as well as in 4QTestament of Qahat and 4QVisions of Amram[a–f]. Such writings, purportedly stemming from ancient heroes, would probably have counted as scripture for many late Second Temple Jews, as concluded in Chapter 2.

Lastly, 4QMessianic Apocalypse is a text which, drawing on Isaiah 61:1, describes an anointed figure and the advent of God's kingdom. Lacking sectarian traits, its significance lies in its reference to resurrection, a theme absent from other DSS in our second and third categories, and in its combination of resurrection, healing, and the kingdom of God. These motifs were later independently conjoined by the authors of Matthew 11:4–5 and Luke 7:22 or their respective sources.[44]

VI New Pseudepigrapha

Now that all the Qumran DSS are available, the largest genre is that under this heading, although many documents are extremely damaged. None, as far as we can tell, are sectarian. Rather, the manuscripts comprise works similar in nature to those long familiar from the Apocrypha and Pseudepigrapha but, unlike them, completely unknown before the discovery of Caves 1–11.[45]

Most were released for the first time in 1991. Not only have they increased the size of our second category of Qumran DSS, therefore, as explained already, but they have also blurred scriptural boundaries with an array of documents deliberately connected with ancient heroes. Among these is 4Qpseudo-Jubilees[a–b] which, expanding on the story of Abraham's near-sacrifice of Isaac in Genesis 22, is reminiscent of Jubilees itself and later Rabbinic texts. Thus, 4Qpseudo-Jubilees[a], 2 2:1–8 reads:

> And Isaac said to Abraham [his father, 'Behold there is the fire and the wood, but where is the lamb] for the burnt-offering?' And Abraham said to [Isaac, his son, 'God will provide a lamb] for himself.' Isaac said to his father, 'T[ie me well'] . . .

Here, it is explained that Isaac agrees to the sacrifice, even requesting his father to bind him tightly.

Just as interesting are compositions linked with Qahat and Moses, as well as with later heroes like Jeremiah, Ezekiel, and Daniel. Thus, 4QTestament of Qahat claims to embody the deathbed wisdom of Moses' grandfather, while 4Qpseudo-Moses[a–e] purportedly contains God's words to Moses about Israel's future schematized history. Or again, 4QApocryphon of Jeremiah A–E recount its namesake's experience in Babylon and Egypt after the sixth-century BCE exile, whereas the text known as New Jerusalem, or NJ for short (1QNJ, 2QNJ, 4QNJ[a–b], 5QNJ, 11QNJ), is based on Ezekiel 40–48 and describes in detail the eschatological Jerusalem.

Linked to Daniel, we find 4Qpseudo-Daniel[a–c]. More specifically, 4Qpseudo-Daniel[a] 3 explains the Babylonian exile's cause:

> The children of Israel chose themselves rather than [God and they sacri]ficed their sons to the demons of idolatry. God was enraged . . . and determined to surrender them to Nebu[chadnezzar, king of Ba]bel . . .

Daniel seems to be presented as the narrator here.[46]

Indeed, as stated earlier, Daniel and other ancient heroes supposedly lie behind most of the forty or so texts in this genre, although their extremely fragmentary state makes it difficult to be sure in every case. Nevertheless, it seems safe to conclude that many of these writings were treated as scripture by late Second Temple Jews with access to them, including members of the Qumran Sect.

VII Miscellaneous Compositions

Some Qumran DSS do not fit into any of the above genres.[47] Among them are various accounts, receipts, and letters (4Q342–359), although doubt has recently been cast on the Qumran origins of some of them. It appears that a number were retrieved from the Murabba'at or Nahal Hever vicinity and subsequently mixed up with Cave 4 material. Nevertheless, six Qumran documents – 4Q343, 4Q345, 4Q348, 4Q350, 4Q355, and 6Q26 – can now be confirmed as examples of such non-literary texts, as can an interesting ostracon from Khirbet Qumran to be considered below.

Rather more unusual is 3QCopper Scroll. It contains a list of riches, inscribed on copper, hidden in sixty or more sites across Palestine. Scholars have disagreed over the years as to whether its semi-cryptic account is fictional or literal and, if the latter, to whom the riches belonged. John Allegro, one of the original DSS research team, embarked on a search for 3QCopper Scroll's riches in 1962 but came away empty-handed. Others have argued that this strange composition should be separated from the Qumran corpus in that it was found set apart from other Cave 3 documents and could have been deposited there after 68 CE.[48] Recently, the view has been gaining ground that 3QCopper Scroll's list was real and, more particularly, it either belonged to the Qumran Community or else constituted a catalogue of Temple treasure deposited shortly before the catastrophe of 70 CE.[49]

A final miscellaneous item is one of two ostraca, or inscribed pottery fragments, recovered in early 1996 from Khirbet Qumran. The ostracon, although damaged, appears to record the transfer of property from 'Honi' to the 'community' (*yahad*) in fulfillment of an oath, thereby providing a new link between the Qumran ruins and the 'community' commended in the literary corpus from surrounding caves. Lines 1–8 of the ostracon read as follows:[50]

1. In year two of the [
2. in Jericho, Honi son of [ ] gave

3. to 'El'azar son of Nahmani [ ]
4. Hisday from Holon [ ]
5. from this day to perpetui[ty]
6. the boundaries of the house and [ ]
7. and the fig trees, the ol[ive tree (?), and]
8. when he fulfilled (his oath) to the Community . . .

Although some doubt has been cast on this transcription, including the occurrence of the word 'community', the official editors have recently reaffirmed its accuracy.[51]

Revising the Qumran–Essene Hypothesis

It is clear that the Qumran DSS, both those detailed above and the biblical, apocryphal, and pseudepigraphical manuscripts considered in an earlier chapter, constitute a diverse literary corpus. The collection should be seen, at least in part, as a cross-section of Jewish literature from late Second Temple Palestine, although within it are texts which appear to have been the sole preserve of a particular religious group. Whilst we must be more cautious than scholars of a previous generation over what belongs to this third category of sectarian DSS, there can be no doubt that a significant proportion of the compositions has a distinctly partisan flavour. That much is evident from the ideology and terminology of such writings, as well as from their idiosyncratic interpretation of scripture. Other works in our second category of Qumran DSS, though not narrowly sectarian in the same way, contain parallel emphases of thought, especially zeal for a correct calendar. Taken as a whole, therefore, the Qumran DSS can be viewed as a partisan library, within which interpretative control was exercised by a minority of sectarian texts. The library was also presumably defined in part by what it excluded, for there is no obvious piece of Hasmonean propaganda, no text clearly linked to the Pharisees, nor any thoroughly hellenized work.[52]

The question which now faces us is whether the Qumran–Essene Hypothesis can be sustained, if necessary with modifications, in response to the full gamut of the collection now available. After all, we have already seen that the haphazard nature of publication before 1991 unwittingly influenced the interpretative framework of scholars. In this regard, we noted earlier that, as long as there seemed little material in our second category of texts, it was reasonable not to pay it too much attention. More concretely, if 4QMMT[a–f] had been published in the

1950s, historians would have appreciated more fully from the outset the role of legal disputes in the group's formation.

Not surprisingly, therefore, the 1991 releases have renewed discussion about the origins and nature of the Qumran Community. Some resultant suggestions are less credible than others, and we shall examine a selection of the more controversial ones in Chapter 7. Here, it is worth considering three responses.

First, García Martínez has argued that the new compositions provide additional support for the Groningen Hypothesis put forward in 1989 by van der Woude and García Martínez himself.[53] He particularly notes that the adoption of a special calendar appears nowhere in the Classical Sources as an Essene characteristic, whereas it features prominently in texts like 4QCalendrical Documents A–H. This disparity, when taken alongside parallels that do exist between the Qumran texts and the Classical Sources, is best explained by supposing that the Qumran Sect was not a body of Essenes proper. It was rather, García Martínez reaffirms, an Essene splinter faction.

Second, Stegemann has revised his earlier formulation of the Qumran–Essene Hypothesis, acknowledging its shortcomings in light of texts like 4QMMT[a–f] and re-evaluations of de Vaux's archaeology.[54] He rejects the theories of Murphy-O'Connor and Davies, as well as the Groningen Hypothesis, because he holds that the Qumran library was too large to have belonged to a schismatic sub-group. Instead, Stegemann proposes that, in the aftermath of the Maccabean revolt in the mid-160s BCE, there were four main groupings in Palestine: (i) the Maccabees themselves; (ii) the Temple establishment; (iii) the Hasideans; and (iv) members of the 'new covenant in the land of Damascus' (CD 6:5). When the existing High Priest was forced out of office by Jonathan Maccabee in 152 BCE, he salvaged a *yahad* ('community' or 'union') which included adherents among the Hasideans, a shadowy group mentioned in 1 Maccabees 2:42, and the 'Damascus' grouping pictured in CD 6:5, 6:19 and 8:21. This *yahad*, according to Stegemann, became the Essenes and, under its leader, the deposed High Priest who was dubbed the 'Teacher of Righteousness', it never accepted the authority of the Maccabees and their Hasmonean successors, nor that of the Temple establishment. However, other members of (iii) and (iv) above became the Pharisees, while the Temple establishment itself came to be known as the Sadducees. For Stegemann, therefore, the Essenes were no peripheral sect but a respected traditionalist movement which, although excluded from political power by the Hasmonean and Temple authorities, had its headquarters in Jerusalem and utilized Khirbet Qumran as a centre for study and manuscript production.

Third, drawing on both the Groningen Hypothesis and Stegemann's work, Boccaccini has recently proposed an 'Enochic/Essene hypothesis'.[55] In his estimation, the Essenes of the Classical Sources represented an Enochic Judaism which flourished in Palestine throughout much of the second half of the Second Temple period and beyond. Its ideas are reflected chiefly in 1 Enoch, but also in Jubilees and the Testaments of the Twelve Patriarchs, emphasizing in particular the notion that God's good creation was corrupted by angelic rebellion. In the mid- to late second century BCE, however, a schism occurred within this broad-based Enochic–Essene movement, giving rise to the isolated community at Qumran under the Teacher of Righteousness. Whilst retaining many of the ideas expressed in the Enochic literature inherited from its parent group, this splinter faction proceeded to produce the Community Rule, Rule of the Congregation, Rule of the Blessings, and other sectarian texts of its own. Central to its worldview, unlike that of its Enochic–Essene predecessors, were a cosmic dualism, the predestination of the individual, and the need for radical separation from other Jews and Gentiles.

None of these positions is likely to persuade most scholars. Although García Martínez correctly stresses the importance of new calendrical material, we saw in the last chapter that the Classical Sources' failure to mention the calendar can be explained differently. Either Philo and Josephus did not know about it or considered it peripheral to their aims in writing. As for Stegemann, he does make some interesting suggestions. He proposes, for example, that no Essenes were literally celibate. Rather, because the movement had such strict marriage regulations, its adherents merely seemed to renounce marriage to outsiders, including Philo and Josephus or their sources. But in other respects, Stegemann's revised Qumran–Essene Hypothesis is very speculative and, for that reason, has not gained a wide following. While his overall reconstruction is possible, including the postulation of four groupings in Palestine by the 160s BCE, there is no compelling evidence rendering it probable. The same objection applies to Boccaccini, for, while certainly ingenious, his 'Enochic/Essene hypothesis' is extremely conjectural. In any case, if the Rule of the Congregation goes back to long before Khirbet Qumran was settled, as now seems the case, his theory as currently expressed cannot stand. Similarly, if a cosmic dualism was as central to the Qumran Community as Boccaccini proposes, it is odd that one copy of the Community Rule from Cave 4 (4QS[d]) lacks the famous passage on the 'two spirits' found in 1QS 3:13–4:14.[56]

Nevertheless, some kind of revised Qumran–Essene Hypothesis seems the most likely candidate to carry DSS research forward. That much is obvious from the failure of any alternative to gain widespread support, as well as the general evidence collated in the last chapter. It also seems the best response to the new materials released in 1991, for nothing has come to light rendering such a revision impossible. Indeed, Cross and Vermes have attempted preliminary revisions of this kind. Cross, for instance, has acknowledged that disputes over the calendar and purity must have contributed to the Qumran group's formation as much as any Zadokite crisis after Jonathan Maccabee's elevation as High Priest in 152 BCE. Vermes, meanwhile, has concluded that disparities now evident between 1QS and 4QS^{b,d} over the role of the 'sons of Zadok' probably reflect changes in the community's authoritative structure.[57]

Yet, further facets of the fresh evidence must be taken seriously for any revised Qumran–Essene Hypothesis to stand the test of time. These include the number of scribal hands now manifest in the Qumran collection as a whole and the striking differences between recensions of some sectarian works just noted. Further issues concern the potential for historical overlaps between the Qumran Community and other Second Temple groupings, as well as the need to reconsider historical allusions in long-known compositions in the light of recently available ones. Let us briefly consider each of these questions in turn.

The multiplicity of scribal hands among the manuscripts awaits satisfactory explanation. There are some cases in which the scribe responsible for one composition has clearly also penned part or all of another. For example, the copyist of 1QS also penned 4QSamuel^a and 4QTestimonia, as well as corrections to 1QIsaiah^a.[58] But such interconnections are rare, even after the 1991 releases, and, if the Qumran collection stemmed from a small religious community, it is difficult to say why. Although the answer may be connected to the likelihood that many manuscripts from our first and second categories were acquired from outside the group, further research is needed.

The release of Cave 4 materials revealed additional copies of important texts, including the long-awaited 4QD^{a–h} (supplementing CD) and the equally anticipated 4QS^{a–j} (adding to 1QS), as well as 4QH^{a–f} (alongside 1QH^{a–b}). Back in 1982, 4QM^{a–g} was published to accompany 1QM and, as in that case, analysis of these parallel exemplars is proving to be at once helpful and problematic.[59] On the one hand, the new manuscripts have provided additional information about the compositions themselves. Thus, 4QD^{a–h} has given us supplementary laws missing from CD, some of which link in with the Classical Sources. For example, a prohibition against a husband 'fornicating' with his wife in 4QD^e is reminiscent of Josephus' statement that married Essenes refrain from sexual intercourse during pregnancy.[60] Or again, strong similarities between the 1QS and 4QD^{a–h} versions of the Penal Code – present also in 4QMiscellaneous

Rules – demonstrate that these texts describe different phases or branches of the same broad movement.

On the problematic side, we have already observed significant divergences between parallel editions. Although their potential for informing us about the growth of the compositions and the community behind them is considerable, it is by no means always clear how they are to be explained. For instance, we saw above that differences between 1QS and 4QS[b,d] over the role of the 'sons of Zadok' could be explained in more than one way. Whilst not undermining the basic Essene link, such recensional variations require further study.

A more general question is how to embed the Qumran DSS within the wider world of late Second Temple Palestine, especially given the corpus' diversity now so evident.[61] We have already learned that the neat distinction formerly made between scriptural and sectarian writings has been blurred by the extent of our second category of texts. And yet the ideological overlap between elements of the latter and some sectarian works suggests that the group behind the Qumran DSS had a long and complex history, dove-tailing to an extent with what eventually became rival groupings. This may be the truth behind Schiffman's recent reassertion, to be unpacked in Chapter 7, that the Qumran Sect was Sadducean in origin, despite his thesis' unsustainability on other grounds.

The Historical Context

Certainly, this latter aspect of Qumran origins requires further investigation. And analysis of historical allusions in recently released texts (e.g. 4QMMT[a–f], 4QApocryphal Psalm and Prayer, 4QCalendrical Document C) will doubtless engender fruitful reconsideration of others in longer-known works (e.g. 1QpHabakkuk, 4QpNahum, 4QpPsalms[a]) and how both might be integrated into a revised Qumran–Essene Hypothesis. Meanwhile, although the Qumran DSS have yielded no historical document in the modern sense, it may be possible to make some general deductions about their broad historical context.[62]

The Qumran–Essene Hypothesis has long posited a second-century BCE origin for the community behind the Qumran DSS on the basis of 1QpHabakkuk and the Damascus Document. We saw earlier that CD 1:5–12 envisages the formation of an embryonic community in the 190s BCE, some 390 years after Nebuchadnezzar's capture of Jerusalem, with the Teacher of Righteousness himself appearing on the scene a further twenty years later.[63] This Teacher of Righteousness and his opponent, the Wicked Priest, also feature prominently in 1QpHabakkuk. The precise identity of the former remains elusive, but most have associated the latter with Jonathan Maccabee after his elevation as High Priest in 152 BCE.[64] Although it is possible that both designations denote several individuals over a period of time, the fact that the 'sons of Zadok' are prominent in some sectarian documents suggests the Zadokite issue, alongside legal disputes of the sort encountered in 4QMMT[a–f], was central to the group's early development.[65]

Indeed, despite the importance of the first century BCE for several new texts like 4QCalendrical Documents C, the dating of other 1991 releases reaffirms the second century BCE as pivotal. 4QMSM and Cave 4 copies of the Rule of the Congregation (4QSE[a–i]), in particular, palaeographically dated to the mid-second century BCE or earlier, provide fairly strong evidence that the group later inhabiting Khirbet Qumran had its origins in the early to mid-second century BCE. Various legal, calendrical, and theological issues certainly faced traditionalists at this time in response to encroaching hellenization (*circa* 200–175 BCE), aspects of Antiochus IV Epiphanes' reign (175–164 BCE), and Jonathan Maccabee's elevation as High Priest (152 BCE). Such issues, as already noted, seem to have informed the likes of Jubilees and portions of Enochic material, both of which have ideological overlaps with many Qumran DSS in our second and third categories.[66] The same formative background presumably explains legal overlaps between some non-sectarian texts and others almost certainly originating within our group. For example, a strict observance of the Sabbath, coupled with condemnation of niece marriage, features in the Damascus Document and fragmentary 4QWays of Righteousness, both normally deemed sectarian, and in 4QLegal Texts A–B, which are not. Whether, at this early stage, our embryonic community constituted Essenes proper, their immediate forebears, or even an Essene splinter faction, remains open to debate. But that its members believed they had ancient origins going back to the Babylonian exile is highly likely in view of CD 1:3–5.

Similarly, there is little doubt that Qumran itself was settled no earlier than John Hyrcanus I's rule (134–104 BCE). If, as just noted, the oldest sectarian documents were composed during the first half of the second century BCE, the initial phases of the community must have been based elsewhere. Because it is mentioned several times in CD and 4QD[a–h], 'Damascus' suggests itself here, with a subsequent relocation to Qumran and/or Jerusalem. Either possibility, or a combination of both, may be reflected in lQS 8:12–16:

> And when these become members of the Community in Israel according to all these rules, they shall separate from the habitation of unjust men and

shall go into the wilderness to prepare there the way of Him; as it is written, *Prepare in the wilderness . . . make straight in the desert a path for our God* (Isa. xl,3). This (path) is the study of the Law which He commanded by the hand of Moses, that they may do according to all that has been revealed from age to age, and as the Prophets have revealed by His Holy Spirit.

This flight to the wilderness could denote a move to Damascus or Qumran, or even a return from either via the desert to Jerusalem. Others have detected in this 1QS passage an indirect reference to a migration from Babylon, referred to cryptically in CD and 4QD[a–h] as 'Damascus'.[67] Unfortunately, we cannot yet judge definitively between these options. Nor is the precise relationship of those at Damascus, Qumran, or Jerusalem with other Essenes in 'camps' elsewhere clear at present.

Nevertheless, archaeological work at Khirbet Qumran shows that our group flourished there in the first-century BCE, with expansion in buildings presumably matching that in numbers at the site and elsewhere. This growth may be related to the changing status of the 'sons of Zadok', noticeable in a comparison of 1QS and 4QS[b,d], as we have seen. More speculatively, we may link an increase in numbers with a decline in use of cryptic script on the assumption that, in the course of the first century BCE, the community became more secure, possibly even bordering on mainstream. Certainly, 1991 saw the release of a significant number of sectarian writings in cryptic script from the second century BCE, including 4QMSM and 4QSE[a–i], whereas this practice seems to have been waning by the mid-first century BCE. Relations with outsiders probably evolved considerably, therefore, with early political rivalry entailing a real danger of physical attack and a concomitant need for encryption. Later hostilities, in contrast, may have been predominantly verbal and theological, lessening the necessity for such secrecy.

In any case, we saw that a careful reading of 4QpNahum informs us that the writer refers to the Pharisees as 'those who seek smooth things' and 'Ephraim', a biblical name which, along with Manasseh, denotes the apostate northern tribes of ancient Israel. Not surprisingly, 'Manasseh' is applied in 4QpNahum 2:1–3:9 and 4QpPsalms[a] 2:18–20 to a group best identified as the Sadducees. As for Alexander Jannaeus, he is dubbed the 'furious young lion' and 'last priest' in 4QpHosea[b] 2:2–3, so that the 'last priests of Jerusalem' in lQpHabakkuk 9:4 are presumably other Hasmoneans. It seems that, in the author's estimation, these rulers were generally a bad lot, although individuals may have been viewed with greater or lesser opprobrium at any given time. If 'King Jonathan' in 4QApocryphal Psalm and Prayer is Alexander Jannaeus, for instance, his promising anti-Pharisaic stance may have inspired this non-sectarian hymn's adoption by the community. Still, according to 1QpHabakkuk, Hasmonean wickedness was to be punished by the 'Kittim' or Romans, viewed as God's instruments for justice. After they took control of Palestine, however, the Romans themselves were vilified as the new archenemies, to be defeated, according to the War Scroll and Book of War, with the advent of God's kingdom. Indeed, the intervention of the Romans in the region in 63 BCE may have been a prime contributor to the changed nature of hostilities with other Jews tentatively suggested in the last paragraph.

Regrettably, sectarian documents do not tell us anything about the group during Phase II (*circa* 1–68 CE). All we know is that its occupation of Khirbet Qumran ended in 68 CE, though the fate of Essenes elsewhere remains a mystery. Roman soldiers put the Qumran Community to flight, using the site as a temporary outpost. Fortunately for us, the sect abandoned its scrolls to posterity in the surrounding caves, where they remained for almost 2,000 years.

The Religious Context

The Qumran DSS of our second and third categories rarely unpack their underlying religious beliefs. This is unsurprising, for Second Temple Jews tended not to formulate a systematic theology. Nonetheless, we can determine the movement's basic world-view and concomitant mode of behaviour, as long as we allow for changes over time and from place to place.[68] Many elements are straightforwardly biblical or comprise developments shared by all Second Temple Jews, whereas others are more idiosyncratic.

Like other Jews, the Qumran Sect knew that Abraham had long ago been singled out for blessing and, most importantly, God had revealed the Torah to his descendants through Moses. After the Babylonian exile, a faithful remnant was preserved, and the community believed that it alone formed that remnant's continuation. Central to its identity was study of the Law, apparently dubbed the 'Book of Meditation' (Hebrew, *sefer he-hagu*) in 1QSa 1:7 and in CD 10:6; 13:2; and 14:8.[69] According to 1QpHabakkuk 7:3–5, more specifically, as we saw above, the Teacher of Righteousness possessed unique insight into the 'mysteries' (Hebrew, *razim*) of the Torah and other scriptures, enabling the sect to comprehend the times in which it lived and to organize its life accordingly. Such special knowledge lies behind the 'hidden things' (*nistarot*) of CD 3:14 and elsewhere, as well as the 'mystery to come' (*raz nihyeh*) of Mysteries

(1Q27, 4Q299–301) and Instruction A (1Q26, 4Q415–418, 432). The Teacher of Righteousness' successors, including the 'sons of Zadok' during some of the group's history, were presumably similarly gifted in the eyes of their followers.

Thus, unlike most of its contemporaries, the Qumran Sect followed a distinctive calendar in which a 364-day year was predominant.[70] Because variations on it feature in Enochic literature and Jubilees, however, as well as in works like 4QCalendrical Documents A–H which are not narrowly sectarian, it was probably adopted by other Second Temple groupings in the late third or second centuries BCE and beyond. This solar-dominated calendar consisted of twelve regular months of thirty days each, plus one additional day at the end of each quarter (12 × 30+4=364), as the following table shows:[71]

	months 1, 4, 7, 10	months 2, 5, 8, 11	months 3, 6, 9, 12
Wednesday	1 8 15 22 29	6 13 20 27	4 11 18 25
Thursday	2 9 16 23 30	7 14 21 28	5 12 19 26
Friday	3 10 17 24	1 8 15 22 29	6 13 20 27
Saturday	4 11 18 25	2 9 16 23 30	7 14 21 28
Sunday	5 12 19 26	3 10 17 24	1 8 15 22 29
Monday	6 13 20 27	4 11 18 25	2 9 16 23 30
Tuesday	7 14 21 28	5 12 19 26	3 10 17 24 31

In this schema, unlike the predominantly lunar system of 354 days adopted by most Jews, the main religious festivals fell on the same day each year, and two additional minor summer feasts were celebrated on the model of the Feast of Weeks at the time of the wheat harvest: the 'Feast of Wine' and 'Feast of Oil'. But the 364-day calendar also rejected two festivals celebrated by the majority of Jews, Purim and Hanukkah, presumably because neither is stipulated by Moses in the Pentateuch, while the latter commemorated the Maccabees' victory in 164 BCE and, by implication, the legitimacy of their Hasmonean successors.[72]

Such calendrical differences explain how, according to 1QpHabakkuk 11:5–8, the Teacher of Righteousness was attacked on the Day of Atonement:

> *Woe to him who causes his neighbours to drink; who pours out his venom to make them drunk that he may gaze on their feasts* (ii, 15).
> Interpreted, this concerns the Wicked Priest who pursued the Teacher of Righteousness to the house of his exile that he might confuse him . . . And

at the time appointed for rest, for the Day of Atonement, he appeared
before them to confuse them . . .

The Wicked Priest did not rest because the date concerned was not his
Day of Atonement. Although calendrical matters may seem tedious to
modern people, therefore, we should not underestimate their significance
in ancient times. After all, its use of Songs of the Sabbath Sacrifice shows
that the Qumran Community believed that it could participate in the
very worship of heaven by adopting the correct calendar.

More mundanely, various officials exercised day-to-day authority,
including the 'Guardian' or 'Master', 'Bursar', and 'council of the community'. These roles certainly differed over time and between branches
of Essenes. In 1QS 6:8–9, for instance, the council of the community is
the whole sect, whereas in 1QS 8:1–4 it consists of twelve lay and three
priestly members. Because the Community Rule nowhere mentions
women, furthermore, it may well be that those at Qumran and some
other Essene settlements consisted solely of celibate males, as scholars
have often assumed, whilst others elsewhere married and had children
according to the rules of the Damascus Document.[73] Alternatively, we
may take up Stegemann's recent suggestion and propose that many
Essenes were indeed sexually abstinent, because strict laws meant that
young men, expectant mothers, divorcees, and priests would *de facto* have
been celibate for much or all of the time. After all, 1QSa 1:9–10 stipulates
marriage at the age of twenty, CD 4:20–21 seems to forbid remarriage
after divorce, and Josephus says that married Essenes did not engage in
intercourse during pregnancy.[74] For different reasons, priestly members
of the community may have undergone periods of sexual abstinence too.
Such restrictions might easily have led outsiders to deduce that the
Essenes had an ideological commitment to a permanent celibacy which,
as Stegemann has proposed, they may not in fact have had.

In any case, the whole movement seems to have gathered annually
under the 'Guardian of all the camps' (CD 14:3–6) to renew its covenant
with God, probably during the Feast of Weeks in the 'third month'
(4QDᵉ).[75] Serious transgressors of the group's laws were expelled and
new members admitted at this time, while others were ranked in accord
with their spiritual progress, as 1QS 2:19–25 describes:

> Thus shall they do, year by year, for as long as the dominion of Belial
> endures. The Priests shall enter first, ranked after one another . . . then
> the Levites; and thirdly, all the people . . . in their Thousands, Hundreds,
> Fifties, and Tens . . . No man shall move down from his place nor move
> up from his allotted position.

Paralleling ancient Israel, the community had priestly, levitical, and lay members, with the latter subdivided into Thousands, Hundreds, Fifties, and Tens (lQS 2:21 and CD 13:1–2) for military purposes. Among its priestly contingent, the sons of Zadok were prominent, as already observed on several occasions, at least for a substantial period of the group's history.

Its special insight into ancient scripture explains the Qumran Sect's devotion to a strict interpretation of the Law.[76] Such commitment led to the stipulation in lQS 8:21–23 that any breach should result in expulsion:

> Every man who enters the Council of Holiness ... who deliberately or through negligence transgresses one word of the Law of Moses ... shall be expelled from the Council of the Community ...

Inspired knowledge also explains how books like Habakkuk were understood to show that the 'end of days' had arrived. Thus, the community believed it constituted the sole locus of truth and divine favour in the final phase of world history. It seems clear that early members of the Qumran Sect were disappointed when the expected end failed to materialize, as we shall see again in Chapter 6.[77] Nevertheless, the conviction that the end was near explains the urgent tone of many sectarian documents, as well as the polemic aimed at non-Essenes. In this connection, it should not be forgotten that Jews outside were free to ally themselves with the sect. That much seems to be inferred by the conciliatory tone of 4QMMT[a–f] which, we mooted earlier, may constitute the 'law' sent by the Teacher of Righteousness to his opponents according to 4QpPsalms[a] 4:9. It is further implied by 1QSa's belief that the final battle between good and evil would present an opportunity for the Jewish masses to join the community.

Despite such freedom, however, the theological determinism of many sectarian compositions is also noticeable, as witnessed already.[78] Even Satan, who tricks the righteous into sin, is under God's control, as far as the author of 1QS 3:21–24 is concerned:

> The Angel of Darkness leads all the children of righteousness astray, and until his end, all their sin, iniquities, wickedness, and all their unlawful deeds are caused by his dominion in accordance with the mysteries of God.

Inherent within this predestined order are the 'way of light' and 'way of darkness'. These opposing forces make their influence felt throughout the universe, according to the spiritual instruction in lQS 4:15–17:

The nature of all the children of men is ruled by these (two spirits) . . .
For God has established the spirits in equal measure until the final age,
and has set everlasting hatred between their divisions.

The conflict between these 'two spirits' rages in the angelic realm, as the
War Scroll makes clear, as much as between and within humans. Only
divine intervention in the final cosmic battle will ensure victory, vindicate
the sect, and lead to cosmic 'renewal' (1QS 4:25).

To that end, the advent of two messianic figures was awaited.[79]
Although the detail of its ideas in this regard doubtless evolved over
time, the Qumran Community believed in both a Priest-Messiah or
'Messiah of Aaron' and a Davidic Messiah or 'Messiah of Israel', with the
latter firmly subordinate to the former.[80] This priestly superiority is
entirely understandable, given scriptural promises to the priesthood and
the fact that the Hebrew *mashiah*, 'anointed (one)', could evoke the High
Priest's anointing in biblical times as much as the Davidic king's. Ample
scriptural warrant further exists for this twofold combination in the
books of Haggai and Zechariah 1–8.[81] Indeed, the two characters are
portrayed in lQS 9:11, with its 'Messiahs of Aaron and Israel', as well as
in lQSa 2:11–22 and probably in the Damascus Document.[82] The
shadowy 'Interpreter of the Law' is another matter, however, for in CD
6:7 he is a figure of the past, whereas in CD 7:18 and 4QFlorilegium
3:12 he seems to arrive in the future.[83] He may be priestly, or he could
be the same as 'the prophet' in 1QS 9:11, whom some scholars identify
as a third messiah.[84] It seems, in any case, that the Qumran Sect's
messianic expectations reflect the fact that, in Israel's ancient past, priests
and kings and, occasionally, prophets could be anointed.

An Essene Community at Qumran

To close our consideration of the Qumran Community's Essene identity,
it is worth pointing to four interrelated factors which, as seen in the
course of this chapter and the last, render preferable the linking of the
DSS from Caves 1–11, the sites of Khirbet Qumran and 'Ein-Feshkha,
and the Essenes portrayed in Philo, Josephus, and Pliny:

(1)   The distinct pottery style of Caves 1–11 was also found during archaeolog-
      ical excavations at Khirbet Qumran and, to a lesser degree, 'Ein-Feshkha.
(2)   An ostracon retrieved from Khirbet Qumran in 1996 probably mentions
      the 'community' (*yahad*) of the sectarian DSS from Caves 1–11 and, in any
      event, mirrors the property transfer commended in 1QS 6:16–23.

(3) Many practices and beliefs are shared by the Essenes of Philo, Josephus, and Pliny and by the group behind the Community Rule and related documents.

(4) There is a clear connection between Pliny's notice of an Essene community near 'Ein-Gedi and Khirbet Qumran's geographical location.

These correspondences require us to posit two broad conclusions. Firstly, against the archaeological background of the Qumran ruins and caves, (1) and (2) can only be adequately explained by deducing that the religious community which owned the contents of Caves 1–11 also employed Khirbet Qumran and 'Ein-Feshkha during the last third of the Second Temple period, even if the earliest phases of its history were based elsewhere. Secondly, given Second Temple history and religion in Palestine at large, (3) and (4) strongly suggest that the group which inhabited Khirbet Qumran and utilized the manuscripts of Caves 1–11 was closely linked with the Essenes of the Classical Sources, however that relationship is to be defined more precisely.

Of course, just how such conclusions are to be unpacked in more detail remains a matter of dispute, whilst how the community envisaged related to other contemporary religious parties is likewise contested. Nevertheless, as scholarship emerges into the twenty-first century, these two basic judgements provide the best framework for understanding the Qumran DSS as a whole. Even if earlier formulations of the Qumran–Essene Hypothesis now seem oversimple in the light of new evidence, these conclusions epitomize their lasting contribution to research.

5

The Dead Sea Scrolls and Judaism

The Nature of the Evidence

The DSS from Qumran – and especially the sectarian documents – provide a glimpse into the life of a religious party with Essene connections which flourished in the late Second Temple period. We can now turn our attention to the wider world of late Second Temple Judaism by placing the Qumran DSS alongside other relevant literature: late biblical material, the Apocrypha and Pseudepigrapha, New Testament, Philo and Josephus, and, to a lesser extent, Rabbinic writings.[1] Afterwards, for the sake of completeness, it will be worthwhile explaining how Judaism developed in the centuries following the Temple's destruction in 70 CE. Then, in the last section of this chapter, we shall briefly consider what impact the DSS might have on modern Judaism.

Beginning with Judaism in Second Temple times, it is important to realize that, in contrast to the Qumran evidence's direct nature, all other sources for the period are marred by limitations of one sort or another.[2] For example, the authorship and date of many books from the Hebrew Bible, Apocrypha, and Pseudepigrapha remain obscure. And even in cases where this problem is less pronounced, it is difficult to be sure whether the perspective of, say, Jubilees, Daniel, or Wisdom was commonplace or marginal. As for the New Testament, although long drawn on for an impression of Judaism in Jesus' day, academic study has shown most of its writings were compiled after 70 CE, as we shall observe more clearly in the next chapter.[3]

A prolific Jewish author in Greek was Philo, who probably lived *circa* 15 BCE to *circa* 50 CE. Looking back to Philo's heading of a Jewish delegation to the Emperor Gaius Caligula in 40 CE, his younger contemporary Josephus described him as 'brother of Alexander the alabarch and no novice in philosophy'.[4] This description highlights Philo's place among the Jewish elite of Alexandria in Egypt.[5] As for his writings, Philo produced numerous interpretative treatises concerning the Law of Moses, as well as others touching on contemporary issues or events. Among the latter are his *On the Embassy to Gaius*, recounting his experiences in the above-mentioned delegation to Caligula, and *On the Contemplative Life* which describes the 'Therapeutae', an Egyptian Jewish sect similar to the Essenes of Palestine.[6] Philo's exegetical works, more generally, marry the Jewish tradition with what he regarded as the best of Greek philosophy, on the assumption that the latter ultimately derived from the former. Further, whilst Jews are required to keep them all literally, Philo was also convinced that God's commandments have a deeper allegorical significance, thus enabling him to link them with Plato's philosophy. His apologetics here are obvious, for Philo wanted to show that Judaism was equal to whatever the non-Jewish world could offer.[7] But just how common this synthesizing philosophical outlook was among other Second Temple Jews, Egyptian or otherwise, remains unclear.

Caution is also required with Josephus who, living from 37 CE until *circa* 100 CE, spent the first half of his life in Jerusalem. Born into a well-to-do priestly family, Josephus was an educated man with a comfortable existence, although it doubtless had its trials and tribulations. One such occasion was his visit to Rome to seek the release of Jewish prisoners, just two years before the outbreak of the First Revolt. Yet, this visit to the imperial capital in 64 CE suggests Josephus was a moderate who, though proud of his Jewish heritage, was content with the status quo of Roman rule in Palestine. After 70 CE, in fact, Josephus settled in Rome as a favourite of the Emperors Vespasian and Titus.[8] Even though he had been a minor leader in the Revolt, he managed to ingratiate himself after capture, apparently predicting correctly that the Roman general in charge of the campaign, Vespasian, would soon become emperor. After his prediction became reality, Josephus subsequently wrote four works from the imperial capital: *Jewish War*, *Jewish Antiquities*, the *Life*, and *Against Apion*.[9] Whilst varying in their subject matter, purpose, and length, these writings try to show *inter alia* that, notwithstanding the war with Rome, the Jews were a peace-loving nation and Judaism a noble religion. Josephus also sought to demonstrate that both he and the Romans had behaved impeccably during the First Revolt, which was largely the fault of a small number of rebels. Unfortunately, both aims, as well as his mixed readership, occasioned considerable, if sporadic, oversimplification and idealization, as we have already seen regarding the

Essenes. Such tendencies particularly obfuscate the Revolt's precise causes, not to mention Josephus' true colours before switching to the Roman side after his imprisonment. Nevertheless, the fact that Josephus lived in Palestine for some thirty years before the Revolt renders him an invaluable source for Second Temple history and religion, although technically he wrote after 70 CE.[10]

As for Rabbinic literature, composed long after 70 CE, it has an even stronger agenda of its own. Among other things, the rabbis who compiled the Mishnah (*circa* 200 CE) and the Babylonian Talmud (*circa* 550 CE) were at pains to establish themselves as the heirs of the Pharisees from the Second Temple period. Although the rabbis doubtless drew on much previously-existing tradition, their overarching aim was to legitimize the religious system developed after 70 CE, as well as their authoritative place within it. Consequently, for example, historians are increasingly reluctant to take at face value the elevated position attributed to the Pharisees in Rabbinic literature, as we shall discover.[11]

Because of these varying limitations, the sources available before the discovery of the Qumran DSS provide neither straightforward descriptions of Second Temple Judaism at large, nor first-hand accounts of specific religious groupings. By utilizing the Qumran documents as a corrective, however, and by combining their evidence with other writings, we can reconstruct some major features of late Second Temple Jewish religion.

Judaism or Judaisms?

Paradoxically, the main inference to be drawn is the impossibility of reducing Second Temple Judaism to a single definition. Apart from anything else, too many gaps remain in the evidence, while what information we do have highlights considerable divergence in practice and belief among the religious groups we have thus far encountered. Each party doubtless believed its outlook was superior, especially the sect behind the Qumran DSS. Nevertheless, we are not in a position to deem any one perspective a truer representation of Judaism than any other. More neutral is the suggestion that each community embodied a particular formulation of what, in its view, constituted being a good Jew amid the complex circumstances of the day. In other words, each community's distinctive characteristics were alternative responses to this basic question – formulated according to the needs and predilections of the group concerned, as well as to the particular religious traditions available to it in a given time and place.

This characterization of Jewish practice and belief has led some scholars to speak of 'Judaisms' in the plural rather than a singular 'Judaism'.[12] Indeed, the array of late Second Temple Jewish identities makes this an attractive proposition, for, apart from the Pharisees, Sadducees, and Essenes, we should not forget about 'revolutionary nationalists' and early Christians.[13] Even the Samaritans could be listed here because, apart from their preference for a Temple on Mount Gerizim, rather than Jerusalem, their distinguishing features were probably no greater than any other Jewish party's.

This overwhelming impression of diversity is exacerbated when we consider Jews in the Diaspora – that is, those dispersed outside the traditional homeland in Palestine. A significant number of Jews descended from earlier exiles had, of course, already been settled for hundreds of years in the former Babylonian empire. In addition, although it has not featured in our inquiry so far, a strong Jewish Diaspora also evolved in other parts of the world during late Second Temple times, as war, commerce, or simple curiosity drove Jews abroad.[14] Such Jewish communities in the Diaspora were spread over too wide an area to form a distinct religious party. Nevertheless, Diaspora Judaism seems to have had a greater tendency to absorb non-Jewish ideas and customs. While this susceptibility should not be exaggerated, Jews in, say, Alexandria or Rome were inclined to assimilate more thoroughly towards Gentile culture and religion than those in Palestine. Philo, the older contemporary of Josephus mentioned above, is an interesting example. Writing from Alexandria in Egypt, he set out to synthesize Jewish and Greek thought. And a similar trait is evident in the slightly earlier book of Wisdom from the Apocrypha, fictitiously ascribed to King Solomon but probably penned in Egypt in the late first century BCE.[15] Like Philo, its author portrays the Jewish hope of life after death in the Greek guise of the soul's immortality, rejecting the notion of a bodily resurrection apparently popular in Palestine.

To sum up so far, the religious parties and tendencies we have encountered in our study up to this point might be described as a collection of Judaisms. Various parallels in practice and belief, as well as the possibility of partially coinciding origins in some cases, allow us to picture them in terms of the overlapping circles of a Venn diagram, rather than as entirely separate entities.[16] Nevertheless, serious divergences meant that each group competed with the others for the attention of late Second Temple Jews. We have already observed that sectarian texts among the Qumran DSS employed insulting nicknames for outsiders (e.g. 'Seekers of Smooth Things' for the Pharisees), while similar rivalry comes across in Acts 23:6–10, where Paul cleverly takes advantage of disputes between Pharisees and Sadducees. Again, 4QApocryphon of Joseph[a] may reflect an anti-Samaritan bias on the part of its anonymous second-century BCE Jewish writer.[17] In such circumstances, no one party constituted a normative or 'orthodox' Judaism, and so the claims of later Rabbinic literature in this regard are inaccurate. In other words, the later rabbis' assumption that the Pharisees represented mainstream Judaism was an anachronistic retrojection onto the past from their own day.[18] Pharisaic piety cannot be equated with the religion of ordinary people in the last two centuries BCE or the first century CE, especially if the Pharisees, despite their frequent popularity with the masses, numbered only some six thousand, as Josephus states. On the other hand, the Sadducees of the Temple establishment, as a small wealthy elite, cannot have been representative either.[19] Nor have we reason to believe that the practices and beliefs of the Essenes were adopted by Jews outside their own membership. Intermittent evidence for the existence of yet other partisan groups only exacerbates this sense of a plurality of Judaisms.[20]

Nevertheless, this evidence for diversity might not be the whole story. We have already observed that membership of the Pharisees, Sadducees, and Essenes numbered no more than several thousand each. Such figures show that, even when combined, they accounted for no more than a minority of the Jewish population in Palestine.[21] Consequently, large numbers did not belong to any religious party, especially if we include Diaspora Jews in the picture. So, what about the ordinary masses of Jewish men, women, and children?[22] It is here that, following E. P. Sanders of Duke University, it may make sense to return to the singular and speak of a 'Common Judaism'.[23] Put another way, setting aside the distinctive elements of named religious parties, the average late Second Temple Jew adhered to a core of practices and beliefs held in common. These had to do with God, with Israel as both land and people, with the Temple in Jerusalem, and, of course, with the Torah as God's ultimate revelation. Since these elements probably constituted four common denominators among all Jews, it is worth saying a few words about the first three, while the Law will receive fuller attention in the next section.

Underlying all Jewish identities in the Second Temple period was a basic belief in the Jewish God. Indeed, Jews were renowned for their monotheistic worship without the use of images, unlike the adherents of other Graeco-Roman cults. But just how this Deity was envisaged could vary considerably. The sectarian Qumran DSS's picture of God, for instance, might seem distant from Philo's philosophical conceptualization. Even so, the adherents of both would have assumed their Deity was the same as the God who had called Abraham, revealed the Torah to Moses, controlled the fate of ancient Israel and Judah, and still guided their descendants, the Jews. Beyond such essentials, many found it unnecessary to speculate further about God's attributes in the way that later generations of Jews and Christians would do.[24] Alongside an elementary belief in God, however, the status of the people of Israel was another indispensable factor.

Primarily, Israel was God's people in the biblical period, so called after one of Abraham's grandsons, Jacob, himself renamed Israel (Genesis 32:28). According to the biblical story, his sons became twelve great tribes who settled in the land which also became known as Israel. Eventually, only the tribes of Judah and Benjamin survived intact and, as explained in Chapter 1, Second Temple Jews believed they were their descendants. They also held that their relationship with God remained special, and hand in hand with that belief went the unique status of the land inhabited by the Israelites of old and their Jewish heirs. Consequently, all Second Temple Jews felt a special bond with the land of Israel – Judaea, Samaria, and Galilee – whether they happened to live in it or not. This link between land and people was one of the driving forces behind both Hasmonean independence and the First Revolt against Rome. But it also remained an important factor when the traditional Jewish homeland was under foreign domination. Thus, during the Roman occupation, Jews from all over the world came on pilgrimage to major religious festivals like the Passover, Feast of Weeks, and Feast of Tabernacles.[25] Such devotion is accurately reflected in Acts 2:9–11, showing that Jews gathered in Jerusalem from far and wide on such occasions.

Of course, the Temple was the centre of religious activity at such times, since it constituted the focus of God's presence on earth in the eyes of most Jews. To safeguard its sanctity, God had ordained a priesthood to perform ritual and sacrifice in accord with his will as revealed in the Torah. Only they were allowed into the Temple's most hallowed parts, while the High Priest alone was permitted to enter the Holy of Holies at its heart once a year on the Day of Atonement. As for ordinary Jews, several sources take it for granted that they paid a special tax which, following the injunctions in Exodus 30:11–16 and Nehemiah 10:32, was contributed annually by adult males for the Temple's upkeep.[26] That the Qumran Sect, convinced the Temple establishment of its day was corrupt, determined that the levy should be paid once in a lifetime only, is an exception proving the rule here.[27] So ingrained was payment of this yearly tax, even among Diaspora Jews who rarely came into contact with the Temple, that the Romans redirected its annual proceeds to the temple of Jupiter in Rome after the defeat of the First Revolt in 70 CE.[28]

The Temple and its precincts were run by the High Priest and other leading priests in Jerusalem. We can compile a list, in fact, of most of the High Priests of the Second Temple period. The main exception concerns the years 159–152 BCE, for Josephus, our major source, remains silent about the incumbent during these years. This may be because there was no High Priest at this time for reasons no longer apparent. Alternatively, some have suggested that the Teacher of Righteousness known from the Qumran DSS held the office until 152 BCE when, as we learned earlier, Jonathan Maccabee bought it from the Seleucids in exchange for military support.[29] Certainty may never be possible on this question. And similarly, it is difficult to grasp the exact nature of the body called in various sources the 'Council' and, later, the 'Sanhedrin'.[30] Allowing for some development over time, it is probably safe to say that this Sanhedrin was Jerusalem's ruling council during late Second Temple times, headed by the High Priest and including other leading priests, as well as prominent Sadducees and Pharisees. Within it, important political and legal decisions were taken, subject to approval, when Palestine was occupied, by the relevant Seleucid or Roman authorities. The extent of the Sanhedrin's power is less than clear, however, especially when it came to executing criminals. We shall see in the next chapter that this issue has been hotly debated by scholars in relation to the trial of Jesus.

Before moving on, it is important to mention two further loci of Jewish worship and study: several additional temples and the synagogue. In the course of the Second Temple period, a small number of competing sanctuaries were set up by individuals or groups. The best known is the one on Mount Gerizim, used by the Samaritans until it was destroyed in the reign of John Hyrcanus.[31] But we also know of a fourth-century BCE temple serving the Jewish troops garrisoned at Elephantine in the upper Nile, as well as a sanctuary in the Transjordan associated with the powerful Tobiad family resident there during the third century BCE. Somewhat later is the temple built in the second century BCE at Leontopolis in Egypt by Onias IV, son of the High Priest Onias III who was deposed from office in Jerusalem in 175 BCE in favour of Jason. This site at Leontopolis operated until 73 CE but, as with the others, it remains unclear just how most Jews viewed its status.[32]

We can be more confident that, in the late Second Temple period, Jews assembled for prayer and study – especially on the Sabbath – in 'prayer houses' or synagogues. At first, such gatherings were particularly pertinent for Jewish communities outside Palestine, for the Jerusalem Temple was too distant to visit regularly. But by the early first century CE, synagogues in Palestine seem to have been becoming increasingly popular, even in Jerusalem.[33] And although we should be cautious about the existence of fixed forms of prayer or worship before 70 CE, the Qumran DSS suggest broad trends may have been establishing themselves in this regard. It is likely, for instance, that the Qumran daily and festival prayers noted in the last chapter had their parallels elsewhere.[34]

The Role of the Torah

Back in Chapter 2, we concluded that late Second Temple Jews drew on an open-ended and wide-ranging body of scriptural works. At the core of such texts was our fourth common denominator shared by all, for it was believed that God had revealed the Torah or Law through Moses to the people of Israel centuries earlier. At the heart of this Torah were rules regarding the Tabernacle – the Temple's predecessor used by the Israelites in the desert – and its priesthood, and a lot more besides.[35] Although the brevity of many commandments necessitated interpretation, the Law nevertheless provided a blueprint for Jewish life. However, many modern people unfamiliar with Judaism's legal tradition find it difficult to grasp. We shall elaborate on it here, therefore, before turning to more speculative doctrinal matters.[36]

Late Second Temple Judaism, like most Graeco-Roman religions, incorporated an elaborate system of worship and sacrifice focused on a central sanctuary, the Jerusalem Temple, whose priesthood was regulated by rules in the Pentateuch. Unusually, the Law also extended its influence into every aspect of ordinary Jewish life. Being a Jew was primarily about living according to God's will as revealed in the Torah. To that extent, Judaism in our period can be described as 'legalistic', that is, concerned with obeying God's laws.

When understood on its own terms, however, Jewish 'legalism' should not be misconstrued as petty or burdensome.[37] The second-century BCE work of Ben Sira serves as an illustration, for praise is heaped upon divine Wisdom, personified as God's helper when the world was created. In Ben Sira 24:23, more particularly, the writer makes an important connection:

> All this is the book of the covenant of the Most High God,
>   the law that Moses commanded us
>   as an inheritance for the congregations of Jacob.

God's very Wisdom is here said to be embodied in the Torah. The only adequate response is to follow its decrees, without any artificial distinction between ritual and ethical commandments. From within such an

Plate 5   *A cistern at Khirbet Qumran, probably split by the earthquake of 31* BCE.
© *Jonathan G. Campbell.*

outlook, all aspects of human life prescribed in the Torah – worshipping
God, loving one's neighbour, punishing the sinner, offering sacrifice,
tithing grain – form one seamless whole. Naturally, therefore, obedience
would normally result in blessing for both community and individual,
whereas disobedience would bring disaster.

All the evidence suggests that late Second Temple Jews accepted the
Torah's divine origin and kept most of its prescriptions much of the
time. Various non-Jewish writers bear this out, commenting on well-
known features of Judaism.[38] The third-century CE Roman historian
Cassius Dio, for example, remarked on Jewish Sabbath observance at the
time of Pompey's conquest of Jerusalem in 63 BCE:[39]

For it [the Temple] was on high ground and was fortified by a wall of its
own, and if they [the Jerusalemites] had continued defending it on all days
alike, he [Pompey] could not have got possession of it. As it was, they
made an exception of what are called the days of Saturn [the Sabbath], and

by doing no work at all on those days afforded the Romans an opportunity
. . . to batter down the wall.

In addition to the Sabbath, several features of Judaism stood out:
imageless worship of the one true God, circumcision of males, abstention
from pork and other dietary regulations, and purity rules to deal with
ritual uncleanness.[40] The latter could be transmitted via corpses, skin
disease, or bodily emissions and, although not necessarily entailing sin,
required ritual washing to restore a state of cleanness. Priests accessing
the Temple had to be particularly attentive to such purity matters, as did
ordinary Jews visiting it during religious festivals.

There can be little doubt that the bulk of the Jewish population kept
these laws, and Josephus recounts an incident under Pontius Pilate
demonstrating this popular piety:[41]

> Pilate . . . introduced into Jerusalem by night . . . the effigies of Caesar
> which are called standards. This proceeding, when day broke, aroused
> immense excitement among the Jews; those on the spot were in conster-
> nation, considering their laws to have been trampled under foot, as those
> laws permit no image to be erected in the city; while the indignation of
> the townspeople stirred the country-folk, who flocked together in crowds.
> Hastening after Pilate to Caesarea, the Jews implored him to remove the
> standards from Jerusalem and to uphold the laws of their ancestors. When
> Pilate refused, they fell prostrate around his house and for five whole days
> and nights remained motionless in that position.
>
> On the ensuing day Pilate took his seat on his tribunal in the great
> stadium and summoning the multitude . . . gave the arranged signal to his
> armed soldiers to surround the Jews . . . Pilate, after threatening to cut
> them down, if they refused to admit Caesar's images, signalled to the
> soldiers to draw their swords. Thereupon the Jews . . . flung themselves in
> a body on the ground, extended their necks, and exclaimed that they were
> ready rather to die than to transgress the law. Overcome with astonishment
> at such intense religious zeal, Pilate gave orders for the immediate removal
> of the standards from Jerusalem.

Despite Pilate's surprise over their reaction to Roman military conven-
tion, the Jews described here were not unrepresentative but epitomized
typical devotion to God's Law. They could not stand by while images of
the divine Caesar on Roman standards were marched into Jerusalem, for
their presence violated the commandment against idolatry in Exodus
20:4 and Deuteronomy 5:8.

Of course, many other laws required interpretation to be obeyed in a
concrete manner. The priests in theory had the ultimate say in such

matters, and this certainly made sense when it came to running the Temple. Different groups of priests could disagree, however, as we saw with regard to the Qumran Community. If 4QMMT[a–f] is any guide, that group's leadership believed the Jerusalem priesthood was in grave error over numerous legal issues concerned with Temple purity. But when it came to everyday life, the priests could not monitor people's private behaviour any more than they could judge whether individuals were loving God with all their heart, as stipulated in Deuteronomy 6:5. In other words, the observance of whole portions of Jewish law was down to ordinary Jews' personal disposition.

The resultant internalization of the Torah by non-priestly Jews may account for the rise of a group like the Pharisees. As explained earlier, they consisted largely of lay persons adept at interpreting the Law independently. Going beyond the basic requirement, they adapted for everyday life purity rules which were not, strictly speaking, applicable to lay people outside the Temple. Moreover, Josephus hints that, when the Pharisees developed their own traditions about how real priests should perform their duties, they clashed with the predominantly Sadducean Temple establishment.[42]

Clearly, then, how the Torah was to be interpreted could provoke serious disagreement, although most Jews apparently tolerated a degree of divergence. Unusually, the Qumran Sect 'separated' (4QMMT[d], line 10) from its contemporaries over contentious legal issues, as we have seen. Whilst others took a more conciliatory line, this extreme case illustrates how resolute Second Temple Jews could be in keeping God's commands, explaining also why so much literature from the period occupies itself with the Law in one way or another.

Nevertheless, as observed at this section's outset, no evidence suggests Jews experienced the Torah's regulations as either trivial or oppressive. Neither was a legal preoccupation inimical to loving God and one's neighbour. Once again, the Qumran DSS's first-hand evidence, as 1QS 11:11–15 illustrates, underlines this:

As for me, if I stumble, the mercies of God shall be my eternal salvation.
If I stagger because of the sin of flesh, my justification shall be by the
  righteousness of God which endures for ever.
When my distress is unleashed He will deliver my soul from the pit and
  will direct my steps to the way.
He will draw me near by His grace, and by His mercy will He bring my
  justification.
He will judge me in the righteousness of His truth and in the greatness of
  His goodness He will pardon all my sins.

The Qumran Community's strict legalism was by no means incompatible with devotion to a loving and merciful God. Nor do we have reason to think that other Jews' commitment to the Torah was any different in this regard.

Theology, Eschatology, Apocalyptic

Alongside a necessary concern with the Torah's legal prescriptions, Second Temple Jewish literature also reflects widespread speculation on a range of theological issues. Unlike the former, however, there was considerable divergence over the extent to which the results of doctrinal speculation were accepted. Put another way, while adherence to the Pentateuch's laws – however they were interpreted – was deemed compulsory, matters of belief remained more fluid. As we have seen, such theological openness meant that, apart from elementary notions about God, Israel, the Temple, and the Torah, most Jews were free to believe more or less what they wished on all kinds of topics. Even if one group held passionately to certain theological convictions, that did not necessarily mean other Jews would have shared those convictions or even been aware of them. Apart from the basic tenets just listed, therefore, especially the Torah's divine origin, late Second Temple Jews held in common very few detailed doctrinal beliefs.

The resultant theological license was further encouraged by the assumption that it was membership of the Jewish community, for the most part attained by birth, which brought redeemed status, not correct belief. Even the Qumran Sect, although judging only its own members true Jews, thought along these lines. For them and others, a person's place within the faithful community was maintained by obedience to the Torah's commands, coupled with the conviction that God would forgive the shortcomings of those loyal to him.

The fact that different Second Temple groups shared a minimal amount of dogma was the corollary of a predominantly legal orientation. It also accounts for the vast array of competing and conflicting theological opinions which arose. Indeed, a variety of doctrines evolved around the foundational notions of God, Israel, the Temple, and the Torah. A few became widespread during the late Second Temple period. It is likely, for example, that most Jews believed in angels and demons by the first century CE. As for life after death, in the eyes of many, this world's injustices required some kind of reversal in the hereafter. According to Josephus, the main dissenters here were the Sadducees.[43] But even with a popular notion like the afterlife, diversity prevailed. As we saw earlier,

Philo envisaged an immortal soul freed from the body, but many Palestinian Jews tended to hope for a physical resurrection.

More exotic doctrinal speculation was the preserve of particular individuals or groups. The existence of the Apocrypha and Pseudepigrapha, as well as similar previously unknown Qumran compositions, shows that speculation about pious folk from the past was rife. In certain quarters, for instance, there was considerable interest in Enoch, mysteriously 'taken' by God without dying according to Genesis 5:24. Thus, the work later known as 1 Enoch, a collection of five once-separate books, is presented as a revelation to its namesake about a range of topics. That numerous Cave 4 copies of four of these books were recovered from Qumran shows that their purported secrets were taken seriously by the community there. All four books probably come from before the latter's formation and encourage the reader in two ways. First, through Enoch's guided tour of the cosmos and its mysteries (in 1 Enoch 17–36), assurances are given that the wicked will perish and the righteous be vindicated, despite contrary appearances. Second, reassurances are made that, notwithstanding the turmoil of the times, history is unfolding in line with what is written on God's heavenly tablets (1 Enoch 93:2). Indeed, numerous details show that the author believed the end of time was near. As for the world's ills, elaborating on the enigmatic story in Genesis 6:1–4, both 1 Enoch 6–16 and Jubilees 10:1–4 maintain that they stem, not so much from Adam and Eve's fall, but from a primordial act of fornication between angelic beings and human females. The offspring of this illicit union took the form of demons which thereafter plagued humanity and will eventually be destroyed in the final battle between good and evil. Given that Enochic traditions and Jubilees probably circulated widely, these ideas would have been known by many Second Temple Jews. We saw earlier that they are reflected in portions of 1QapGenesis which, like the traditions of 1 Enoch and Jubilees, was also probably inherited by the Qumran Sect from outside. Similarly, 4QSongs of the Sage may mirror the notion of angelic–human offspring by speaking negatively of the 'bastards'.

In contrast, belief in the Teacher of Righteousness' special status was a distinguishing mark of the Qumran Community. This conviction was doubtless passionately held and explained enthusiastically to newcomers. Even so, it seems to have taken a back seat in comparison to more urgent legal matters. Certainly, it was the correct application of purity rules to the Temple and priesthood which 4QMMT[a–f] sought to impart to its addressees, even though their formulation probably derived from the Teacher of Righteousness, his associates, or their successors.

More generally, varied theological opinions also form the background to late Second Temple hopes for the future. Scholars tend to employ the term 'eschatology', derived from the Greek adjective *eschatos* (meaning 'last'), when referring to such expectations and, as in other areas, a spectrum of views was tolerated.[44] This meant that, apart from a general belief that something good was ultimately in store for God's people, no one set of eschatological beliefs was universally current among Jews in the last two centuries BCE or the first century CE.[45]

Thus, the second-century BCE work Ben Sira, anticipating an improved version of the current state of affairs, looks forward to the arrival of an ideal High Priest. Some of the stories in Daniel, in contrast, compiled in the middle of Antiochus IV's persecutions during the 160s BCE, await imminent divine intervention. The dramatic and supernatural elements in this sort of eschatology are often described as 'apocalyptic'. In this manner, portions of 1 Enoch variously foresee an imminent vindication for the upright, a renewed heaven and earth, a new Jerusalem, the advent of a messianic figure, and a reversion to creation's primordial bliss.[46] Such features often appear in the literary genre known as the 'apocalypse', a name stemming from the Greek *apocalypsis* ('revelation') and denoting any text purporting to be a direct revelation from God or an angel. Parts of 1 Enoch and Daniel certainly fall into this generic class and also reflect apocalyptic themes. It should be made clear, however, that some apocalypses incorporate little that is 'apocalyptic' (e.g. Jubilees), while other writings not set in the form of the apocalypse do contain considerable 'apocalyptic' material (e.g. War Scroll). Although many scholars do not do so, therefore, it is most accurate to think of the genre of the apocalypse, on the one hand, and 'apocalyptic' imagery, on the other, as overlapping but distinct entities.[47]

The arrival of an eschatological figure was sometimes expected to improve the lot of God's people.[48] Once again, though, variety is evident. In 1 Maccabees, because the Maccabee brothers and, by implication, their Hasmonean successors have individually already fulfilled the role, the only concrete expectation of this type is the vague promise of a future 'prophet' (1 Maccabees 14:41). In the Psalms of Solomon, conversely, written soon after Pompey's capture of Jerusalem in 63 BCE, the author looks to a new Davidic king who will purify the Jewish nation and free Jerusalem from Roman control. The figure concerned can be described as a 'Messiah', as long as it is remembered that the term simply means 'anointed (one)' and connotated no clearly defined notion in late Second Temple times. As seen in relation to Qumran, almost any servant of God could be described as 'anointed', including priestly and prophetic figures, as well as a descendant of David.[49] Only later did 'the Messiah' come to designate a fixed identity, as both Judaism and Christianity developed after the Temple's destruction.[50] In some Jewish texts written before 70 CE, in contrast, no anointed figure features at all, the relevant eschatological or apocalyptic functions being attributed directly to God. Still further removed from such notions is the book of Wisdom. Containing virtually nothing eschatological, let alone apocalyptic, its writer looks forward in good Platonic fashion to the soul's release from the body at death.

The Torah Takes Over

The contrast between the binding status of the Torah's laws and the open-ended nature of much doctrinal speculation continued to be a feature of Judaism after Second Temple times.[51] However, the defeat of the First Revolt against Rome in 70 CE, coupled with the failure of the Second Revolt in 135 CE, provoked a crisis of a sort that had not been experienced since the Babylonians destroyed Jerusalem in 587 BCE. More precisely, the Temple and the priesthood were no longer able to function properly and, without these institutions, many of the Pentateuch's prescriptions were unworkable. Sacrifice could not be offered, for instance, nor could certain purificatory rites be performed. In the face of these losses, Judaism had to reorient itself in order to survive.[52]

The form such reorientation took may seem surprising at first. Essentially, the vacuum created by the demise of the Temple and its priests was filled by a devotion to the Torah even more wholehearted than that which had obtained beforehand. This meant that lay Jews, in particular, could continue obeying the Law in those areas requiring neither a visit to the Temple nor the aid of the priesthood. Legal observance thus retained its place at the heart of Jewish spirituality, while matters theological remained secondary. Nevertheless, over time, Judaism underwent a process of transformation at a deeper level. Though it takes us beyond the world of the Qumran DSS, it is worth looking briefly at what happened.

First, let us consider changes brought about by Jerusalem's fall. From 70 CE, we hear less and less of the Sadducees, presumably because the destruction of the city and its Temple ended their power and wealth. The Qumran Community, as we saw in Chapter 4, was put to flight in 68 CE and, because they are nowhere clearly mentioned in Rabbinic sources, we may conclude that related Essene groups elsewhere died out too. As for the 'revolutionary nationalists', their humiliating defeat at Roman hands precluded them from contributing to Jewish renewal afterwards.

With the demise of the Sadducees, Essenes, and revolutionary nationalists, as well as the general chaos which must have engulfed many ordinary Jewish lives, it was left to a small group of rabbis to rescue the situation. They reshaped Jewish religion over a period of one hundred and fifty years, though their precise historical origins are unclear. As for the term 'rabbi', the word means 'teacher' in Rabbinic literature and became the standard designation for a religious leader, as the principal Second Temple figures, the priests, receded into the background. Derived from the Hebrew *rav*, 'great', the word could also operate simply as an ordinary term of respect, especially before 70 CE. It is likely, therefore, that its few occurrences in first-century CE literature denote 'sir' rather than the title 'rabbi'.[53]

Rabbinic documents from 200 CE onwards describe the rabbis in idealized terms. Thus, their founder, Yohanan ben Zakkai, smuggled into Yavneh (or Jamnia) from Jerusalem in a coffin while under Roman siege, is said to have headed a team of Torah experts who were heirs to the Pharisees.[54] Some elements in this story are clearly anachronistic or even legendary. Nevertheless, a core of early Rabbinic teachers did establish themselves in Yavneh to the north-west of Jerusalem, moving to Usha in Galilee during the second century CE. As for the alleged Pharisaic connection, it no doubt contains a strong element of truth, for many of the later rabbis' legal positions are similar to those attributed in the Qumran DSS to the sect's enemies, who definitely included the Pharisees.[55] Hence, we may surmise that, on the one hand, Yohanan ben Zakkai and his colleagues took as their starting point for renewal the elements of Common Judaism outlined earlier. On the other hand, with the Temple and priesthood defunct, they had to concentrate, like the Pharisees before them, on laws which applied to the everyday lives of lay people. But unlike the Pharisees, who had been able to benefit from the Temple when necessary, they found a way of making such day-to-day matters flourish as Judaism's mainstay.

One of the ways they did this was through the synagogue. Although late Second Temple Jews met for public reading of the Torah in prayer-houses or synagogues, it was only with the Temple's demise that the institution came into its own, as Jewish communities throughout the world slowly made it an indispensable focal point of worship and learning. As long as the Temple had stood, too much competing emphasis on the synagogue was thought both unnecessary and inappropriate. But after 70 CE, the partial borrowing of Temple language and imagery in synagogal liturgy and furniture helped the rabbis rescue Judaism and, in time, consolidate the community.[56]

Most creatively, the rabbis after 70 CE set about redefining the scope of the Torah. The end result was embodied in the Mishnah, a compilation from *circa* 200 CE consisting mostly of legal debate.[57] Indeed, the underlying notion of the Torah's essence finds expression in one of the Mishnah's few theological tractates, Avot (meaning 'Ancestors'). An abridged version of Avot 1:1–18 reads as follows:[58]

1. Moses received the Law from Sinai and committed it to Joshua, and Joshua to the elders, and the elders to the Prophets; and the Prophets committed it to the men of the Great Synagogue. They said three things: Be deliberate in judgement, raise up many disciples, and make a fence around the Law.

2. Simeon the Just was of the remnants of the Great Synagogue. He used to say: By three things is the world sustained: by the Law, by the [Temple-]service, and by deeds of loving-kindness.

3. Antigonus of Soko received [the Law] from Simeon the Just ... 4. Jose b. Joezer of Zeredah and Jose b. Johanan of Jerusalem received [the Law] from them ... 6. Joshua b. Perahyah and Nittai the Arbelite received [the Law] from them ... 8. Judah b. Tabbai and Simeon b. Shetah received [the Law] from them ... 10. Shemaiah and Abtalion received [the Law] from them ... 12. Hillel and Shammai received [the Law] from them. Hillel said: Be of the disciples of Aaron, loving peace and pursuing peace, loving mankind and bringing them nigh to the Law ...

This passage begins straightforwardly by recalling that, after Moses received the Law, it was entrusted to successive biblical generations. However, from the 'men of the Great Synagogue', the writer proceeds to post-biblical teachers, culminating in Avot 2:1 with Rabbi Judah, the compiler of the Mishnah itself in around 200 CE. While statements associated with these names in Avot 1–2 are mostly theological, their pronouncements elsewhere in the Mishnah are overwhelmingly legal.[59]

The implications of this are more far-reaching than might at first sight appear, especially when combined with other Rabbinic evidence. Essentially, alongside the Pentateuch or Written Torah in the form of what would eventually become the Masoretic Text (MT), the rabbis thought that God had revealed to Moses a concomitant Oral Torah. Passed on through the centuries, it was eventually written down in the Mishnah and, subsequently, the Babylonian Talmud (*circa* 550 CE). The Oral Torah, in addition to laws purportedly uttered by Moses himself, contained legal rulings made by the rabbis after 70 CE, thereby imbuing them with a kind of Mosaic authority by association. The resultant notion of the 'Dual Torah', made up of both Written and Oral parts, constitutes Rabbinic Judaism's most innovative feature.[60] There is no evidence, in fact, that Second Temple Jews held such a notion. Neither the Pharisees with their distinctive 'regulations' nor the 'hidden things' of some sectarian DSS from Qumran should be understood in that way.[61]

In common with Second Temple times, though, doctrinal matters were less pressing for the rabbis. Apart from Judaism's primary theological foundations, which now included belief in the bodily resurrection of the dead, Jews remained free to speculate.[62] For instance, some believed that Abraham, the founding father of both Israelites and Jews, had kept the whole Torah – even though he had lived before its revelation to Moses. Others pondered the place of the Gentiles in the divine scheme of things. But little attempt was made to harmonize contradictory viewpoints on such matters which, as a result, can often be found side by side in Rabbinic literature. Despite a universal expectation that God would one day restore his people's fortunes, a similar open-endedness applied to eschatology. Although a standard hope for the advent of an anointed Davidic figure took shape, the Messiah's precise characteristics and activities remained open to debate.[63]

Moreover, there is little that can be described as apocalyptic in Rabbinic texts. Many Second Temple Jews, in contrast, had been prone to think in apocalyptic terms, as the proliferation of apocalyptic themes in the period's literature demonstrates. But with the defeat of the First Revolt, in which such notions had played a significant part, the rabbis of Yavneh rejected apocalyptic ideas, although other Jews found this change of heart more difficult. That reluctance explains the appearance of works like 4 Ezra and 2 Baruch in around 100 CE.[64] Defeat of the Second Revolt in 135 BCE, however, also convinced many ordinary Jews of the dangers of the apocalyptic imagination, thereby slowly bringing the Jewish majority under the sway of Rabbinic Judaism from the third century onwards.[65] Without ceasing to believe that God would rescue his people one day, it now seemed best to leave the matter entirely in his hands. What counted in the meantime was devotion to the Written and Oral Torah as interpreted by the Rabbinic authorities.

Indeed, between the publication of the Mishnah (*circa* 200 CE) and the appearance of the Babylonian Talmud (*circa* 550 CE), Jewish life gradually took on a new homogeneity. Not only was everyone agreed that keeping the Torah's legal prescriptions was Judaism's mainstay but, with the rise to prominence of the rabbis and their interpretation of the Law, broad agreement was eventually reached on how to obey it in practice. From around the fourth or fifth century CE, therefore, we can begin to speak of a truly normative Rabbinic Judaism, although alternatives continued to exist in various forms right up to the Middle Ages and beyond.[66]

The Dead Sea Scrolls and Modern Judaism

We have just seen that it was largely through the notion of the Dual Torah that the rabbis managed to salvage Judaism's post-70 CE predicament. By the time of the Babylonian Talmud, this Dual Torah had eclipsed the practical need for a Temple or priesthood, for the most sacred Jewish rite was now study of the Law itself.[67] Biblical heroes like Moses or David, accordingly, are portrayed in Rabbinic literature as Torah scholars, while even God is presented on occasion as student of the Torah *par excellence*.[68]

This religious system served the Jewish community well for over a millennium, so that, despite sporadic persecution, Jewish spirituality flourished under Roman, Christian, and Islamic rule. In the Middle Ages, for example, Jewish philosophy and mysticism retained their distinctiveness through the ongoing role of the Dual Torah.[69] However, the situation changed dramatically from the late 1700s, as Jews adjusted in markedly different ways to life in the modern world. To complete this chapter's overview, it is worth elucidating a little on this overt return to diversity. And although most experts shy away from it, we shall then tentatively broach the subject of the DSS's relevance for Judaism today.

Rather as in Second Temple times, modern Jews have responded divergently to complex circumstances. Among several factors eliciting different responses, the fruits of historical study have been important. We saw back in Chapter 2, for example, that most nineteenth-century scholars came to question the Pentateuch's Mosaic origins. In reaction to this and other issues, Judaism split into a number of denominations from the early 1800s onwards. Allowing for a little oversimplification, and though all are not present in every part of the world with a Jewish community, they continue to exist today across a six-fold axis from the most traditional to the most progressive: ultra-Orthodox, Orthodox, Conservative, Reform, Reconstructionist, and Humanistic. The most traditional are ultra-Orthodox Jews, the majority of whom trace their origins back to the late eighteenth-century Hasidic revival of Eastern Europe and whose outlook is still framed entirely by the Dual Torah; at the opposite extreme, Reconstructionist and Humanistic Jews see Judaism as an evolving human civilization, in which God and the Torah are mythical elements. These two ends of the spectrum account for a relatively small proportion of global Jewry. In between, the Orthodox, Conservative, and Reform camps encompass most Jews, and each attempts to formulate an effective compromise with the modern world.[70]

Yet, even among these groupings considerable differences remain. At the top of the list comes the Torah. Whilst Orthodox Jews still uphold its divine origin, Reform Judaism qualifies such belief by acknowledging the results of academic study. For the former, the Pentateuch's laws in the form of the MT and their elaboration in the Talmud remain obligatory divine commands, and the fruits of scholarship are held at arm's length. Reform Jews, however, modify the revelatory status of the Torah and Talmud by accepting that historical and cultural circumstances shaped ancient traditions as much as the divine will. Conservative Judaism takes up a midway position – generally holding, like the Orthodox, to traditional religious practice but embracing, like Reform Jews, the results of historical study.

These divergent standpoints give rise to opposing views on many practical issues. Day-to-day adherence to the Written and Oral Law is the most obvious one. Thus, Orthodoxy maintains that the whole gamut of ancient dietary rules should be followed because of their divine authority, and Conservatives are similarly observant in practice. Reform Jews, on the other hand, encourage only those who find such rules meaningful today to follow them. More topically, a parallel split is evident over the role of women. It makes little sense for Orthodox synagogues to ordain female rabbis, for instance, since the Talmud assumes that men alone are obliged to obey the full range of God's commandments. But within Reform and, to a lesser degree, Conservative Judaism, this issue is not so problematic, for a more creative and selective approach to the past is allowable.[71]

Now, it would be wrong to suggest that the Qumran DSS unequivocally support one manifestation of modern Judaism rather than another. Neither do they easily connect to contentious issues, like the role of women, for such questions did not confront Second Temple Jews in the way that they nowadays challenge all major world religions. Yet, it would be equally wrong to say that these important documents from antiquity contribute nothing. Two observations stand out.

The first has to do with historicity, and the Qumran DSS have a dual lesson here. On the one hand, the biblical DSS have made it difficult to uphold the MT's traditional priority, as we have seen, let alone the Pentateuch's Mosaic authorship. Not only have they endorsed the general conclusions of earlier biblical scholarship that most books, including the Pentateuch in its final form, were penned between *circa* 550 and 300 BCE, but they have also shown that multiple editions of individual books probably existed from the outset. These included what later came to be called the MT but, as confirmed by relevant manuscripts from Murabba'at and Nahal Hever, only after 70 CE did that particular edition come to predominate among Jews.[72] Simultaneously, even if later

Rabbinic writings preserve many individual Second Temple traditions, including Pharisaic legal decisions, the Pharisees can no longer be thought of as the guardians of mainstream Second Temple Judaism in a direct line going backwards to an Oral Law revealed to Moses and forwards to the Mishnah and Babylonian Talmud.[73] On the contrary, the sectarian Qumran DSS have helped reconstruct a picture of Judaism in the last two centuries BCE and the first century CE which is quite different: the Pharisees were one among several small religious parties with distinctive traditions over and above the elements of 'Common Judaism'. Although they may often have been favoured by the ordinary people, that is a long way from the Rabbinic portrait. Not least, no Second Temple evidence survives to show that the Pharisees viewed their own special 'regulations' as an Oral Law of Mosaic origin.

Inasmuch as contemporary debates between Orthodox, Conservative, and Reform Judaism centre on such historical questions, the Qumran DSS sit more comfortably with a Conservative or Reform position than an Orthodox one. This much must be conceded, for their evidence heightens the fluidity of late Second Temple Judaism, even if Jews in the last two centuries BCE and the first century CE were themselves unaware of the full extent of that fluidity. Having long accepted that the Pentateuch took shape soon after 550 BCE following a long period of growth, therefore, Conservative and Reform Jews will not be too disturbed to discover now that many biblical writings existed in divergent editions from the start and that the Rabbinic picture of the Pharisees is anachronistic. Yet, there is more at stake than mere historicity. This explains why modern Orthodox Judaism tends to keep such historical conclusions at arm's length.

Here, we must turn to our second observation which concerns Judaism's very nature. The Orthodox position encourages the belief that at the heart of Jewish practice lies legislation revealed by God to Moses on Mount Sinai in a literal sense. As such, the Pentateuch's laws and their elaboration in the Talmud are absolutes which, notwithstanding an inherent degree of flexibility, cannot be annulled. This approach furnishes Orthodoxy with a consistency and certainty which many people feel is a necessary part of any religion worth its salt. But it also means that its ability to adapt Jewish practice and belief has limitations. For example, there is little scope for dealing with the possibility that the ancient writers' cultural background led them to frame their legislation in an inherently sexist manner. Thus, despite recent Orthodox adaptations regarding rites and roles for women, the official position remains more or less unchanged.[74]

From a Reform or Conservative perspective, such absolutes were shattered in the nineteenth century, when scholars concluded that a literal understanding of the Pentateuch's Mosaic authorship was unsustainable. The notion of a revelatory corpus had to be tempered with the realization that Jewish traditions had evolved considerably over the centuries – in biblical times, in the Second Temple period, in the Rabbinic age and beyond. With no fixed revelatory point in a literal sense, it could be seen that each new generation had in fact always reshaped earlier traditions to a degree only apparent with modern academic study of the Hebrew Bible, Second Temple Judaism, and the Rabbinic period. Although such historical conclusions inevitably relativize past practices and beliefs, they endow Reform Judaism and, to a lesser extent, Conservative Judaism with a capacity to remould ancient traditions and create new ones. For example, the Reform synagogue ordained its first female rabbi in 1972, while Conservatives followed suit in 1984.[75]

Yet, the DSS from Caves 1–11 make it crystal clear that both the Qumran Community and other Second Temple Jews believed God had literally revealed his Torah to Moses during the second millennium BCE – even if the Torah, for them, extended only to the Written Pentateuch and not, as with the rabbis after 70 CE, to the Oral Law. In contrast to our first observation, therefore, and notwithstanding the fact that modern scholars find no historical evidence to support the tradition of Mosaic authorship, the modern Orthodox position in this regard remains closest to late Second Temple Jewish belief.

6

Christianity Reconsidered

A Century of New Testament Study[1]

Historical and literary investigation into the New Testament has been going on for well over a century, and one of its fruits is the daunting body of academic literature that now exists on each New Testament book. Nonetheless, although experts continue to disagree on innumerable points of detail, many lessons about the nature of Jesus' ministry and about early Christianity have been learned.[2]

Lack of space rules out even the briefest survey of such scholarship, nor can we analyse in detail particular New Testament passages. However, several points can be distilled which will help us understand in the next two sections the similarities and differences between the Qumran DSS, on the one hand, and Jesus and early Christianity, on the other. We shall then be in a position, especially in view of the light shed in the last chapter on Second Temple Judaism at large, to ask what caused Jews and Christians to part company by the end of the first century CE. That done, the possible impact of the contents of Caves 1–11 on modern Christianity will be considered.

The first general point to be gleaned from over one hundred years of study concerns the original composition dates of the books of the New Testament. On the basis of details in the text ordinarily passed over by the general reader, nearly all experts would accept that much of the literature, even that drawing on older sources, reached its final edition after 70 CE.[3] As with the Old Testament, therefore, it has been necessary to revise the traditional dates of authorship accepted by religious authorities for centuries. An example from Luke's Gospel will illustrate what is involved. The words attributed to Jesus in Luke 19:41–44, rather than a future prediction from his own lips, seem to reflect a time when the defeat of the First Revolt of the Jews against Rome had already happened. As such, the passage must stem from after 70 CE, for we know that Christians subsequently interpreted the Temple's destruction as a sign of divine disfavour on the majority of Jews who had not become Christians. Consequently, even if Luke's Gospel preserves the real words of Jesus elsewhere, in its present form it was completed as a whole after 70 CE.[4]

A similar conclusion is likely with regard to the composition date of Mark and inescapable when it comes to Matthew, John, the book of Acts, and many letters in the New Testament.[5] Included among the latter, several epistles traditionally believed to be the handiwork of Paul were almost certainly written after his death: Colossians, 2 Thessalonians, 1–2 Timothy, Titus, and Hebrews. The main factor pointing in this direction is the theological disparity between them and other letters also attributed to Paul: Romans, 1–2 Corinthians, Galatians, Ephesians, Philippians, 1 Thessalonians, and Philemon. Most agree that the best way of explaining this doctrinal incongruity is to suppose that only these last eight were penned by Paul himself during the 40s and 50s CE. Consequently, they make up the earliest New Testament evidence for Christianity. As for the other letters, inasmuch as we saw in Chapter 2 that the pseudonymous association of a work with a past hero was not uncommon among late Second Temple Jews, we should not be surprised to see a parallel phenomenon developing among early Christians in the late first and second centuries CE.

Our second general point comes as a corollary of what has just been described: the New Testament is not of one mind.[6] Certain motifs, it is true, are common or even universal, the most obvious being the centrality of Jesus. But even here diversity is prevalent, for Jesus' precise role is not everywhere the same. In the early chapters of Acts, for example, he is a messianic prophet rejected by the people, vindicated through resurrection, and now ready to return in glory as God's viceroy. In Paul's letter to the Romans, in contrast, greater significance is given to Jesus' death as the means of salvation for the individual believer. Such differences occurred as ideas developed independently among Christians in different locations. Naturally, the churches over the centuries have tended to play down the divergences in favour of the real similarities that also exist between New Testament books. But historians find it more fruitful to highlight variation and a further illustration may help. Some New Testament passages, like 1 Corinthians 15:22–25 or 1 Thessalonians 4:15–18, demonstrate that the first Christians expected Jesus to return soon in apocalyptic splendour as part of the divine plan of salvation. After several decades, though, Christians were faced with the fact that such expectations had not materialized. The resultant adjustment in outlook is reflected clearly in 2 Peter 3:3–10, and it is worth citing part of the passage:

> ³First of all you must understand this, that in the last days scoffers will come, scoffing and indulging their own lusts ⁴and saying, 'Where is the promise of his [Jesus'] coming? For ever since our ancestors died, all things continue as they were from the beginning of creation!'
>
> . . . ⁸But do not ignore this one fact, beloved, that with the Lord one day is like a thousand years, and a thousand years are like one day.

Although the author believes in theory that Jesus could reappear at any moment, the fervour of earlier writings has waned. Hence, in 2 Peter, we see early second-century Christians coming to terms with the idea that they might have to wait some time for Jesus' return.[7]

Our third and final point has to do with what can be known of the historical Jesus himself and the early Christians who lived in the 30s, 40s, and 50s CE. Given the late and varied nature of most New Testament books, what is said about Jesus and the apostles in the Gospels and Acts cannot always be taken at face value. But complete scepticism is not in order. By carefully reading between the lines of the Gospels, it is possible to recover an outline of the historical Jesus, while several sermons incorporated into Acts 2–4 probably contain accurate recollections of the earliest Christian message. Likewise, the genuine Pauline letters provide us, not only with direct access to Paul's own ideas, but also with indirect clues as to the thought of his contemporaries and predecessors. So, to Jesus and early Christianity and the relationship of both to the Qumran DSS we may now turn.

Was Jesus an Essene?

Over the past hundred years or so, there have been many attempts to trace the life and work of Jesus of Nazareth. The main source for such reconstructions has, of course, been the New Testament, even though the oldest substantial witnesses we possess are in the form of copies from the third and fourth centuries CE.[8] The Gospel of Thomas, similarly complete only in a fourth-century manuscript, is now also widely thought to contain some authentic Jesus sayings.[9] However, José O'Callaghan's suggestion that scraps of several New Testament books were found in Cave 7 at Qumran has been rejected by all experts in the field, including the proposal that Mark 6:52–53 has survived in the form of 7Q5.[10] The latter is a small fragment of twenty Greek letters, half of which are unclear. Without fresh evidence to substantiate the claim, therefore, the equation of 7Q5 with a portion of Mark is no more than a remote theoretical possibility which need not detain us.[11]

It is not practicable to present an exhaustive survey of the numerous versions of the historical Jesus that have been proffered over the years.[12] With hindsight, however, it is interesting to note that a rather naive optimism at the beginning of the last century had given way to an equally unrealistic scepticism by the mid-twentieth century.[13] Fortunately, in the last thirty years a cautious optimism has come to dominate academic study of the life and work of Jesus. Among several important scholars in the English-speaking world are Geza Vermes of Oxford University, already mentioned in connection with the Qumran DSS, and E. P. Sanders of Duke University.[14] These and others agree that some facts are recoverable, although a biography of Jesus in the modern sense is beyond reach. Two prominent features of recent reconstructions, for example, are Jesus' thorough Jewishness and his message's essentially eschatological character. For readers unfamiliar with this kind of New Testament study, it is worth outlining in a little detail the picture of Jesus' ministry that emerges from the ancient sources with a high degree of probability.

Most concur that Jesus was born just before Herod the Great died in 4 BCE (see Matthew 2:1–2) and was executed while Pontius Pilate was Prefect of Judaea between 26 and 36 CE (note Mark 15:1). If the statement in Luke 3:23 that Jesus was 'about thirty years old' is to be believed, then he embarked on his public ministry in the late 20s CE after encountering John the Baptist's eschatological message of repentance.[15] With John's execution, Jesus became an itinerant preacher and healer in his own right. As a Jew, he doubtless accepted the main elements of Common Judaism, including the requirement to obey the Torah's commandments. Several Gospel stories show this was indeed the case, like the account in Mark 1:42–44 of Jesus' exhortation to a healed leper:

> [42]Immediately the leprosy left him, and he was made clean. [43]After sternly warning him he sent him away at once, [44]saying to him, 'See that you say nothing to anyone; but go, show yourself to the priest, and offer for your cleansing what Moses commanded, as a testimony to them.'

Whatever is to be made of the secrecy imposed on the former leper, Jesus sent him to be ritually cleansed by a priest because this was required by the Torah after leprosy. However, the story's wider context also implies that Jesus' main concern was to instill in people a renewed faith in God, particularly among those excluded because of disease, poverty, or sin. Such devotion was especially apt in view of the imminent arrival of the kingdom of God. This phrase is not defined in the Gospels, but Jesus seems to have employed it to designate the impending advent of God's kingly rule, bringing salvation for his people and the defeat of evil. There is no evidence that Jesus engaged in direct political or military action, for the power of God about to be unleashed on the world deemed it unnecessary. What the people experienced as exorcisms, healings, and other miracles through his ministry, though, were signs that God's kingdom was near. It was this eschatological fervour that constituted the driving force behind Jesus' role as the proclaimer of 'good news', rather than any particular belief about his own identity.

After working in Galilee, Jesus spent the last phase of his ministry, which probably lasted about one year in total, in Judaea. At the time of one of the busiest Jewish festivals, the Passover, Jesus was arrested in Jerusalem. What exactly happened next is hotly debated by scholars.[16] At a superficial level, the Gospel 'Passion Narratives' (Matthew 26–27; Mark 14–15; Luke 22–23; John 18–19) explain his subsequent execution as a result of doctrinal disputes with the Jewish religious leaders of the time. But this presentation most likely reflects religious rivalry between Jews and Christians long after Jesus' death. Certainly, there is nothing about Jesus' message itself which would have provoked such outrage. The real cause was probably rather mundane, therefore, for both Josephus and Acts testify that several independently-minded spiritual leaders were dealt with harshly during the 40s and 50s CE for the sake of political expediency.[17] And earlier, of course, John the Baptist had met with a similar fate. As in all these cases, Jesus seems to have been killed by the authorities, not because of his religious message *per se*, but to avoid the risk of social upheaval. Both Roman and Jewish rulers feared unrest, in other words, either as a consequence of Jesus' popularity in general or, more particularly, because of the volatility of Jerusalem and its crowds during the Passover.

Lack of space precludes adding further details to this bare reconstruction which, in any case, would require us to choose between dissenting scholarly opinions. Even what has just been presented is not acceptable to all, for Jesus' commitment to Common Judaism, as well as his eschatological outlook, are rejected in certain quarters.[18] Nevertheless, the above outline makes it unlikely that Jesus was an Essene, given what we have already learned from the Qumran DSS. But this does not mean there were no similarities between Jesus' message and that of the Essenes.[19] The most noticeable link is a common note of repentance against a background of eschatological urgency. This finds expression in

lQS's exhortation to keep the sect's interpretation of the Law in antici-
pation of imminent divine intervention, for example, as well as in Jesus'
call to believe the 'good news' of the impending advent of the kingdom.
Both outlooks share an 'already-but-not-yet' attitude in that salvation has
been tasted but will not be fully experienced until its consummation at
the end of time. Jesus' approach to the arrival of God's kingdom,
therefore, once thought to be entirely original, can in fact be seen to be
thoroughly embedded within the diverse world of late Second Temple
Judaism.

With this kind of general parallel, however, the similarities between
Jesus and the Qumran DSS end. Thus, while Jesus doubtless shared the
common Jewish attachment to the Torah, we have no evidence that he
cared for the sort of supererogatory piety of the Essenes, nor the
application of purity laws to life outside the Temple that appears in
varying degrees to have preoccupied the Pharisees. The fact that Jesus
preached openly to the Jewish crowds, moreover, is contrary to the
Essene secrecy evident in the sectarian DSS and in Josephus. In addition,
Jesus worked towards the end of the period during which the Essenes
existed and this chronological factor militates against identifying Jesus
simply as an Essene.

Jesus might just possibly have had an association with the Essenes
before he embarked on his ministry, ceasing to be one of their number
when he began to preach and heal. But the truth is we know next to
nothing about Jesus before his public career. The birth narratives in
Matthew 1:18–2:23 and Luke 1:5–2:40, as well as the report about Jesus
as a boy in Luke 2:41–52, are clearly legendary. Indeed, with the story
of Mary's miraculous conception, we can compare Suetonius' account of
Augustus Caesar's supernatural origin.[20] As for Jesus' precocity in Luke
2:41–52, Josephus boasts of his own talents as a fourteen-year-old in
what may have been a standard literary motif of the time:[21]

> While . . . about fourteen years old, I won universal applause for my love
> of letters; insomuch that the chief priests and the leading men of the city
> [of Jerusalem] used constantly to come to me for precise information on
> some particular in our ordinances.

These fanciful parallels suggest Jesus' religious experiences before his
ministry are destined to remain unknown to us.

A better case for an Essene link can be made in relation to Jesus'
forerunner, John the Baptist.[22] The limited information we have about
this man comes mainly from Mark 1:4–8, Matthew 3:1–12, and Luke
3:1–20. All three agree that John lived in the desert 'preaching a baptism

of repentance for the forgiveness of sins' (Mark 1:4) and that his work prepared the way for Jesus. Like Jesus and the Essenes, John appears to have had a heightened eschatological sense of his message's urgency. More significantly, he lived in the desert and engaged in baptismal rituals in a manner reminiscent of the purificatory rites enjoined in the Qumran DSS. On the basis of Luke 1:80, it could even be suggested that John the Baptist was adopted by the Essenes as a child, a practice certainly mentioned by Josephus.[23] Once more, however, caution is in order. Although it is possible that he had previously been a member of the Qumran Sect, by the time he was carrying out the work ascribed to him in the Gospels, John could no longer have been an Essene. As with Jesus, the public nature of his proclamation is in stark contrast to their preference for secrecy. And when it comes to the common connection with the wilderness, we noted back in Chapter 1 that the Judaean desert functioned as a sanctuary for various religious and political groups throughout Second Temple times and beyond.

To sum up, the testimony of the Qumran DSS, when set alongside an informed reading of the Gospels, forces us to conclude that Jesus was not an Essene. Neither did John the Baptist belong to the Essene movement – at least, not while engaged in his public preaching mission. At the same time, the luxury afforded by the documents from Caves 1–11 has shown up significant parallels between the message of the Qumran DSS, on the one hand, and the ministries of Jesus and his forerunner, on the other. Taken together, these overlaps demonstrate just how Jewish John and Jesus must have been. There is certainly nothing to suggest that either intended to found a new religion abrogating any of the main elements of Common Judaism. On the contrary, both are best understood when placed fully within the world of late Second Temple Judaism in Palestine.

The Dead Sea Scrolls and Early Christianity

A similar evaluation of the evidence holds for the relationship between the Qumran DSS and early Christianity after Jesus' death. Despite real parallels, it is clear that the early Christians were not Essenes. Apart from any other factor, like John the Baptist and Jesus, the Christian movement arose at the end of the period during which the group utilizing Caves 1–11 flourished. The early Christians also engaged in open preaching among Jews – and eventually Gentiles – in a way that separates them from the Essenes. Furthermore, the main distinguishing feature of early Christianity was its emphasis on Jesus of Nazareth, whereas there are no references to Jesus in the sectarian DSS from Qumran, nor anything clear in the classical accounts of Philo, Josephus, and Pliny.[24] As for names featuring cryptically in the documents from Qumran, we saw in Chapters 3 and 4 that they are best set against the background of the second and first centuries BCE.[25] It can safely be stated, therefore, that, despite recent contrary claims, no New Testament character is mentioned in any of the Qumran DSS. Nor are there grounds for directly linking the two communities by way of common historical events, as we shall see more fully in the next chapter.

Nevertheless, a comparison of the Qumran DSS and the writings of the New Testament does show up a number of interesting parallels. Of all the religious groupings current in late Second Temple times, the early Christians may well have had most in common with the Essenes. It is worth spelling out two overlaps of a general nature and three which are more specific.

The first has already been touched on, for, as will be clear by now, both the Qumran Community and the early Christians had a strong eschatological-cum-apocalyptic orientation. Each believed in its own way that God was on the verge of intervening in human affairs. This theme constitutes a thread through the Gospels, Acts, and genuine letters of Paul, on the one hand, as well as through sectarian DSS from Qumran like 4QMMT[a–f], the Damascus Document, and War Scroll, on the other. Furthermore, both communities experienced a crisis when the end of the world failed to materialize. Just as 2 Peter 3:3–10 sought to reassure Christians that history was still on course, so lQpHabakkuk 7:5–8 had dealt with a similar problem nearly two hundred years earlier:

> For there shall be yet another vision concerning the appointed time. It shall tell of the end and shall not lie (ii, 3a).
>
> Interpreted, this means that the final age shall be prolonged, and shall exceed all that the Prophets have said; for the mysteries of God are astounding.

This first-century BCE Qumran writer, however, unlike his early second-century CE Christian counterpart, went on to exhort his readers to persevere in their obedience to the sect's interpretation of the Law.

Several items of vocabulary mark a second general overlap. It has long been noted that the Hebrew term in the Community Rule often translated as 'the Congregation' (Hebrew, *ha-rabbim*, meaning literally 'the Many') is similar to Paul's 'the majority' (Greek, *tōn pleionōn*) in 2 Corinthians 2:6. Again, the designation 'overseer' or 'bishop' (Greek, *episkopos*) in some New Testament books (e.g. Philippians 1:1) seems equivalent to the 'Guardian' or 'Overseer' (Hebrew, *mevaqqer*) of the Qumran texts (see 1QS 6:12). Or again, various eschatological titles applied to Jesus throughout much of the New Testament, such as 'prophet', 'christ', and 'son of God', clearly have their counterparts within the range of messianic titles employed in the Qumran documents (e.g. 1QS 9:11; 1QSa 2:11–12).[26] Overall, such terminological links strongly suggest that many early Christian turns of phrase were originally Hebrew or Aramaic expressions subsequently translated into Greek as the church grew beyond the confines of Palestine.[27] They also demonstrate that, like John the Baptist and Jesus before them, the first generation or two of Christians were thoroughly embedded within the world of late Second Temple Judaism.

Besides these general similarities, some closer parallels also exist. Bible interpretation, in particular, is a noticeable feature of both the early Christians and the Essenes. Just as we categorized a whole class of Qumran literature on the basis of its utilization of scripture, so many New Testament writings expound the contents of the Old Testament in terms of the first century CE rather than the time of the original authors. Scattered through the Gospels, for instance, scriptural references are adduced to support Jesus' proclamation that the Kingdom of God is near, as in the citation of Isaiah 42:1–4 in Matthew 12:18–21. Other New Testament works cite biblical verses to lend weight to the early Christian message. In Acts 2:14–17, for example, Peter explains to the crowd that Joel 2:28–32 has been fulfilled in the glossolalia of the early Christians:

[14]But Peter . . . raised his voice and addressed them, 'Men of Judea and all who live in Jerusalem, let this be known to you, and listen to what I say. [15]Indeed, these are not drunk, as you suppose, for it is only nine o'clock in the morning. [16]No, this is what was spoken through the prophet Joel:

[17]In the last days it will be, God declares, that I will pour out my spirit upon all flesh, and your sons and your daughters shall prophesy, and your young men shall see visions, and your old men shall dream dreams.'

This Christian parallel to the Qumran treatment of the Old Testament shows that similar assumptions underlay usage of scripture in both communities.

Here and there, in fact, the same scriptural passage is employed. Habakkuk 2:4, for instance, is cited and interpreted in both 1Qp-

Habakkuk 7:17–8:1–3 and Galatians 3:11–12, as the following arrangement indicates:

<table>
<tr><td>

[11] *1QpHabakkuk 7:17–8:3*
[*But the righteous shall live by his faith*] (ii, 4b).
Interpreted, this concerns all those who observe the law in the House of Judah, whom God will deliver from the House of Judgement because of their suffering and because of their faith in the Teacher of Righteousness.

</td><td>

Galatians 3:11–12 (NRSV)
[11]Now it is evident that no one is justified before God by the law; for 'The one who is righteous will live by faith'. [12]But the law does not rest on faith; on the contrary, 'Whoever does the works of the law will live by them.'

</td></tr>
</table>

Closer scrutiny, however, shows that the same biblical text was handled differently by the authors in question. Despite similar assumptions about scripture at a general level, the two communities' distinctive messages encouraged divergent interpretations of the same concrete passages. Thus, Habakkuk 2:4 is used by Paul to bolster his contention that trust in God is distinct from the secondary matter of obedience to the Torah's rules. The Qumran author, on the other hand, employs the same verse to emphasize that true faith and practical adherence to the sect's interpretation of the Law are one and the same.

Another link between the early Christians and those at Qumran concerns doctrinal speculation about individuals. For instance, both chose the figure of Melchizedek, 'priest of God Most High' according to Genesis 14:18, as an object for theological reflection. The New Testament letter to the Hebrews appeals to him typologically as a basis for viewing Jesus as a heavenly High Priest, even though, like Melchizedek, he was not descended from the priestly line of Aaron. In 11QMelchizedek, the same ancient figure is equated with the Archangel Michael and predicted to defeat Satan at the end of time.[28] For this author, both Melchizedek and other angels are called *'elohim*, the regular Hebrew word for 'God'. However, because certain obscure Old Testament passages, like Exodus 21:6 and Psalm 8:6, use the term to mean 'judge' or 'angel', Melchizedek's designation as *'elohim* does not denote his literal divinity but merely his eschatological role as a supernatural judge on behalf of God.

More generally, the figure envisaged in 11QMelchizedek is the biblical Melchizedek himself, albeit conflated with the Archangel Michael of Daniel 12:1. Hebrews, in contrast, draws on the figure of Melchizedek as nothing more than a type in relation to Jesus' status. Despite striking similarities, therefore, the treatment of Melchizedek by the Essenes and by the early Christians was different. This is hardly surprising, for we learned in the last chapter that numerous past heroes could be subjected to doctrinal speculation in a variety of ways in the last two or three centuries BCE and the first century CE.[29]

Unique to both the Qumran DSS community and the early Christians was a focus on their respective founders, the Teacher of Righteousness and Jesus. Attachment to these special individuals was one of the features which marked out the two religious movements as distinct from each other, as well as from the other Jewish parties that flourished in the late Second Temple period. Here too, though, what seems to be an exact parallel at first sight fails to remain so under closer scrutiny. For those at Qumran, the Teacher had a vital but restricted role both as founder and as an inspired interpreter of the Law, while at least two further future messianic figures seem to have been expected.[30] But for the early Christians, Jesus subsumed within his person all such roles. We can turn again to Hebrews to illustrate this, for the writer portrays Jesus as both Davidic Messiah and as the high-priestly figure *par excellence*.[31]

A final important link between the Qumran Community and early Christianity has to do with a common aspect of organization attested nowhere else in the late Second Temple period. According to Acts 2–5, the early Christians in Jerusalem practiced a kind of communal ownership. Acts 4:32 implies that each drew from a central fund according to need:

> Now the whole group of those who believed were of one heart and soul, and no one claimed private ownership of any possessions, but everything they owned was held in common.

This description is remarkably close to what is commended in the Community Rule. Furthermore, as with the Essenes, it seems that some Christians retained private property, for Paul assumes as much in 1 Corinthians 16:2. This more relaxed arrangement parallels CD 14:12–13, stipulating that members contribute only a proportion of their income to a common fund.

What then are we to make of these substantial overlaps between early Christianity and the religious group behind the Qumran DSS, especially the organizational parallels in property matters just noted? We have already seen that it is not possible to equate the two communities. It is possible, however, that some individuals joining the early Christian movement had an acquaintance with the Essenes and their practices;

some may even have been former members. This could explain the similarities in organization described above. A few scholars, indeed, have argued that, from the days of Herod the Great, there was an Essene Quarter in the south-western part of Jerusalem which, by the first century CE, happened to be in close proximity to the earliest Christian community.[32] Unfortunately, the evidence only amounts to Josephus' reference to an 'Essene Gate' in Jerusalem and his statement that Herod looked favourably on the Essenes at the start of his reign.[33] While some Essenes probably did live in Jerusalem, as in other towns in Palestine, the existence of a special Essene Quarter next to the first Christian meeting-place requires much more proof. Equally plausible in the mean-time is the suggestion that, despite Essene secrecy, the generality of their organizational practice had become common knowledge and that, for want of a better model, early Christians adopted some aspects of it and adapted them to their own needs.

Yet, when it comes to the shared eschatological zeal, the parallel scriptural interpretation, and speculation on particular figures, a broader explanation is in order. In short, the two communities developed along similar lines in certain respects because they were both zealous Jewish sects springing from the world of late Second Temple Judaism in Palestine. The prime impact of the sectarian DSS on our understanding of early Christianity, therefore, is to show that the early Christians were essentially another Second Temple Jewish party which came into being during the first century CE. Although some New Testament scholars by the mid-1900s were beginning to see that this might well be the case, it is only as familiarity with the Qumran DSS has increased in recent decades that such a conclusion has become obvious to most working in the field.[34] Nearly all New Testament experts would now accept this reconstruction, although a few – older studies continuing in circulation and more recent ones – still conclude that Jesus or the first Christians had broken with Common Judaism in some fundamental way.[35]

In reality, the Qumran DSS have taught us that Jesus' already-but-not-yet eschatology would not have taken him outside the confines of Common Judaism, either in his own mind or that of other Second Temple Jews; and the same applies immediately after Jesus' death to his followers' theological speculation about his central role in God's plan. In that case, the main distinguishing feature of the first Christians was simply that, alongside a basic adherence to Common Judaism, they assigned a vital place in the divine schema to Jesus of Nazareth and believed he would soon return in apocalyptic splendour. They also tried to persuade other Jews of his special anointed role and, not surprisingly, the term 'messiah' was applied to him. Given Jesus' unique standing among early Jewish Christians, moreover, that word soon became a title, 'the Messiah', which was then translated into Greek as 'the Christ' which, in turn, became a kind of surname in the designation 'Jesus Christ'.

From Jewish Prophet to Gentile God[36]

The above description applies to the early Christian movement as it took shape in and around Jerusalem during the second quarter of the first century CE. From a careful reading of Acts 1–5 and the genuine letters of Paul, it can be deduced that, as well as believing in Jesus and his imminent return, its members continued to worship at the Temple, to keep the Sabbath, to adhere to the Torah's dietary and purity rules, and to circumcise their sons. Indeed, as the Qumran DSS have demonstrated in relation to the Essenes, a strong eschatological outlook, coupled with devotion to a particular figure, did not imply any fundamental break with Common Judaism, even when the majority of other Jews disagreed.

So, how and when did Christianity become a religious tradition separate from Judaism? Here, we must turn more closely to the Apostle Paul who, after his own conversion in the early 30s CE, engaged in missionary activity outside Palestine for some thirty years.[37] More concretely, he introduced one critical innovation which, given the lasting impact of his work, slowly transformed the early Christian movement from an entirely Jewish phenomenon into a fully-fledged Gentile religion by *circa* 100 CE. Paul argued, in short, that non-Jews should be allowed to enter the Christian community without converting to Judaism – that is, without adopting the full range of Jewish religious practices derived from the Torah, including circumcision for males. In so doing, he was doubtless driven by his own conversion experience which had convinced him of his calling to be an apostle to the Gentiles, as emphasized in Galatians 1:13–17 and Romans 1:1–6; he was probably also aware that his missionary success would be curtailed if adult male converts had to undergo the unpleasant rite of circumcision. According to Galatians 2, however, Paul's plea for the admittance of Gentiles as Gentiles was initially opposed by leaders of the Jerusalem church. Such opposition alone shows that this development had not been envisaged by Jesus or the first Christians.[38]

Nevertheless, in the mid- to late 40s CE, a compromise was reached at the so-called Council of Jerusalem described in Galatians 2:1–10 and Acts 15:6–21. Although these two accounts cannot be completely reconciled, it appears that the Jerusalem apostles decided to concentrate their efforts on bringing Jews into the Christian fold, while Paul was able to continue working among Gentiles without requiring full conversion to Common Judaism. In Galatians 2:7–9, he describes this arrangement in his own words:

> [7]On the contrary, when they saw that I had been entrusted with the gospel for the uncircumcised, just as Peter has been entrusted with the gospel for the circumcised . . . [9]and when James and Cephas and John, who were acknowledged pillars, recognized the grace that had been given to me, they gave to Barnabas and me the right hand of fellowship, agreeing that we should go to the Gentiles and they to the circumcised.

Presumably, pending Jesus' imminent return, both sides deemed this compromise acceptable and, as it transpired, Paul's missionary efforts outside Palestine had considerable success. He was no doubt helped by the prior existence of sizable numbers of 'God-fearers' – sympathetic Gentiles who, without formally converting, had already attached themselves to synagogues in Asia Minor, Greece, and elsewhere.[39]

Yet, faced with mixed Jewish–Gentile congregations in the Diaspora, Paul had to strike a careful balance as to his main religious focus. Since only a minority of his converts were Jews with a commitment to Common Judaism, he did this by concentrating on Jesus, the single unifying element among all who had responded to his message in Galatia, Corinth, and the other urban centres he visited. It was through his doctrinal reflections on Jesus over three decades, therefore, that Paul sought to build up these young congregations without alienating either the Jewish or Gentile side. In Galatians 2:19–21 and 5:24–25, for example, he expounds the benefits to the Christian who has died and risen with Jesus by virtue of being 'in Christ'. Such theological elaboration is comparable to that found in other late Second Temple Jewish writings. We saw earlier how 1 Enoch enlarges on the figure of Enoch, while the sectarian Qumran texts give a special place to the Teacher of Righteousness.

Thus, Paul included in Philippians 2:6–11 an early Christian hymn which describes Jesus Christ:

> [6]who, though he was in the form of God, did not regard equality with
>   God as something to be exploited,
> [7]but emptied himself, taking the form of a slave, being born in human
>   likeness.
> And being found in human form, [8]he humbled himself and became
>   obedient to the point of death – even death on a cross.

⁹Therefore God also highly exalted him and gave him the name that is
above every name,

¹⁰so that at the name of Jesus every knee should bend, in heaven and on
earth and under the earth,

¹¹and every tongue should confess that Jesus Christ is Lord, to the glory
of God the Father.

Jesus is on the verge of divinity here.[40] However, as with Melchizedek's
designation as 'elohim in 11QMelchizedek, the language used falls short
of full deification, for, as long as Jewish monotheism prevailed in the
background, this was impossible. With that proviso, it was permissible to
employ hyperbolic language to describe figures like Enoch, Melchizedek,
the Teacher of Righteousness, or Jesus, deemed by their respective
devotees to have a special function in the divine plan.[41]

Nevertheless, Paul's admission of Gentiles as Gentiles into the communities he founded meant that increasing numbers of converts had no
attachment to Common Judaism. According to Galatians 3:27–28, in
fact, mystical union with Jesus rendered other distinctions – including
that between Jew and Gentile – of no consequence. In other words, the
Jewishness of Jewish Christians was not of great significance. Although
such Jewish Christians were free to obey the detail of the Torah if they
wished, Paul insisted that Gentile Christians were not compelled to do
so. Not surprisingly, as the body of Gentile Christians grew, Jewish
Christians who kept the Law had less and less in common with them.
Not only, therefore, did Jewish Christians outside Palestine get little
encouragement to remain committed to Common Judaism, but, without
the requirement to convert, Gentile Christians increasingly saw the
Torah merely as a source of spiritual lessons from the past.[42]

This potentially fractious state of affairs may have been sustainable in
the short term, as all Christians – both Jewish and Gentile – awaited
Jesus' return in the first few decades after his crucifixion. But Jesus failed
to come back as expected. Moreover, after Paul's own death in the early
60s CE, further developments meant that, by circa 100 CE, most Christians
belonged to a religious tradition separate from Judaism. Whilst the seeds
of this eventual split were sown by Paul, as argued already, another factor
precipitated the final rupture: the destruction of the Jerusalem Temple
in 70 CE. This event pushed non-Christian Jews and Gentile Christians
in opposite directions, leaving Jewish Christians caught in the middle.
Thus, the Temple's demise was interpreted by Gentile Christians as
divine retribution on the majority of Jews who had not accepted the
gospel. This interpretation is already found in Luke 19:41–44, as noted
earlier, and was elaborated in Christian writings of the second century

CE and afterwards to show that God had abrogated Judaism and founded Christianity instead.[43] For Jews, in contrast, the calamity of 70 CE created a situation in which all were expected to rally round those elements of Common Judaism which could continue without the Temple. That enterprise, as learned in the last chapter, led ultimately to the dominance of Rabbinic Judaism from around the fourth century CE onwards.

In these complex and fraught circumstances, Jewish Christians faced an impossible dilemma, for they were increasingly viewed as aberrant by both non-Christian Jews and Gentile Christians alike. That scenario seems to lie behind the Rabbinic denouncement of 'heretics' in parts of the Jewish liturgy probably dating to the late first or early second century CE; it likewise informs the lambasting of the Pharisees in Matthew 23, where Jesus' words represent an indirect attack by the author on the Rabbinic authorities of his own day.[44] Such pressures will have led some Jewish Christians to abandon their faith in favour of full involvement in the synagogue, while others probably opted to attach themselves to Gentile Christianity. As for those who remained within Jewish Christianity, they found themselves increasingly cut off from the wider world of non-Christian Judaism.

Overall, it is not surprising that Jewish Christians entered into terminal decline after 70 CE and had disappeared altogether by the end of the fourth century CE.[45] In fact, although certainly closest to Jesus and the first Christians in terms of historical development, no first-hand evidence from Jewish Christianity has survived. To understand it, we have been dependent mainly on what can be gleaned from Paul's letters and from Acts – both penned, of course, from the viewpoint of Gentile Christianity. Indeed, if the New Testament is any guide, most Gentile Christian writers of the late first and early second centuries CE concerned themselves with doctrinal speculation about Jesus. Such a preoccupation is reflected in 1–2 Timothy and 1–2 Peter, in which Christian identity is framed in an increasingly non-Jewish way. This process reached a climax by the time of the Gospel of John. Stemming from around 100 CE, it frequently refers negatively to 'the Jews' as though they formed an entity completely separate from the author and his readers.

Gentile Christianity's divorce from its parent, Jewish Christianity, had a momentous effect on the theology of Gentile Christians. Essentially, hyperbolic words and motifs which had not previously implied Jesus' deity, because set within the monotheism of Common Judaism, were now taken to indicate literal divinity. We know, for instance, that Paul's letters were circulating as an authoritative body of texts by the early second century CE, as evidenced in the reference to them as such in the late 2 Peter 3:15–16. Various statements within that Pauline corpus easily lent themselves to an interpretation which rendered Jesus divine – with the hymn of Philippians 2:6–11, cited above, a good case in point.

Once such passages were read in this way, new writings could make what was now thought to be Jesus' true identity even more explicit. The Gospel of John and 1 John are the only New Testament books which have taken this bold step and elaborated their doctrinal positions accordingly.[46] John 1:1–4, equating Jesus with God's eternal Word, is the best known example:

> [1]In the beginning was the Word, and the Word was with God, and the Word was God. [2]He was in the beginning with God. [3]All things came into being through him, and without him not one thing came into being. What has come into being [4]in him was life, and the life was the light of all people.

For the writer here and his community, Jesus Christ is clearly divine. And outside the New Testament, the roughly contemporaneous letters of Ignatius (*circa* 35–*circa* 107 CE), Bishop of Antioch, assume the same.[47] The Gentile Christians concerned, however, were almost certainly unaware of how much this theological innovation violated Jewish notions of God, seeing it instead as inherent all along in Jesus' own ministry and in earlier authors like Paul. But for the diminishing body of Jewish Christians who remained beyond 70 CE, as well as for the emerging Rabbinic movement, such a doctrine compromised traditional monotheism and transformed Gentile Christianity into an independent non-Jewish religion.

Of course, it is not for historians arbitrarily to approve any of these Jewish or Christian positions of the late first and early second centuries CE. More neutral is the supposition that each side was responding to the complex circumstances of the day, as seemed appropriate. In any case, we have concluded that it was the setting aside of the main elements of Common Judaism, rather than speculation about Jesus' status, which was the primary cause of the eventual parting of the ways between Jews and Christians.[48] As has hopefully come across, the Qumran DSS have indirectly provided much of the relevant framework for grasping this fact. Not least, they highlight the Law's priority in all forms of late Second Temple Judaism over against secondary matters of theological speculation. It was primarily the abandonment of the former, therefore, not doctrinal elaboration about Jesus in itself, which divided the Gentile Christian movement from Judaism in a process which began with Paul and was exacerbated by the Temple's destruction.[49] Only once this split had become irreversible, towards the end of the first or beginning of the second century CE, did the theology of Gentile Christians evolve in ways that would have been unthinkable within the Jewish tradition.

The Dead Sea Scrolls and the Church Today

In subsequent centuries, although Jewish Christians died out, Gentile Christianity developed even further. In the area of dogma, the Nicene Creed (325 CE), the Apostles' Creed (*circa* 390 CE), and the Chalcedonian Definition (451 CE) provided a core of beliefs to which all Christians were supposed to adhere.[50] Thus, doctrines like the Incarnation and Trinity received detailed exposition and became essential elements of Christian orthodoxy. Naturally, it was thought that such beliefs, if not spelled out explicitly in the New Testament, were at least implied in its pages. This assumption remained the norm when the Christian world split into East (Orthodox) and West (Catholic) in the eleventh century and with the schismatic effects of the Protestant Reformation during the fifteenth and sixteenth centuries.[51]

With the advent of modern academic study, however, the presumption that a fully developed Christianity could be found in the New Testament began to be questioned. At the same time, new knowledge was coming from other quarters. As outlined in Chapter 2, analysis of the Old Testament overturned many traditional notions of authorship and date, while challenges of a different sort emanated from Darwin and Freud.[52] As a result, from the nineteenth century, most Christian churches spawned a spectrum of theological wings within existing denominations. The resultant fault lines can be characterized in traditional–progressive terms and continue to exist in varying degrees inside the Roman Catholic and Anglican Churches, for example, as well as within and between Protestant groups.[53] Consequently, Christians now take up contradictory positions on a number of contentious subjects, only some of which – like the ordination of women or the place of homosexual people within the community – hit the headlines of the press from time to time.[54]

The Qumran DSS do not address such specific issues, as hardly needs to be stated. Nor do they impinge directly on the validity of this or that type of modern Christianity. Nevertheless, such a valuable collection of Jewish literature from a group which lived at the time of Jesus and the first Christians may, in combination with other evidence from the period, have a bearing on contemporary Christian identity. Despite the reluctance of most DSS scholars to broach such matters, therefore, three related observations are in order.

First, although the Qumran DSS do not link up directly with early

Christian personalities or events, we have seen that their contribution to our understanding of the wider world of late Second Temple Judaism indirectly casts light upon early Christianity. Analysis of the Qumran Community, with its combination of 'legalism' and belief in the Teacher of Righteousness, for instance, helped us conclude that there is no reason to think that the first Christians intended to break with Common Judaism. Where New Testament writings assume otherwise, they almost certainly reflect a situation prevailing after the success of Paul's missionary activity, when that split was already on the way to becoming a *fait accompli*. By the end of the first century CE, indeed, the Gentile Christian movement began to lose sight of its Jewish origins and even started to misapprehend the nature of Judaism. That much can be gleaned by reading between the lines of John's Gospel, and the suffering of the Jews in Christendom in later centuries can largely be explained as a result of this tragic misunderstanding.[55] More positively, recent academic study of late Second Temple Judaism, including the Qumran DSS, is one of a range of factors which has encouraged modern Christians to rediscover their Jewish origins.[56] This, in turn, has contributed to a welcome improvement in relations between Jews and Christians over the last fifty years.

Second, however, the Qumran DSS have highlighted the overwhelming diversity of late Second Temple Jewish religion. Although Jesus and the first Christians were certainly part of that flux, it is difficult for the historian – or, indeed, the informed theologian – to privilege as special in some way the early Christian manifestations of Second Temple tradition without engaging in special pleading of one kind or another. In any case, like the Qumran Sect before them, the Christian movement underwent significant changes in the course of the first century CE, as we have just seen in relation to the aftermath of Paul's Gentile mission. Thus, for anyone seeking guidance from the New Testament – or, theoretically speaking, from the sectarian Qumran DSS – such shifting religious sands create a serious practical problem. In other words, because the ancient writers were not of one mind, modern Christians wishing to distill definitive lessons from the New Testament may find themselves in something of a dilemma.[57] As noted at the end of our last chapter, a parallel dilemma faces Jews who are aware of the results of scholarly analysis of sacred Jewish texts, for the traditions of the past are inevitably relativized by academic study. As was suggested in that case, so a conservative approach to Christian scripture and tradition is rendered less sustainable than a more overtly selective and creative outlook. This is because rigorous historical analysis tends to deprive the believer of a clear-cut ancient archetype and, therefore, of the ability to see modern issues of belief and practice in black-and-white biblical terms.

Returning more specifically to the Qumran DSS, a third observation may add a constructive twist to what has just been stated. It concerns the religious imagination of the Essenes, particularly evident in the sect's interpretation of scripture. lQpHabakkuk 11:9–15, for instance, illustrates a masterful control of biblical sources:

> *You have filled yourself with ignominy more than with glory. Drink also, and stagger! The cup of the Lord's right hand shall come round to you and shame shall come on your glory* (ii, 16).
> Interpreted, this concerns the Priest whose ignominy was greater than his glory. For he did not circumcise the foreskin of his heart, and he walked in the ways of drunkenness that he might quench his thirst. But the cup of the wrath of God shall confuse him . . .

Each biblical phrase has a counterpart in the commentary. Thus, *You have filled yourself . . . with glory* is applied to 'the Priest whose ignominy was greater than his glory', while *Drink also, and stagger!* denotes his drunkenness as a sign of impiety and *The cup of the Lord's right hand* prefigures the Wicked Priest's punishment. But what about 'For he did not circumcise the foreskin of his heart'? In the biblical citation, lQp-Habakkuk reflects the LXX's *Drink and stagger* as a way of emphasizing the subject's wickedness. However, the MT here reads 'Drink and show your uncircumcision', uncircumcision being another metaphor for impiety. As it happens, 'stagger' and 'show your uncircumcision' look similar in Hebrew and this explains the discrepancy – presumably accidental – between the MT and LXX.

Yet, it is more interesting to note that the author of lQpHabakkuk was unencumbered by the existence of such conflicting readings. He employed both creatively for his own purposes. This sort of creativity, in terms of both practice and belief, informs a lot more of the sectarian DSS from Qumran than might at first sight appear, for neither the Torah nor books like Isaiah or Habakkuk came ready-interpreted from God. Even if the Teacher of Righteousness and other leaders were not fully aware of the extent of their own imaginative contribution, there may very well be a lesson here for modern Jews and Christians. In other words, it may be that the array of religious traditions that have flourished in the past, often all the more bewildering and contradictory for being subjected to academic analysis, presents an opportunity for the spiritual imagination. Indeed, it is arguable that, like the writer of 1QpHabakkuk,

Jews and Christians throughout the ages have always creatively selected and reshaped existing tradition in order to make sense of the circumstances of their own day. If so, then an unaltering adherence to the religious past has been a very rare thing indeed.

7

Controversy and Conspiracy

Three Recent Counter-Theories

We have seen that a broad consensus has emerged within the world of DSS research over the past fifty years. The best way of explaining the ruins at Qumran and the manuscripts in Caves 1–11 is to connect both with the Essenes of Philo, Josephus, and Pliny. This hypothesis enables us to account for most of the evidence in a consistent manner, including those Qumran DSS released for the first time in 1991. It also allows us to paint a picture of the religious community utilizing Khirbet Qumran, as well as the state of the biblical text available to its members and, presumably, other Jews elsewhere. Furthermore, the Qumran DSS help us enter more fully than ever before into the world of late Second Temple Judaism at large and that of nascent Christianity.

Nevertheless, whilst the majority of experts would accept such general conclusions, it must be remembered that within the resultant consensus are many variations and disagreements on points of detail. We saw earlier, for example, that some view the Qumran Community as a splinter group which seceded from its Essene parent body. Others have tried to counteract this trend by reworking a direct identification of the Qumran Sect with the Essenes.[1] Vigorous debate on issues like these will doubtless continue for the foreseeable future, and this is just one factor making the Qumran DSS such a fascinating subject area.

However, several proposals of late have either dispensed with any Essene connection at all or else doubted the link between Khirbet Qumran and the documents from surrounding caves. In this section, therefore, we shall review a revival of the Sadducean hypothesis, a radical theory of Qumran origins presented in a new translation of the manuscripts, and a proposal linking the Qumran DSS with the well-to-do of Jerusalem. In the following section, several alternative theories about the function of the Qumran site itself will be evaluated. The remainder of the chapter will then examine three sensational proposals that have received much media attention. Finally, we shall close with a brief consideration of why Jewish documents which are some 2,000 years old have been the object of such intense popular fascination for over five decades.

I Resurrecting the Sadducees

One challenge to the Qumran–Essene Hypothesis has come from Lawrence Schiffman of New York University. For some time, he has promoted the theory that the Qumran Community was a group with strong Sadducean links.[2] Schiffman's evidence includes the fact that some sectarian DSS lay stress on the 'sons of Zadok' (Hebrew, *bene Tsadoq*), an epithet likely related to the name 'Sadducees' (*Tsaddukim*).[3] More particularly, he highlights legal positions advanced in both the sectarian DSS from Qumran and the Mishnah.

The Mishnah is a lengthy work of over sixty tractates or books, and it was compiled around 200 CE, although many of its traditions are older. Essentially, it applies the Pentateuch's laws to the shifting circumstances of everyday life and, as part of its programme, contains a tractate called Yadaim which deals with matters of ritual purity. One of its sections purports to recall some legal conflicts between the Pharisees and Sadducees of Second Temple times. Yadaim 4:7, in particular, is worth noting:[4]

> The Sadducees say, We cry out against you, O ye Pharisees, for ye declare clean an unbroken stream of liquid. The Pharisees say, We cry out against you, O ye Sadducees, for ye declare clean a channel of water that flows from a burial ground.

The Mishnah's language here can seem inaccessible to the unpracticed reader. But the point at issue concerns how ritual impurity is transmitted. In the first sentence, we are told that the Sadducees believed impurity could be transmitted from an unclean pot into which liquid was being poured, back up the stream of water, into the clean dish from which the liquid was being emptied. The Pharisees, apparently, disagreed. While the subject might seem uninteresting to many modern people, Schiffman notes that the legal stance attributed to the Sadducees by the Mishnah also features in the central Qumran text known as 4QMMT[a–f].[5]

[5]Also, concerning streams (of liquid), we say that they have no [6]purity, and that such streams do not separate the impure from the [7]pure. For the liquid of streams and that in the receptacle are alike, [8]being one liquid.

Schiffman is right to detect agreement between the Yadaim tractate and 4QMMT[a–f] here and elsewhere. Joseph Baumgarten, moreover, had earlier pointed out similar parallels between later Rabbinic law and the Temple Scroll.[6]

On several counts, however, it does not necessarily follow that the Qumran Sect was Sadducean, as proposed by Schiffman. Apart from anything else, we saw earlier that other elements can be isolated showing superficial links between the Qumran DSS, on the one hand, and the Pharisees or even the 'revolutionary nationalists', on the other.[7] This should come as no surprise, for, just as modern Jewish or Christian denominations overlap in certain respects, so too presumably did religious groupings in Palestine in the last two centuries BCE and first century CE – as was suggested, indeed, by our Venn diagram imagery in a previous chapter.[8] Such occasional agreements are insufficient in themselves to identify the Qumran Community as Sadducean.

Schiffman, nevertheless, has reaffirmed his position in a 1994 book, albeit a little more cautiously than in previous publications.[9] Given legal parallels of the kind exemplified above, he traces the Qumran Sect to a nucleus of Sadducean dissidents opposed to Jonathan Maccabee's accession to the High Priesthood in 152 BCE. Although they subsequently developed in distinctive ways, that Sadducean link, Schiffman argues, should predominate in debates about the community's origins and identity, whilst the apparent similarities with the Essenes of the Classical Sources highlighted by other scholars require reassessment.[10]

Schiffman has failed to persuade most experts for three main reasons. First, several elements present in some sectarian Qumran DSS – including belief in angels and resurrection of the dead – were rejected by the Sadducees according to Josephus. Those behind the documents were either not Sadducees at all, therefore, or had moved so far beyond a Sadducean starting-point that an original connection tells us little of their fully-fledged identity. Second, Schiffman underplays the cumulative evidence linking the Qumran DSS with the Essenes of the Classical Sources. As observed in Chapter 3, most have been swayed by the consistent nature of such overlaps which outweigh real but intermittent links with Sadducees, Pharisees, or revolutionary nationalists. Third, Schiffman alleges that other scholars have misread the Qumran DSS over the years by relating them almost exclusively to early Christianity instead of the history of Judaism.[11] Although this may be true of much popular coverage, as we shall learn presently, even a brief scan of academic works listed in earlier chapters of this book demonstrates that the charge is unfair.

II Wise, Abegg, and Cook

Three scholars published a new translation of the non-biblical Qumran DSS in 1996.[12] In their introduction, M. Wise, M. Abegg, and E. Cook engage in a critique of the Qumran–Essene Hypothesis, dubbed by them the 'Standard Model'. They also posit an embryonic replacement theory which sees both Sadducean and Essene elements in the manuscripts.

More precisely, the authors claim the Standard Model has three principal strands: (i) the Qumran Community's Essene identity; (ii) its anti-Hasmonean stance; and (iii) Khirbet Qumran as its headquarters. Each of these strands entails serious problems for Wise, Abegg, and Cook, especially after the 1991 releases. Contradictions between the Qumran documents and the Classical Sources call into question the narrowly Essene origin of the former, for instance, while what is probably praise for Alexander Jannaeus in 4QApocryphal Psalm and Prayer challenges the group's supposed anti-Hasmonean convictions. Furthermore, archaeological work at Khirbet Qumran cannot confirm its status as the headquarters of the Essene movement, especially not for the second-century BCE.

We have met some of these difficulties before, of course, concluding that they do not necessarily rule out a version of the Qumran–Essene Hypothesis.[13] Wise, Abegg, and Cook, however, have put forward the beginnings of a radically different proposal. For them, new texts like 4QMMT[a–f] and 4QCalendrical Document C, as well as older ones viewed in a new light, point to the first century BCE for the origin of the Qumran Community. Thus, the Teacher of Righteousness welcomed the pro-Sadducean policies of the first-century BCE ruler Alexander Jannaeus, as implied by apparent praise of the latter figure in 4QApocryphal Psalm and Prayer. But the Teacher of Righteousness' followers fell out of favour when the Pharisees gained influence after Alexandra Salome became queen in 76 BCE. It is the resultant situation, rather than Jonathan Maccabee's rise to power in the second century BCE, which informs long-known documents like 1QpHabakkuk and 4QpNahum.[14] Indeed, Josephus speaks revealingly about this fraught period:[15]

> [The Pharisees] became . . . the real administrators of the state, at liberty to banish and to recall . . . whom they would . . . [and] they proceeded to

kill whomsoever they would. The most eminent of the citizens thus imperilled sought refuge with Aristobulus [Hyrcanus II's brother], who persuaded his mother [Salome] to spare their lives . . . [but if necessary] to expel them from the city.

Wise, Abegg, and Cook argue that the Teacher of Righteousness' exile to Khirbet Qumran is best understood against the Pharisaic activity of the 70s BCE reported here. The Wicked Priest, in that case, is Salome's son, the Pharisee-supporting Hyrcanus II.

By way of evaluation, Wise, Abegg, and Cook make a number of useful suggestions, pointing out more clearly than most scholars, for example, that the Qumran Sect must have been thoroughly intertwined with wider political and religious circumstances, including those of the first century BCE. In other respects, though, they artificially represent the Standard Model and its three strands as some kind of monolith which must either stand or fall in its entirety. No consideration is given to how the Qumran–Essene Hypothesis might be sensibly adjusted in response to the 1991 releases. After all, such a revision linking the Classical Sources, the manuscripts of Caves 1–11, and Khirbet Qumran would not have to insist that the latter site was the movement's head-quarters for a full 150 years. Nor is there acknowledgment by Wise, Abegg, and Cook that their alternative might have problems of its own. Thus, a settlement at Qumran in *circa* 76 BCE does not tally with the archaeological evidence any more than de Vaux's second-century BCE reconstruction. More seriously, we learned earlier that very recent pub-lication of fragments from the early to mid-second century BCE seems to reaffirm that period as pivotal for the formation of what became the Qumran Community, whatever important first-century BCE develop-ments also occurred.[16]

III Did the Dead Sea Scrolls come from Jerusalem?

Professor Norman Golb of Chicago University has posed a third chal-lenge to the Qumran–Essene Hypothesis.[17] In his view, no Essenes lived at Qumran at all, for, as we shall see in the next section, he has argued that the site was a fortress unconnected with any religious sect. Nor is the hotchpotch of texts from the nearby caves to be identified as an Essene library. Rather, echoing a much earlier suggestion, the literature constitutes the random contents of Jerusalem libraries taken to the caves for safety just before the city's fall to the Romans in 70 CE.[18]

So, what arguments does Golb adduce in favour of his thesis? Three are worth highlighting. First, he believes the Qumran DSS collection is too large and diverse to have been one religious party's property. Most documents, indeed, are not sectarian but consist of books from the Hebrew Bible, Apocrypha, and Pseudepigrapha, as well as other works apparently circulating widely. As for the so-called sectarian texts, they advocate contradictory views on a range of issues like marriage and, according to Golb, cannot represent the single viewpoint required by the Qumran–Essene Hypothesis. Moreover, the presence of a supposedly sectarian composition, Songs of the Sabbath Sacrifice, in both Caves 4 and 11 (4QShirShab and 11QShirShab) and at the rebel stronghold of Masada confirms, for him, that the documents were employed by Jews of different persuasions. In Golb's judgement, therefore, the Qumran DSS stemmed from the Temple library and the private collections of wealthy individuals from Jerusalem, with the books secreted in the caves as the Romans advanced on the city. Naturally, it is pointless to harmonize the contradictory elements of such a haphazard collection, as many have erroneously attempted to do.

Second, Golb dismisses the evidence of Pliny the Elder as irrelevant, for this ancient author set his description of the Essenes in the present tense. Since his work was published in 77 CE, by which time Khirbet Qumran had been destroyed, Pliny's Essenes must have been resident somewhere else. A third objection raised by Golb concerns the apparent lack within the collection of accounts and other domestic documents which would have been essential if the Qumran DSS belonged to an independent religious sect which existed for over a century.

Golb has expanded his thesis in a lengthy book appearing in 1995.[19] However, he does not appreciate the complexity of the new 1991 releases. He assumes, for instance, that the 'Jonathan' of 4QApocryphal Psalm and Prayer must be Alexander Jannaeus (whose Hebrew name was Jonathan) and that this constitutes another nail in the coffin of the Qumran–Essene Hypothesis which takes it for granted that the Hasmoneans were the sect's enemies.[20] But Golb seems unaware that this 'Jonathan' could just as easily be Jonathan Maccabee, as others have suggested.[21] Similarly, though it is now clear that some non-literary manuscripts among 4Q342–359 came from Murabba'at or Nahal Hever, a few were certainly retrieved from Cave 4.[22] Hence, one of Golb's objections to the Qumran–Essene Hypothesis vanishes. Furthermore, his other objections have not persuaded scholars, not least because Golb fails to treat alternative viewpoints with sufficient seriousness.

Thus, the fact that Pliny's description is in the present tense does not outweigh the dramatic, if general, nature of his testimony. Since Pliny freely admits to incorporating sources into his *Natural History*, it is wise to conclude simply that he drew on an account of the Essenes written before the Qumran settlement was abandoned in 68 CE. As for Golb's most serious point, that the diverse nature of the Qumran literary corpus precludes ascribing it to any one group of late Second Temple Jews, several factors make his theory a less likely explanation than that which was proffered in Chapters 3 and 4.

Firstly, the fact that much of the collection consists of widespread biblical, apocryphal, and pseudepigraphal works is only to be expected, for these books were the common heritage of all Second Temple Jews. Apart from anything else, the Qumran Community would have required its own copies of such material so that, through its leaders' interpretative skills, it could persuade insiders and outsiders alike of the validity of its beliefs and practices. Secondly, aside from popular books (like Genesis, Deuteronomy, Isaiah, Psalms, Enochic texts, or Jubilees), most scriptural works are extant in only a few samples. In contrast, multiple copies of writings like 4QMMT[a-f], the Damascus Document, and Community Rule have survived, clearly confirming the collection's partisan nature. Despite real differences or even contradictions among some of these sectarian DSS, furthermore, the thread of distinctive emphases binding them together is more substantial than Golb allows, as observed in Chapter 4.[23]

Thirdly, the suggestion that, as the Roman siege began, Jerusalem's best and brightest slipped out of the city with hundreds of documents and carried them all the way to Qumran has struck most scholars as implausible. Preferable by far is the supposition that the contents of Caves 1–11 were linked to the site of Qumran which, for a considerable time during the late Second Temple period, was used by some kind of Essene community.

Fortress, Villa, or 'Entrepôt'?

As if pre-empting the last section's final point, Golb and others have argued for a re-evaluation of the Khirbet Qumran site itself. We shall briefly examine three recent propositions.[24]

I Khirbet Qumran as a fortress

Golb has allied his theory about the Qumran DSS with an alternative evaluation of Khirbet Qumran.[25] The location, he alleges, was not inhabited by a religious community but was a fortress without any connection to the manuscripts of Caves 1–11. Golb certainly has on his side the general fact that the Hasmoneans built other fortifications in the region, such as the fortresses at Masada and Macherus on either side of the Dead Sea. More specifically, he points to several features of the Qumran settlement which seem to back his case. Not only were the buildings surrounded by substantial walls and serviced by an extensive water system, but a tower also stood at their centre. The fact that the site was destroyed by military attack, moreover, acts as a further pointer to its own military use.

Actually, this theory is not entirely new. Back in the late 1940s, de Vaux thought that Khirbet Qumran had been a fortress unconnected with the Cave 1 documents. But he soon changed his mind after further excavations, and his revised conclusion still holds good.[26] Apart from anything else, if Qumran was a fortress, it was a bad one. Its walls, for instance, are not thick enough for effective defense, while the design of the water-supply would have laid it open to attack. In these circumstances, the tower could only have offered temporary sanctuary to its inhabitants. As for Golb's deduction from Khirbet Qumran's destruction, we have no reason to think Roman soldiers restricted their attacks to military installations. Due to these and other objections, in fact, no eminent scholar has seen fit to follow Golb in concluding that Khirbet Qumran was primarily a fortress.

II Khirbet Qumran as a villa

Another theory about the nature of the Qumran ruins has been proposed by an archaeologist, Pauline Donceel-Voûte, whilst preparing with Robert Donceel the final excavation reports never completed by de Vaux. Although their report too now seems to have been delayed indefinitely, Donceel-Voûte, like Golb, has concluded that the Qumran settlement was not occupied by a religious community. But unlike Golb, she thinks it was a villa.[27] Central to her argument is the identity of the location known as Locus 30.[28] The remains discovered there in the 1950s included debris from a collapsed first storey, among them bits of brick and plaster. Their shape allowed de Vaux to piece together what he identified as the table and benches of a 'scriptorium' or writing-room. Donceel-Voûte, however, has proposed that the reconstructed artifacts were more likely to have been dining furniture. Khirbet Qumran, on this hypothesis, was a wealthy person's villa and the upper level of Locus 30 functioned as a dining-room. Accordingly, de Vaux's writing-table was really a type of reclining sofa common in Graeco-Roman times. What were previously thought to be inkwells must similarly have been some other dining utensil.[29]

Once more, the evidence is more convincing when interpreted differently. The main item of furniture from Locus 30, as de Vaux reconstructed it, was 50 centimetres wide, 70 centimetres high, and several metres long. If it had been a reclining couch, it would have been unique in the ancient world, for such sofas were normally much wider. Indeed, it would have been difficult not to fall off this narrow piece of furniture which, according to a recent study, would not have been strong enough to cope with such usage anyway.[30] In short, de Vaux's characterization of Khirbet Qumran as a religious settlement and of Locus 30 as some kind of 'scriptorium' remains the best explanation to date.

III Khirbet Qumran as a commercial entrepôt

A third identification for Khirbet Qumran in opposition to the general consensus is that of A. Crown and L. Cansdale.[31] These two scholars have argued that the site was a commercial centre or 'entrepôt' set alongside a major regional trade route. Again, their suggestion remains unconvincing. Not only is there no evidence for an ancient trade route in close proximity to Qumran, but the location also lacks the remains of the accommodation and storage facilities that would have been required for such an enterprise. Needless to say, Crown and Cansdale's proposition has not gained supporters.

To summarize so far, it should not be thought that every aspect of the theories presented by Crown and Cansdale, Donceel-Voûte, Golb, Schiffman, or Wise, Abegg, and Cook is simply untenable. On the contrary, these are able scholars, some of whose individual suggestions on particular facets of the data are plausible. The main argument against their hypotheses is simply the persuasiveness of a wide variety of other factors, whose cumulative force they have not treated sufficiently seriously. In light of the evidence amassed earlier on, in other words, the best option still seems to be a version of the Qumran–Essene Hypothesis championed in Chapters 3 and 4, linking together the DSS from Caves 1–11, the buildings of Khirbet Qumran and 'Ein-Feshkha, and the Essenes of Philo, Josephus, and Pliny.

The Qumran Dead Sea Scrolls and the Vatican

Renewed scholarly interest in the Qumran DSS, as exemplified in the controversial theories just described, was inspired largely by the fresh texts of 1991. However, the manuscripts have also attracted a lot of media attention over the past decade. Numerous sensationalist books have likewise claimed to shed new light of one sort or another on the nature of the corpus and, by implication, on Second Temple Judaism and early Christianity. Space will not allow an exhaustive account of all these proposals, but we can consider three of the most significant ones in this and the next two sections.

Back in 1991, two journalists, Michael Baigent and Richard Leigh, caused a sensation when, just before the new Cave 4 releases, they published a work provocatively entitled *The Dead Sea Scrolls Deception*.[32] The authors set themselves three major tasks. Most straightforwardly, they provided an account of the DSS discovery and how the Qumran–Essene Hypothesis emerged as a scholarly consensus in the 1950s and 1960s. Because we have already reviewed the relevant data, this aspect of their work requires no further comment.

Secondly, the journalists went on to disclose that the Qumran–Essene Hypothesis was the result of a conspiracy to suppress material threatening the Christian tradition.[33] To those with little or no prior knowledge, their argument could appear convincing, for Baigent and Leigh draw on several factors which are true. Thus, the reader of their book is informed of the delay in publishing Cave 4 material and the restrictions on access before 1991. It is also explained that most members of the early editorial team were or became Roman Catholic and had an association with the Ecole Biblique et Archéologique Française de Jérusalem. This institution, it is pointed out, operated under the auspices of the Vatican in Rome.

On the basis of these observations, all more or less sound in themselves, Baigent and Leigh founded their main accusation: the Vatican directed de Vaux's editorial team and was at pains to control the interpretation of the Qumran DSS to protect traditional Christianity. To that end, they further charged, the Qumran–Essene Hypothesis' main function was artificially to separate the contents of Caves 1–11, both chronologically and theologically, from early Christianity. Moreover, Cave 4 material was withheld over the years to prevent the damage to Christian belief which would have resulted if certain texts had entered the public domain.

Those who have followed the thread of this book so far may suspect that the real delusion in *The Dead Sea Scrolls Deception* is the conspiracy theory propagated by the authors. But in view of the book's wide publicity, it is worth spelling out why its contents cannot stand. Of the many criticisms that could be made, three are fatal to the journalists' conspiracy theory.

First, Baigent and Leigh do not fully appreciate that some elements in the Qumran–Essene Hypothesis derived from scholars outside the narrow clique headed by de Vaux. Geza Vermes, for example, was the first to argue seriously that the Wicked Priest of lQpHabakkuk was Jonathan Maccabee. He was, at the same time, a vociferous critic of the editorial team's scandalous publication record before the release of Cave 4 documents in 1991.

Second, contrary to the impression given by Baigent and Leigh, the Ecole Biblique has a world-wide reputation for academic study of the Bible. Indeed, the institute's journal, *Revue Biblique*, remains at the cutting edge of modern research.[34] It produces articles representing a range of opinions from a variety of scholars – whatever their personal religious convictions – on all major aspects of Old Testament, Second Temple Jewish, and early Christian history. When it comes to scholarly freedom and integrity, therefore, neither the Ecole Biblique nor the *Revue Biblique* can be portrayed as under the Vatican's thumb.

Third, *The Dead Sea Scrolls Deception*'s conspiracy theory is further undermined by the fact that several proposals contrary to the Qumran–Essene Hypothesis have emanated from Roman Catholics. We briefly observed earlier, for instance, that a Spanish Jesuit, José O'Callaghan, identified some Cave 7 fragments with portions of the New Testament.[35] Similarly, Father Joseph Fitzmyer of the Catholic University of America, Washington DC, has been among those who criticized the original editorial team for failing to publish quickly.[36] These Catholic scholars cannot be characterized as toeing a Vatican line. Consequently, we must conclude that, whatever the real shortcomings of de Vaux and others, Baigent and Leigh's theory of a Vatican cover-up is unsustainable.

The same negative judgement has to be passed on Baigent and Leigh's third major theme concerning the true identity of the Qumran Community. Their views in this regard are derived mainly from Robert Eisenman of California State University, whose name crops up frequently in their book. To his position, therefore, we may now turn.

The Qumran Scrolls and James the Just

For over fifteen years, Eisenman has been trying to persuade scholars that the Teacher of Righteousness was really James the brother of Jesus who, according to Josephus, was executed by the High Priest Ananus in 62 CE. This Ananus was the Wicked Priest of lQpHabakkuk, in Eisenman's view, while the Liar of the Damascus Document was the Apostle Paul. The Gospels were composed in the second century CE, long after Paul's transformation of Christianity, for, reinterpreting Jesus' death as a universal atoning sacrifice, Paul had successfully remodelled the movement into something peaceable which was acceptable to the authorities. Virtually nothing can be known of the historical Jesus, therefore, except that his execution was politically motivated.[37]

Nevertheless, Eisenman believes he can deduce that Christianity before Paul was legalistic, nationalistic, and xenophobic. It emerged from a broad Zealot movement which can be traced back centuries and also incorporated the community at Khirbet Qumran. Central to the argument is 1QpHabakkuk 11:3–8. This passage, interpreting Habakkuk 2:15, was cited earlier but is worth repeating:[38]

> *Woe to him who causes his neighbours to drink; who pours out his venom to make them drunk that he may gaze on their feasts* (ii, 15).
> Interpreted, this concerns the Wicked Priest who pursued the Teacher of Righteousness to the house of his exile that he might confuse him with his venomous fury. And at the time appointed for rest, for the Day of Atonement, he appeared before them to confuse them, and to cause them to stumble on the Day of Fasting, their Sabbath of repose.

Although the ancient author may have had others in mind as well, we concluded in Chapters 3 and 4 that the Wicked Priest and Teacher of Righteousness primarily denoted the second-century BCE founder of the Qumran Sect and his opponent, Jonathan Maccabee. In that case, the 'house of his exile' refers to either Qumran or, more likely, some earlier outpost used before that site was settled.[39]

However, Eisenman equates it with Jerusalem. Although that is not impossible, he then proceeds to link lQpHabakkuk 11:3–8 with Josephus' account of the execution of James the brother of Jesus, a character known in later Christian tradition as 'James the Just':[40]

> ... Ananus thought that he had a favourable opportunity because Festus was dead and Albinus was still on the way. And so he convened the judges of the Sanhedrin and brought before them a man named James, the brother of Jesus who was called the Christ, and certain others. He accused them of having transgressed the law and delivered them up to be stoned.

The incident described here is set in 62 CE, just after the rule of the Procurator Porcius Festus but before the arrival of Clodius Albinus. In these circumstances, the new High Priest, Ananus, attempted to assert his authority by picking on James, the leader of Jerusalem's small and relatively unimportant Jewish–Christian community.[41] Eisenman maintains that this event is reflected in 1QpHabakkuk 11:3–8. But without corroborative support, there is no basis for such an interpretation, let alone for taking the passage as the foundation for other elements in his imaginative theory.

Eisenman, in 1992, along with Michael Wise of Chicago University, produced the first widely available edition of the newly released Cave 4 documents.[42] Although the Hebrew and Aramaic texts and their English translations are reasonably accurate, the accompanying comments reflect Eisenman's idiosyncratic interpretation. One composition calls for particular attention, 4QRule of War, fragment 5. Eisenman holds that the work refers to the messiah's violent death, translating the relevant portion as follows:[43]

> . . . Isaiah the Prophet, ['The thickets of the forest] will be fell[ed with an axe] (2) [and Lebanon shall f]all [by a mighty one.] A staff shall rise from the root of Jesse, [and a Planting from his roots will bear fruit.'] (3) . . . the branch of David. They will enter into Judgement with . . . (4) and they will put to death the Leader of the Community, the Bran[ch of David] (this might also be read, depending on the context, 'and the Leader of the Community, the Bran[ch of David'] will put him to death) . . . (5) and with woundings, and the (high) priest will command . . . (6) [the sl]ai[n of the] Kitti[m] . . .

While bracketing an alternative rendering, Eisenman maintains that this passage supports his thesis that a broad Zealot movement, informing both the Qumran Community and early Christianity, expected a messianic figure to undergo a political execution. Although there is no other evidence to suggest any late Second Temple Jews thought in this way, Eisenman had been prominent in earlier press reports in the first flurry of excitement after the 1991 releases.[44] He had argued, in particular, that 4QRule of War showed the Qumran Community and the early Christians shared a belief in the messiah's death.

However, though the ambiguous form of the relevant verb means Eisenman's translation is theoretically possible, Vermes' rendering makes better sense:

> [As it is written in . . .] Isaiah the Prophet, *[The thickets of the forest] will be cut [down with an axe and Lebanon by a majestic one will f]all. And there shall come forth a shoot from the stump of Jesse* [. . .] the Branch of David and they will enter into judgement with [. . .] the Prince of the

> Congregation, the Br[anch of David] will kill him [. . . by strok]es and by wounds. And a Priest [of renown?] will command [. . . the s]lai[n] of the Kitti[m . . .]

Justification for this translation comes from other fragments of 4QRule of War and the context of the Isaiah 10:34 citation. Both have the victory of God's anointed over his enemies in view, not his death. Indeed, this is the overwhelming picture emerging from all Second Temple Jewish texts anticipating the advent of a messianic figure modelled on King David. It is reasonable, therefore, to suppose that the Christian emphasis on the messiah's death was formulated after Jesus' execution had taken place.

More generally, Eisenman dismisses out of hand the cumulative force of carbon dating, palaeography, and archaeology.[45] While no one denies the limitations of such techniques, their overall impact is fatal to his argument. We learned earlier that these methods point generally to the first century BCE as the period during which the Qumran Community flourished. More significantly, as mentioned back in Chapter 3, the most recent carbon dating has ruled out a first-century CE setting for 1QpHabakkuk.[46]

Finally, one more fragment deserves comment, for 4QApocryphon of Daniel contains language remarkably close to Luke 1:32, 35. The Qumran document, damaged in places, reads as follows:

> I . . . dwelt on him. he fell down before the throne . . . O [K]ing, you are angry for ever and your years . . . your vision and all. For ever you . . . [the gre]at ones. An oppression will come to the earth . . . a great massacre in the provinces . . . the king of Assyria [and E]gypt . . . he will be great on earth . . . will make and all will see . . . he will be called (or: call himself) [gran]d . . . and by his name he will be designated (or: designate himself). II The son of God he will be proclaimed (or: proclaim himself) and the son of the Most High they will call him. Like the sparks of the vision, so will be their kingdom. They will reign for years on the earth and they will trample all. People will trample people (cf. Dan. vii, 23) and one province another province . . . until the people of God will arise and all will rest from the sword. Their (the people of God's) kingdom will be an eternal kingdom (cf. Dan. vii, 27) and all their path will be in truth. They will jud[ge] the earth in truth and all will make peace. The sword will cease from the earth, and all the provinces will pay homage to them. The Great God (cf. Dan. ii, 45) is their helper. He will wage war for them. He will give peoples into their hands and all of them (the peoples) He will cast before them (the people of God). Their dominion will be an eternal dominion (Dan. vii, 14) and all the boundaries of . . .

The verbal similarities with Luke's Gospel are real enough, although they were known to the scholarly world over twenty-five years ago.[47] However, the identity of the 'son of God' is unclear. Eisenman, not surprisingly, has linked the passage to his theory of Christian origins, but more sober suggestions have been made.

The figure could be understood positively as an angelic being (like the supernatural hero of 11QMelchizedek) or as the Messiah of David expected in some Qumran DSS. In fact, since 2 Samuel 7:14 refers to King David (and his descendants) as God's son, this would not be unusual in a late Second Temple Jewish context. Alternatively, 'son of God' could be understood negatively as some idolatrous divine pretender, either from the past (like Antiochus IV) or anticipated in the future. Because the document draws heavily on Daniel 7, where this motif is prominent, the second is perhaps more likely. Anyhow, either is preferable to linking the text to Eisenman's unconvincing theory.

An Hypothesis Too Far!

An even more sensational theory has come from Barbara Thiering of the University of Sydney, Australia. Although she had previously written several useful articles on the Qumran world, in 1992 she produced a book called *Jesus the Man: A New Interpretation from the Dead Sea Scrolls*.[48] To those with a basic familiarity with the Qumran DSS, it is difficult to avoid the conclusion that her book's contents belong to the realms of fantasy. For others, however, the provocative title, combined with detailed appendices and lengthy footnotes, gives the work a semblance of hefty scholarship. In view of the publicity it received, therefore, we shall explain why Thiering's thesis is untenable.

Essential to Thiering, as also to Eisenman, is her insistence that the sectarian Qumran DSS pertain chiefly to the last one hundred years of Second Temple history. In other words, 1QpHabakkuk and related works have to do with people and events of the first century CE, not, as argued in Chapters 3 and 4, the second and first centuries BCE. To justify this claim, Thiering re-dates the sectarian writings, stating that palaeographical datings ascribed to individual documents should be given a wider berth of fifty years or so to account for potentially misleading factors. For instance, some first-century CE scribes may have deliberately written in an old-fashioned hand, whilst a false impression of antiquity could be given if a text were penned by a scribe still in training under an older master.

Upon these shaky foundations, Thiering proceeds to discredit the main elements of the scholarly consensus. The reference to the Wicked Priest in lQpHabakkuk 8:9–10 constitutes a good example. As we saw earlier, because he was 'called by the name of truth when he first arose' but fell from grace when he 'ruled over Israel', Jonathan Maccabee seems to have been the primary referent here. Yet, for Thiering, 'Israel' means the Qumran Community, not the whole of the Jewish people, while 'truth' denotes its special teaching, rather than general uprightness. The crucifixion described in 4QpNahum 1 is similarly relocated by Thiering to the first century CE, as a version of Pontius Pilate's reaction to the protest over Roman standards bearing Caesar's image. We cited the relevant passage from Josephus in Chapter 5 and, because he records that Pilate quietly withdrew his troops without exacting punishment, Alexander Jannaeus' cruel action in the first century BCE remains the best background for understanding 4QpNahum 1.[49]

Thiering, nevertheless, continues to construct a first-century CE setting for the main sectarian DSS from Qumran. Thus, the opponent of the Wicked Priest and hero of the Qumran Sect, the Teacher of Righteousness, is equated with John the Baptist. This identification is based on the fact that the Hebrew word for 'teacher', *moreh*, could, grammatically speaking, be taken as 'sprinkler' in the sense of baptizer. According to Thiering, John became the leader of an Essene movement which incorporated traditional and 'liberal' wings in tension with each other. John himself belonged to the traditional side and believed the end of the world was near. Because he thereby threatened the religious and political status quo, Herod Antipas had him executed in 31 CE.

Before his death, however, the Essene movement experienced serious internal conflict. Tension between the Torah-centred traditionalists and the less rigorous 'liberal' side is reflected in lQpHabakkuk 11:5–8, where we learn that, as noted in Chapter 4, the Teacher of Righteousness was pursued by the Wicked Priest.[50] In Thiering's opinion, the latter was none other than Jesus of Nazareth. The tearing of the heavens in Mark 1:9–11, she argues, is a cryptic reference to the same dispute:

[9]In those days Jesus came from Nazareth of Galilee and was baptized by John in the Jordan. [10]And just as he was coming up out of the water, he saw the heavens torn apart and the Spirit descending like a dove on him. [11]And a voice came from heaven, 'You are my Son, the Beloved; with you I am well pleased.'

On the basis of this sort of decodifying interpretation, Thiering claims to be able to reconstruct Jesus' life in remarkable detail. Gospel references to Galilee and Jerusalem, accordingly, are not taken at face value but, for her, denote the Judaean desert and Qumran. Moreover, married to Mary Magdalene, Jesus was an illegitimate descendent of King David, whom the sect expected to ascend Israel's royal throne. He led the 'liberal' wing within the Essene movement and was less Torah-oriented and less nationalistic than the faction of John the Baptist.

To cut a long story short, Jesus went too far even for his own supporters when, although a Davidic descendent himself, he dressed in the apparel of the High Priest – an incident which Thiering claims to be able to recover from the transfiguration story in Mark 9:2–8. This and earlier misdemeanours, intolerable to traditionalists, explain why Jesus is dubbed the Wicked Priest in lQpHabakkuk. After a further disappointment, Judas Iscariot betrayed Jesus as a potential insurgent to Pontius Pilate. Thereupon, the Prefect of all Judaea rode out to Qumran for the trial of Jesus who was crucified just outside the settlement. As if that were not enough, on the basis of Mark 15:36's reference to the 'sour wine' offered to him at his crucifixion, Thiering surmises that Jesus was not killed by this ordeal. He was merely rendered unconscious and, after burial in Cave 8, was revived with herbs. He then stayed at Qumran for a period, separated from Mary Magdalene, married a second wife, and accompanied Paul on his missionary work. Eventually, Jesus ended up in Rome, where he is presumed to have died an old man.

To those who have worked their way through preceding chapters, it should be clear that Thiering's hypothesis is pure fantasy. In case any doubts remain, however, it is worth highlighting three reasons for this negative judgement. Firstly, while it is good to question current theories and re-evaluate existing evidence, Thiering's attempt to cast doubt on the work of others amounts to special pleading. She wrongly assumes, for example, that the inexact nature of the science of palaeography necessarily favours her younger dates for some Qumran DSS. In reality, allowing an extra fifty years' latitude could just as easily lead in the opposite direction, at least in some instances. In any case, Accelerator Mass Spectrometry tests conducted in 1991 showed that the Qumran DSS collection centres chiefly on the first century BCE, while those of 1994 demonstrated specifically that 1QpHabakkuk was penned no later than the first century BCE.[51]

Secondly, persons mentioned by name in the sectarian documents clearly point in the same direction. 4QpNahum 1:2–3, as observed several times before now, mentions an Antiochus and a Demetrius who are almost certainly Antiochus IV and Demetrius III of the second and first centuries BCE, respectively. Among the texts released for the first time in 1991, furthermore, we saw also that 4QCalendar C lists, among others, the first-century BCE figures of Salome Alexandra and Aemilius

Scaurus. In contrast, no concrete historical figure from the first century CE is named in any sectarian DSS. It makes sense, therefore, to look for the identity of those referred to cryptically – like the Teacher of Righteousness and the Wicked Priest – within the same time frame.

Finally, Thiering's supposed emulation of lQpHabakkuk's use of scripture in her own reading of the Gospels is thoroughly misguided. A document like lQpHabakkuk is often, quite reasonably, dubbed a Pesher or Commentary by scholars, because it follows each biblical citation with an interpretation introduced by the Hebrew word *pesher* ('interpretation'). Persons and events mentioned in the former are reapplied imaginatively to the author's time in the latter, as noted earlier.[52] However, the writers of lQpHabakkuk or 4QpNahum spell out their interpretations of the scriptural text quite straightforwardly; they did not intend their own compositions to be treated as cryptic works by future generations. The same point applies to the Gospels. They too claim various Old Testament passages have found their fulfillment in Jesus. But we have no evidence whatsoever to suggest that the writers shaped their accounts so as to conceal under the surface additional data which only Thiering has been able to decipher. In reality, a more sober account of both the Qumran DSS and the Gospels is preferable by far. The cumulative evidence, indeed, makes it impossible to take Thiering's conclusions seriously.[53]

The Fascination of the Qumran Scrolls

Sensationalist speculation about the significance of the Qumran DSS did not begin with the musings of Baigent and Leigh, Thiering, or other recent authors. Indeed, ever since their discovery, these remarkable documents from the Judaean desert have been subjected to outlandish interpretations.

When it comes to Eisenman's hypothesis and the conspiracy theory of Baigent and Leigh, in fact, many of their ideas replicate those put forward in the 1950s and 1960s by the American critic Edmund Wilson and the British scholar John Allegro. Thus, Wilson wrote an article for the *New Yorker* in 1955 and later in the same year published a book entitled *The Scrolls from the Dead Sea*.[54] Popularizing the more circumspect views of a French scholar, André Dupont-Sommer of the Sorbonne University, Wilson maintained that the small team of scholars in control of the Qumran texts was withholding information about beliefs hitherto thought uniquely Christian.[55] There is, of course, a grain of truth in this, for indirect parallels with the Qumran DSS, as learned in the previous chapter, show just how Jewish Jesus and the early Christians were. But Wilson had more dramatic links in mind, such as belief in a messianic death and resurrection. To date, no such documents have come to light, even after the 1991 releases.

Similar ideas were put forward, albeit in a less dramatic fashion, by John Allegro, one of the original band of Qumran scholars, in three lectures on British radio in 1956. He maintained that the manuscripts contained references paralleled in later Christian doctrine, including a messianic crucifixion and resurrection in association with the first century BCE.[56] This caused something of a media sensation, for, whatever Allegro's intentions, it was assumed that his comments were damaging to Christianity by implying that what happened to Jesus was less than unique. In any case, other team members publicly denied all such claims about the contents of the ancient documents, while Allegro went on to elaborate ever more fanciful theories about the Qumran DSS and their relationship to Christianity.[57] Ultimately, he destroyed his academic credibility with the publication of his infamous book *The Sacred Mushroom and the Cross*, a fantasy linking early Christian tradition with hallucinogenic mushrooms![58]

As for his notion that some Qumran DSS refer to a crucifixion and other 'Christian' ideas, Allegro must have had in mind 4QpNahum, the two damaged documents considered above (4QRule of War and 4QApocryphon of Daniel), and 4QMessianic Apocalypse. Now that all the manuscripts and fragments are available, nothing else has come to light that could be construed in this way. However, whilst these works do mention crucifixion, death, a 'son of God', and resurrection, respectively, earlier discussions have shown it would be inaccurate to interpret them along the lines of Allegro, Wilson or, more recently, Eisenman. With the benefit of hindsight, therefore, it is no wonder relations between Allegro and his fellow team members in the 1950s deteriorated, nor is it surprising that contemporary scholars have failed to take seriously more recent suggestions of a similar nature. On the other hand, if the material concerned had been fully published at the time, the energy expended on recurrently sensationalizing the subject could have been redirected to more rewarding endeavour.

Yet, even back in 1910, with the publication of the Cairo copies of the Damascus Document found in 1897, the *New York Times* ran a sensational Christmas Day story claiming that the manuscripts described 'personages believed to be Christ, John the Baptist, and the Apostle Paul'![59] This announcement did not reflect the views of the man who knew most about the manuscripts, the Cambridge scholar Solomon Schechter.[60] Yet, it did receive support from George Margoliouth of the

British Museum, who thought that the Damascus Document's 'Messiah of Aaron' was none other than John the Baptist, while the Teacher of Righteousness was Jesus and the Scoffer was Paul. The media have lapped up similar reports ever since, with the help of the occasional renegade scholar.

Is there a rational explanation for this apparently limitless propensity to link the Qumran DSS with Jesus and Christianity in what, after fifty years of research, is a rather credulous manner? Part of the answer may lie in the fact that the Christian religion in its various forms has saturated the culture of Western Europe and North America for hundreds of years, coupled with traditional views of the Bible, Jesus, and ancient Judaism. Accordingly, most people throughout the centuries have assumed, and still assume, that Jesus and the early Christians were the most important players in the world of their time. It would seem natural from this perspective to assume that any new evidence about the late Second Temple period would most likely have something to do with them.

Even with the rise of academic study of the Bible, many at first found it difficult to put on hold pervasive assumptions derived from the dominance of orthodox forms of Christianity throughout the centuries. For example, late nineteenth- and early twentieth-century studies of Judaism in the time of Jesus, when produced by Christians, were often tinged with traditional caricatures of Jewish religion deriving from the polemics of the pre-modern age.[61] Fortunately, scholars nowadays are more aware of the potential their presuppositions have for affecting academic analysis. This does not mean that they need to stop being Jewish or Christian or of any other persuasion, however, for the realization of the danger is half the battle. Put another way, when scholars are able to acknowledge their preconceptions and predilections, they can in large measure ensure they are held in check or overridden in the course of their work. The rise of progressive versions of Judaism and Christianity from the nineteenth century onwards has also helped. Although the adherents of these forms of Jewish and Christian religion remain a minority in most parts of the world, their existence has provided forms of religious expression more easily able to accept historical scholarship, even when its results conflict with more traditional religious convictions.

Most non-specialists, it has to be said, remain unaware of such developments. This applies to both those who are religious and those who are not. The latter, indeed, just like everyone else, tend to pick up pictures of Judaism and Christianity derived from the days before historical research encouraged a more complex and less black-and-white understanding. Of course, when knowledge in all areas of the sciences and humanities is growing, it is not surprising that the results of academic study in the field of religion are not widely known. The reticence of many professional academics to explain their work to a general audience only makes things worse.

It also often means that journalists – even when trying their best to be neutral and objective – are unaware of the uncritical, not to say traditional, framework within which they operate when it comes to religious matters. An article in *The Independent* newspaper in September 1992, for example, was headed 'Scroll Fragment Challenges Basic Tenet of Christianity'. Despite this heading, its discussion of 4QApocryphon of Daniel, a fragmentary work considered above, stated quite sensibly that its reference to a 'son of God' probably denoted some divine pretender who would rule the last human empire before the advent of God's kingdom. Mixed in with such sober judgement, however, and without really explaining why, it was also suggested that 4QApocryphon of Daniel might challenge 'the fundamental Christian belief that Jesus was the unique Son of God'.[62] It does nothing of the sort, of course, for the phrase 'son of God' would not have meant God the Son (i.e. the Second Person of the Trinity), as the article's words imply here, to Jews or Christians before 70 CE. Rather, historical research, as concluded in Chapter 6, strongly suggests this Christian belief only emerged in embryonic form towards the end of the first century CE as Jews and Christians parted company.

Indeed, in shedding considerable, albeit indirect, light on early Christianity, study of the Qumran DSS has played a vital role in helping scholars come to such conclusions. We saw, for example, that it was Gentile Christians' detachment from the Law, rather than belief in Jesus' special role in and of itself, which precipitated the break between Judaism and Christianity towards the end of the first century CE.[63] Furthermore, the early Jewish Christian movement was originally one of several parties within late Second Temple Judaism. The Qumran documents have provided us with clear testimony on this point: they too reflect a religious community which, although at a different time and in a different way, married devotion to the central core of Common Judaism with an eschatological attachment to a religious leader rejected by others.

Most remarkably, the Qumran DSS have allowed the sort of direct access to the practices and beliefs of an Essene community previously thought unimaginable. As the only first-hand evidence from a religious party flourishing in late Second Temple times, we have learned much about the group's origins and character and have been able to catch a glimpse of its attitude towards outsiders. By combining the evidence of the manuscripts with other literature from the period, Second Temple

Judaism now seems infinitely more complex and varied than scholars envisaged even a few decades ago. Moreover, this richness impacts on the nature of the Old Testament itself, for the luxury afforded by the discovery of biblical, apocryphal, and pseudepigraphal manuscripts among the DSS has revealed a hitherto undreamed of fluidity in the text and content of the scriptures.

Scholars are still reeling in response to the vast array of ancient documents they now have at their disposal, especially after the release of fresh Cave 4 material in 1991. Although, as we learned earlier, the publication of outstanding texts now proceeds apace, it will take some time to analyse these new compositions in depth and relate them more precisely to those that have been in the public domain for much longer. In the decades to come, therefore, we can look forward to the emergence of an ever more subtle understanding of the Essene community at Qumran and its relationship with other Jews, as well as further insights into the nature of late Second Temple Judaism as a whole, what preceded in earlier centuries, and what followed in the Rabbinic period.

Meanwhile, if this book about the Qumran DSS succeeds in disseminating more widely just how radically the fruits of academic study of the Hebrew Scriptures, Second Temple Judaism, and early Christianity can shape an informed view of the past, it will achieve its aim.

Plate 6   *South-easterly view over the Khirbet Qumran ruins.*
© *Jonathan G. Campbell.*

Appendix
Important Qumran Dead Sea Scrolls

The following catalogues by genre important Qumran DSS of the second and third categories defined in Chapter 1; it does not include manuscripts of the first category (i.e. books from the Hebrew Bible, Apocrypha, or Pseudepigrapha). The titles employed are generally those of the 'Provisional List of Documents from the Judean Desert' in *EDSS*. Within each genre, works are arranged as far as possible according to the order adopted in Chapter 4's generic survey.

Rules

4QMSM	Midrash on the Book of Moses	4Q249
4QMMT^{a–f}	Some Precepts of the Law	4Q394–399
1QS, 4QS^{a–j}, 5QS	Community Rule	1QS, 4Q255–264, 5Q11
CD, 4QD^{a–h}, 5QD, 6QD	Damascus Document	CD, 4Q266–273, 5Q12, 6Q15
4QWords of the Sage	Words of the Sage to Sons of the Dawn	4Q298
4QRebukes	Register of Rebukes	4Q477
4QMiscellaneous Rules	Miscellaneous Rules	4Q265
1QM, 4QM^{a–g}	War Scroll	1QM, 4Q491–497
4QBook of War, 11QBook of War	Book of War	4Q285, 11Q14
1QSa, 4QSE^{a–i}	Rule of the Congregation	1Q28a, 4Q249a–i
1QSb	Rule of the Blessings	1Q28b
4QPolemical Fragment	Polemical Fragment	4Q471a

4QCommunal Ceremony	Communal Ceremony	4Q275
4QFour Lots	Four Lots	4Q279
4QHarvesting	Harvesting	4Q284a
4QPurities A–C	Purities A–C	4Q274, 276–277, 278
4QLegal Texts A–C	Legal Texts A–C	4Q251, 264a, 472a
4QT, 11QT[a–c]	Temple Scroll	4Q524, 11Q19–21

Hymns and Poems

1QH[a], 1QH[b], 4QH[a–f]	Hymns Scroll	1QH[a], 1Q35, 4Q427–432
4QHymnic Fragment	Hymnic Fragment	4Q255recto
11QApocryphal Psalms C	Apocryphal Psalms C	11Q11
4QApocryphal Lamentations A–B	Apocryphal Lamentations A–B	4Q179, 4Q501
4QShirShab, 11QShirShab	Songs of the Sabbath Sacrifice	4Q400–407, 11Q17
11QApocryphal Psalms A, 4QApocryphal Psalms B	Apocryphal Psalms A–B	11Q5, 4Q88
4QNon-canonical Psalms A–B	Non-canonical Psalms A–B	4Q380–381
4QApocryphal Psalm and Prayer	Apocryphal Psalm and Prayer	4Q448

Calendars, Liturgies, Prayers

4QLuminaries[a–c]	Words of the Luminaries	4Q504–506
4QDaily Prayers	Daily Prayers	4Q503
4QLiturgical Prayers	Liturgical Prayers	4Q34bis
4QFestival Prayers[a–c]	Festival Prayers	4Q507–509
4QCurses	Curses	4Q280
4QBlessings[a–e]	Blessings	4Q286–290
4QWorks of God	Works of God	4Q392
4QCommunal Confession	Communal Confession	4Q393
4QPersonal Prayer	Personal Prayer	4Q443
4QIncantation	Incantation	4Q444
4QPurification Liturgy	Purification Liturgy	4Q284
4QRitual Purifications A–B	Ritual Purifications A–B	4Q414, 512
4QRitual of Marriage	Ritual of Marriage	4Q502
4QPhases of the Moon	Phases of the Moon	4Q317
4QCalendrical Documents A–H	Calendrical Documents A–H	4Q320–330

4QCalendrical Signs	Calendrical Signs	4Q319
4QZodiology	Zodiology and Brontology	4Q318
4QHoroscope and Physiognomy	Horoscope and Physiognomy	4Q186, 561
4QOrder of Service	Order of Service	4Q334
4QLiturgical Work A	Liturgical Work A	4Q409
4QExorcism	Exorcism	4Q560

Wisdom Literature

1QMysteries, 4QMysteries[a-c]	Mysteries	1Q27, 4Q299–301
1QInstruction A, 4QInstruction A[a-e] 4QInstruction B	Instructions A–B	1Q26, 4Q415–418a, 419, 423
4QComposition concerning Divine Providence	Composition concerning Divine Providence	4Q413
4QWays of Righteousness[a-b]	Ways of Righteousness	4Q420–421
4QInstruction-like Work	Instruction-like Work	4Q424
4QSongs of the Sage[a-b]	Songs of the Sage	4Q510–511
4QBless, My Soul[a-e]	Bless, My Soul	4Q434–438
4QBeatitudes	Beatitudes	4Q525
4QAdmonitary Parable	Admonitory Parable	4Q302
4QWiles	Wiles of the Wicked Woman	4Q184
4QSapiential Work	Sapiential Work	4Q185

Scriptural Interpretation

1QpHabakkuk	Pesher on Habakkuk	1QpHabakkuk
4QpIsaiah[a-e]	Pesher on Isaiah	4Q161–165
4QpHosea[a-b]	Pesher on Hosea	4Q166–167
1QpMicah, 4QpMicah	Pesher on Micah	1Q14, 4Q168
1QpZephaniah, 4QpZephaniah	Pesher on Zephaniah	1Q15, 4Q170
1QpPsalms, 4QpPsalms[a-b]	Pesher on Psalms	1Q16, 4Q171, 173
4QpNahum	Pesher on Nahum	4Q169
4QpApocalypse of Weeks	Pesher on the Apocalypse of Weeks	4Q247
4QGenesis Commentaries A–D	Genesis Commentaries A–D	4Q252–254a
4QAges of Creation A–B	Ages of Creation A–B	4Q180–181

4QFlorilegium	Florilegium	4Q174
4QTestimonia	Testimonia	4Q175
4QCatenae A–B	Catenae A–B	4Q177, 182
11QMelchizedek	Melchizedek	11Q13
4QOrdinances[a–c]	Ordinances	4Q159, 513–514
4QRP[a–e]	Reworked Pentateuch	4Q158, 364–367
1QapGenesis	Genesis Apocryphon	1QapGenesis
4QBiblical Chronology	Biblical Chronology	4Q559
4QMessianic Apocalypse	Messianic Apocalypse	4Q521
4QConsolations	Consolations	4Q176
4QParaphrase	Paraphrase of Genesis-Exodus	4Q422

New Pseudepigrapha

4QtgJob, 11QtgJob	Targum of Job	4Q157, 11Q10
4QtgLeviticus	Targum of Leviticus	4Q156
4Qpseudo-Jubilees[a–c]	Pseudo-Jubilees	4Q225–227
4QText with Citation of Jubilees	Text with Citation of Jubilees	4Q228
4QPrayer of Enosh	Prayer of Enosh	4Q369
1QBook of Giants, 2QBook of Giants, 4QBook of Giants[a–e], 6QBook of Giants	Book of Giants	1Q23, 2Q26, 4Q203, 530–533, 6Q8
4QAdmonition based on the Flood	Admonition based on the Flood	4Q370
1QBook of Noah, 4QBook of Noah, 6QBook of Noah	Book of Noah	1Q19, 4Q534, 6Q19
4QWords of Michael	Words of Michael	4Q529
1QAramaic Levi, 4QAramaic Levi[a–e]	Aramaic Levi	1Q21, 4Q213, 213a–b, 214, 214b
4QTestament of Naphtali	Testament of Naphtali	4Q215
4QApocryphon of Joseph[a–c]	Apocryphon of Joseph	4Q371–373
4QTestament of Qahat	Testament of Qahat	4Q542
4QVisions of Amram[a–f]	Visions of Amram	4Q543–548
4QText mentioning Hur and Miriam	Text mentioning Hur and Miriam	4Q549
1QWords of Moses	Words of Moses	1Q22

4QDiscourse on the Exodus and Conquest	Discourse on the Exodus and Conquest	4Q374
1QApocryphon of Moses, 4QApocryphon of Moses[a-c]	Apocryphon of Moses	1Q29, 4Q375–376, 408
4QApocryphal Pentatuech A–B	Apocryphal Pentatuech A–B	4Q368, 377
4QProphecy of Joshua	Prophecy of Joshua	4Q522
4QApocryphon of Joshua[a-b]	Apocryphon of Joshua	4Q378–379
4QVision of Samuel	Vision of Samuel	4Q160
4QParaphrase of Kings	Paraphrase of Kings	4Q382
4QElisha Apocryphon	Elisha Apocryphon	4Q381a
4QFragment mentioning Zedekiah	Fragment mentioning Zedekiah	4Q470
4QNarrative C	Narrative C	4Q462
4QApocryphon of Jeremiah A–E	Apocryphon of Jeremiah A–E	4Q383–384, 385b, 387b, 389a
1QNJ, 2QNJ, 4QNJ[a-b], 5QNJ, 11QNJ	New Jerusalem	1Q32, 2Q24, 4Q554–555, 5Q15, 11Q18
4Qpseudo-Ezekiel[a-e]	Pseudo-Ezekiel	4Q385–388, 391
4QHistorical Text A	Historical Text A	4Q248
4QPrayer of Nabonidus	Prayer of Nabonidus	4Q242
4Qpseudo-Daniel[a-c]	Pseudo-Daniel	4Q243–245
4QApocryphon of Daniel	Apocryphon of Daniel	4Q246
4QFour Kingdoms[a-b]	Four Kingdoms	4Q552–553
4Qproto-Esther	Proto-Esther	4Q550

Miscellaneous Compositions

4Q343, 345, 348, 350, 355, 6Q26	Various Economic Documents	4Q343, 345, 348, 350, 355, 6Q26
4QTwo Ways	Two Ways	4Q473
4QList of Netinim	List of Netinim	4Q340
4QList of False Prophets	List of False Prophets	4Q339
Ostracon	Ostracon	Ostracon

Further Reading

1. Introductions to the Qumran DSS and the Essenes

F. García Martínez, J. L. Barrera, *The People of the Dead Sea Scrolls*, Leiden (1995).

H. Shanks, *The Mystery and Meaning of the Dead Sea Scrolls*, London (1998).

H. Stegemann, *The Library of Qumran*, Grand Rapids/Leiden (1998).

J. C. VanderKam, *The Dead Sea Scrolls Today*, London (1994).

G. Vermes, *An Introduction to The Complete Dead Sea Scrolls*, London (1999).

2. English Translations of the Qumran DSS

J. H. Charlesworth (ed.), *The Dead Sea Scrolls: Hebrew, Aramaic, and Greek Texts with English Translations*, Volumes 1–4B, Tübingen/Louisville (1994–1999).

F. García Martínez, *The Dead Sea Scrolls Translated: The Qumran Texts in English*, Leiden (1996).

F. García Martínez, E. J. C. Tigchelaar, *The Dead Sea Scrolls Study Edition*, Volumes I–II, Leiden (1997–1998).

M. Knibb, *The Qumran Community*, Cambridge (1987).

G. Vermes, *The Complete Dead Sea Scrolls in English*, London (1997).

M. Wise, M. Abegg, E. Cook, *The Dead Sea Scrolls: A New Translation*, New York (1996).

3. English Translations of Related Works

Holy Bible: New Revised Standard Version, New York (1989).

J. H. Charlesworth (ed.), *The Old Testament Pseudepigrapha*, Volumes I–II, London (1983–1985).

F. H. Colson, M. Whitaker, *Philo*, I–X, Cambridge Mass. (1929–1943).

H. Danby, *The Mishnah*, Oxford (1933).

I. Epstein (ed.), *The Babylonian Talmud*, I–XXXV, London (1935–1952).

H. F. D. Sparks, *The Apocryphal Old Testament*, Oxford (1984).

H. StJ. Thackery, R. Marcus, L. Feldman, *Josephus*, I–X, Cambridge Mass. (1926–1955).

G. Vermes, M. Goodman, *The Essenes according to the Classical Sources*, Sheffield (1989).

4. The Qumran DSS in Hebrew, Aramaic, and Greek

Discoveries in the Judaean Desert, I–XXXVIII, Oxford (1955–2001).

J. H. Charlesworth (ed.), *The Dead Sea Scrolls: Hebrew, Aramaic, and Greek Texts with English Translations*, Volumes 1–4B, Tübingen/Louisville (1994–1999).

F. García Martínez, E. J. C. Tigchelaar, *The Dead Sea Scrolls Study Edition*, Volumes I–II, Leiden (1997–1998).

5. Dictionaries, Encyclopedias, Atlases

F. L. Cross, E. A. Livingstone (eds.), *Oxford Dictionary of the Christian Church*, Oxford (1997).

D. N. Freedman (ed.), *Anchor Bible Dictionary*, Volumes I–VI, New York (1992).

D. N. Freedman (ed.), *Eerdmans Dictionary of the Bible*, Grand Rapids (2001).

B. M. Metzger, M. D. Coogan (eds.), *The Oxford Companion to the Bible*, Oxford (1993).

G. Parker (ed.), *The Times Atlas of World History*, London (1993).

J. B. Pritchard (ed.), *The Times Atlas of the Bible*, London (1987).

L. H. Schiffman, J. C. VanderKam (eds.), *Encyclopedia of the Dead Sea Scrolls*, Volumes I–II, New York (2000).

R. J. Zwi Werblowsky, G. Wigoder (eds.), *Oxford Dictionary of the Jewish Religion*, Oxford (1997).

6. Detailed Studies

J. M. G. Barclay, *Jews in the Mediterranean Diaspora*, Edinburgh (1996).

M. Bernstein and others (eds.), *Legal Texts and Legal Issues*, Leiden (1997).

O. Betz, R. Riesner, *Jesus, Qumran and the Vatican*, London (1994).

G. Boccaccini, *Beyond the Essene Hypothesis: The Parting of the Ways between Qumran and Enochic Judaism*, Grand Rapids/Cambridge (1998).

G. J. Brooke (ed.), *Temple Scroll Studies*, Sheffield (1989).

G. J. Brooke (ed.), *New Qumran Texts and Studies*, Leiden (1994).

J. G. Campbell, *The Use of Scripture in the Damascus Document 1–8, 19–20*, Berlin (1995).

R. P. Carroll, *Wolf in the Sheepfold: the Bible as Problematic for Theology*, London (1997).

M. Casey, *From Jewish Prophet to Gentile God: the Origins and Development of New Testament Christology*, Cambridge (1991).

J. H. Charlesworth (ed.), *Jesus and the Dead Sea Scrolls*, New York (1990).

R. J. Coggins, *Introducing the Old Testament*, Oxford (2001).

P. R. Davies, *Behind the Essenes: History and Ideology in the Dead Sea Scrolls*, Atlanta (1987).

P. R. Davies, *Sects and Scrolls: Essays on Qumran and Related Topics*, Atlanta (1996).

J. D. G. Dunn, *The Theology of Paul the Apostle*, Grand Rapids/Cambridge (1998).

B. D. Ehrman, *The New Testament: A Historical Introduction to the Early Christian Writings*, Oxford (2000).

P. W. Flint, J. C. VanderKam (eds.), *The Dead Sea Scrolls After Fifty Years: A Comprehensive Assessment*, Volumes I–II, Leiden (1998–1999).

N. Golb, *Who Wrote the Dead Sea Scrolls?*, London (1995).

M. Goodman, *The Roman World: 44 BC–AD 180*, London (1997).

L. L. Grabbe, *Judaism from Cyrus to Hadrian*, Edinburgh (1992).

L. L. Grabbe, *Judaic Religion in the Second Temple Period*, London (2000).

A. Hastings (ed.), *A World History of Christianity*, London (1999).

W. Horbury, *Jewish Messianism and the Cult of Christ*, London (1998).

W. Horbury (ed.), *Hebrew Study from Ezra to Ben-Yehudah*, Edinburgh (1999).

W. Horbury and others (eds.), *The Cambridge History of Judaism*, Volume III, Cambridge (1999).

T. H. Lim and others (eds.), *The Dead Sea Scrolls in their Historical Context*, Edinburgh (2000).

J. Murphy-O'Connor, *Paul and Qumran*, New York (1990).

J. Neusner, *Torah Through the Ages*, London (1990).

J. Neusner, *Judaism in Modern Times: an Introduction and Reader*, Oxford (1995).

M. A. Powell, *The Jesus Debate*, London (1998).

E. Qimron, *The Hebrew of the Dead Sea Scrolls*, Atlanta (1986).

T. Rajak, *Josephus: The Historian and His Society*, London (1983).

J. Sacks, *One People? Tradition, Modernity and Jewish Unity*, London (1993).

E.P Sanders, *Judaism: Practice and Belief 63 BCE – 66 CE*, London (1992).

D. F. Sawyer, *Women and Religion in the First Christian Centuries*, London (1996).

L. H. Schiffman, *Sectarian Law and the Dead Sea Scrolls*, Chico (1983).

L. H. Schiffman, *Reclaiming the Dead Sea Scrolls: Their True Meaning for Judaism and Christianity*, New York (1994).

E. Schürer, G. Vermes and others, *The History of the Jewish People in the Age of Jesus Christ*, Volumes I–III.2, Edinburgh (1973–1987).

H. Shanks (ed.), *Ancient Israel: a Short History from Abraham to the Roman Destruction of the Temple*, London (1989).

H. Shanks (ed.), *Christianity and Rabbinic Judaism*, London (1993).

J. A. Soggin, *An Introduction to the Old Testament*, London (1989).

J. A. Soggin, *An Introduction to the History of Israel and Judah*, London (1999).

G. Stemberger, *Introduction to the Talmud and Midrash*, Edinburgh (1996).

E. Tov, *Textual Criticism of the Hebrew Bible*, Minneapolis/Assen (1992).

E. Ulrich, *The Dead Sea Scrolls and the Origins of the Bible*, Grand Rapids/ Cambridge (1999).

R. de Vaux, *Archaeology and the Dead Sea Scrolls*, Oxford (1973).

G. Vermes, *The Religion of Jesus the Jew*, London (1993).

M. Whittaker, *Jews and Christians: Graeco-Roman Views*, Cambridge (1984).

Notes

Chapter 1

1 See Map 2. 'Khirbet' is Arabic for 'ruin of'.
2 For convenience, we shall employ 'Palestine' as equivalent to the vague 'Holy Land'. Historically, the name comes from the Latin word Palaestina and, before that, from Philistia, the territory of the Philistines. In the Roman period, Palaestina was used with qualifying terms to designate differing overlapping regions at different times.
3 A summary can be found under the entry by W. W. Fields, 'Discovery and Purchase' in L. H. Schiffman, J. C. VanderKam (eds.), *Encyclopedia of the Dead Sea Scrolls*, Volumes I–II, New York (2000). Hereafter, this encyclopedia is abbreviated to *EDSS*.
4 J. C. Trever, *The Untold Story of Qumran*, New Jersey (1965), gives more information, as does his *The Dead Sea Scrolls: A Personal Account*, Grand Rapids (1977). See also M. Burrows, *The Dead Sea Scrolls*, New York (1955).
5 In the Syrian Orthodox Church, a Metropolitan is a kind of archbishop.
6 M. Burrows and others, *The Dead Sea Scrolls of St. Mark's Monastery*, I–II, New Haven (1950–1951).
7 With perseverance, the work was unrolled and published in N. Avigad, Y. Yadin, *A Genesis Apocryphon*, Jerusalem (1956).
8 The codex – the form of the modern book – became popular with Christians from the second century CE and more widely from the fourth century CE. Jews to this day retain the scroll form for the liturgical use of sacred texts in the synagogue.
9 BCE (Before the Common Era) and CE (Common Era) are used in preference to BC and AD but refer to the same periods of time.
10 E. L. Sukenik, *The Dead Sea Scrolls of the Hebrew University*, Jerusalem (1954–5).

11   The Shrine includes the Metropolitan's scrolls, for, after taking them to
     America in 1949 for safekeeping and then offering them for sale in the
     Wall Street Journal, in 1954 he unwittingly sold them back to Israel
     through a middleman for $250,000.

12   The news was further broadcast by W. F. Albright in the *Bulletin of the
     American Schools of Oriental Research* 100 (April, 1948), p. 3.

13   D. Barthélemy, J. T. Milik, *Qumran Cave 1*, Oxford (DJD I: 1955). In
     some early volumes, the series is entitled 'Discoveries in the Judaean
     Desert of Jordan' (DJDJ).

14   See Map 3.

15   De Vaux never completed a final archaeological report, and neither have
     those recently charged with the task by the Ecole Biblique, P. Donceel-
     Voûte and R. Donceel. The best record remains, therefore, R. de Vaux,
     Archaeology and the Dead Sea Scrolls, Oxford (1973). For an overview, see J.
     Patrich, 'Archaeology' in *EDSS*.

16   See J. A. Sanders, *The Psalms Scroll of Qumran Cave 11*, Oxford (DJDJ IV:
     1965), as well as J. P. M. van der Ploeg and others, *Le Targum de Job de la
     grotte XI de Qumrân*, Leiden (1971), and D. N. Freedman, K. A. Matthews,
     The Paleo-Hebrew Leviticus Scroll (11QpaleoLev), Winona Lake (1985).

17   His impressive study was published in Hebrew in 1977 and then in English
     as *The Temple Scroll*, I–III, Jerusalem (1983). See now also E. Qimron, *The
     Temple Scroll: A Critical Edition with Extensive Reconstructions*, Beer Sheva/
     Jerusalem (1996).

18   According to the fourth-century CE church historian Eusebius, a Greek
     scriptural translation was found near Jericho in the early third century CE
     (*Ecclesiastical History*, VI xvi I). Around 800 CE, the Nestorian Patriarch
     Timotheus I also reported manuscript finds near Jericho. See again W. W.
     Fields, 'Discovery and Purchase' in *EDSS*.

19   The First Revolt against Rome (66–70 CE) and the Second Revolt against
     Rome (132–135 CE), as well as the much earlier Maccabean Revolt (mid-
     160s BCE), should be carefully distinguished. All three will reappear in
     Chapter 3.

20   In this usage, 'apocryphon' denotes any scripture-like book which failed to
     enter Jewish or Christian Bibles after 70 CE. The plural designation
     'Apocrypha' is explained below.

21   Generally, we shall use titles suggested by the up-to-date 'Provisional List
     of Documents from the Judean Desert' in *EDSS*. But these sometimes
     differ from the names employed in other recent studies, including G.
     Vermes, *The Complete Dead Sea Scrolls in English*, London (1997). The
     latter volume is hereafter abbreviated to *CDSSE*.

22   The sheer number of damaged writings, in fact, may suggest Cave 4 was a
     genizah, a place for discarding worn-out sacred texts.

23   No works from the New Testament were found, despite contrary claims.
     This absence will be picked up again in Chapter 6.

24   For more details, see J. M. Baumgarten, 'Damascus Document' in *EDSS*.

25   He wrote in the *Jewish Quarterly Review* (of which he was then editor),

beginning with 'Scholarship and the Hoax of Recent Discoveries', *Jewish Quarterly Review* 39 (1949), pp. 337–63.

26   A useful overview of Second Temple Judaism is J. C. VanderKam, *An Introduction to Early Judaism*, Grand Rapids (2001).

27   The first six chapters of H. Shanks (ed.), *Ancient Israel: A Short History from Abraham to the Roman Destruction of the Temple*, London (1989), offer an academic outline of biblical history. For more detail, see J. A. Soggin, *An Introduction to the History of Israel and Judah*, London (1999).

28   For more on the surrounding cultures of Egypt, Mesopotamia, Greece, and Rome, see L. de Blois, R. J. van der Spek, *An Introduction to the Ancient World*, London/New York (1997).

29   The First Temple, as historians call it, was probably completed in 927 BCE but was subsequently destroyed by the Babylonians in 587 BCE.

30   This incident is recounted by Philo in *On the Embassy to Gaius*, 31–42. All Philo's works are translated in F. H. Colson, M. Whitaker, *Philo*, I–X, Cambridge Mass. (1929–1943).

31   For these later centuries, see also H. Shanks (ed.), *Ancient Israel: A Short History from Abraham to the Roman Destruction of the Temple*, London (1989), chapter 7–8.

32   See further J. J. Scullion, 'God (OT)' in D. N. Freedman (ed.), *Anchor Bible Dictionary*, Volumes I–VI, New York (1992). Hereafter, this dictionary is abbreviated to *ABD*.

33   See C. Martone, 'Publication' in *EDSS*.

34   M. Baillet and others, *Les Petites Grottes de Qumrân*, Oxford (DJDJ III: 1962).

35   G. Vermes, *The Dead Sea Scrolls: Qumran in Perspective*, London (1977), p. 23f.

36   See J. M. Allegro, A. A. Anderson, *Qumran Cave 4, I (4Q158–4Q186)*, Oxford (DJDJ V: 1968) and the critical 114-page review by J. Strugnell, 'Notes en marge du Volume V des *Discoveries in the Judaean Desert of Jordan*', *Revue de Qumrân* 7 (1969–71), pp. 163–276. The next volume was R. de Vaux, J. T. Milik, *Qumrân Grotte 4, II: I Archéologie; II Tefillin, Mezuzot et Targum (4Q128–4Q157)*, Oxford (DJD VI: 1977).

37   A third volume, however, did appear while he was editor-in-chief: M. Baillet, *Qumrân Grotte 4, III (4Q482–4Q520)*, Oxford (DJD VII: 1982).

38   This incident is recounted in G. Vermes, *An Introduction to the Complete Dead Sea Scrolls*, London (1999), p. 7; the present author, one of his postgraduate students at the time, attended the conference. To be fair, a collection of non-Qumranic material was prepared while Strugnell was editor-in-chief: E. Tov, *The Greek Minor Prophets Scroll from Nahal Hever (8HevXIIgr)*, Oxford (DJD VIII: 1990).

39   The story appeared in *Ha-aretz* on 9 November 1990. An English version can be read in H. Shanks (ed.), *Understanding the Dead Sea Scrolls*, London (1993), pp. 260–63.

40   B. Z. Wacholder, M. Abegg, *A Preliminary Edition of the Unpublished Dead*

Sea Scrolls: the Hebrew and Aramaic Texts from Cave 4, fascicle 1, Washington (1991).

41 R. H. Eisenman, J. M. Robinson, *A Facsimile Edition of the Dead Sea Scrolls*, I–II, Washington (1991).

42 For the former, see E. Tov (ed.), *The Dead Sea Scrolls on Microfiche*, Leiden (1992) and *A Companion Volume to the Dead Sea Scrolls Microfiche Edition*, Leiden (1995), as well as G. J. Brooke (ed.), *The Allegro Qumran Collection*, Leiden (1996). For the latter, see T. Lim and others, *The Dead Sea Scrolls Reference Library*, I–II, Oxford/Leiden (1997, 1999).

43 The DJD(J) series now includes: P. W. Skehan and others, *Qumran Cave 4, IV: Paleo-Hebrew and Greek Biblical Manuscripts*, Oxford (DJD IX: 1992); E. Qimron, J. Strugnell, *Qumran Cave 4, V: Miqsat, Ma'ase ha-Torah*, Oxford (DJD X: 1994); C. Newsom, E. Schuller (eds.), *Qumran Cave 4, VI: Poetical and Liturgical Texts – Part 1*, Oxford (DJD XI: 1998); E. Ulrich, F. M. Cross, *Qumran Cave 4, VII: Genesis to Numbers*, Oxford (DJD XII: 1994); H. Attridge and others, *Qumran Cave 4, VIII: Parabiblical Texts – Part 1*, Oxford (DJD XIII: 1994); E. Ulrich, F. M. Cross (eds.), *Qumran Cave 4, IX: Deuteronomy, Joshua, Judges, Kings*, Oxford (DJD XIV: 1995); E. Ulrich (ed.), *Qumran Cave 4, X: The Prophets*, Oxford (DJD XV: 1997); E. Ulrich and others, *Qumran Cave 4, XI: Psalms to Chronicles*, Oxford (DJD XVI: 2000); J. M. Baumgarten, *Qumran Cave 4, XIII: The Damascus Document (4Q266–273)*, Oxford (DJD XVIII: 1996); M. Broshi and others, *Qumran Cave 4, XIV: Parabiblical Texts – Part 2*, Oxford (DJD XIX: 1995); and U. Glessmer, *Qumran Cave 4, XII* (DJD XXI: 2001); J. Fitzmyer (ed), *Qumran Cave 4, XV: Sapiential Texts – Part 1*, Oxford (DJD XX: 1997); J. VanderKam (ed.), *Qumran Cave 4, XVII: Parabiblical Texts – Part 3*, Oxford (DJD XXII: 1996); F. García Martínez and others (eds.), *Qumran Cave 11, II: 11Q2–18, 11Q20–31*, Oxford (DJD XXIII: 1998); E. Puech (ed.), *Qumran Cave 4, XVIII: Textes hébreux (4Q521–528, 4Q576–579)*, Oxford (DJD XXV: 1998); P. S. Alexander and G. Vermes, *Qumran Cave 4, XIX: Serekh ha-Yahad and Two Related Texts*, Oxford (DJD XXVI: 1998); E. Chazon and others, *Qumran Cave 4, XX: Poetical and Liturgical Texts – Part 2*, Oxford (DJD XXIX: 1999); D. Dimant, *Parabiblical Texts – Part 4*, Oxford (DJD XXX: 2001); E. Puech, *Qumran Cave 4, XXII* (DJD XXXI: 2001); T. Elgvin and others, *Qumran Cave 4, XXIV: Sapiential Texts – Part 2*, Oxford (DJD XXXIV: 1999); J. Baumgarten and others, *Qumran Cave 4, XXV: Halakhic Texts*, Oxford (DJD XXXV: 1999); S. J. Pfann and others, *Qumran Cave 4, XXVI: Cryptic Texts and Miscellanea – Part 1*, Oxford (DJD XXXVI: 2000); J. H. Charlesworth and others, *Miscellaneous Texts from the Judaean Desert*, Oxford (DJD XXXVIII: 2000).

44 See further S. J. Pfann, 'Archaeological Surveys' in *EDSS*.

45 See Map 2. 'Wadi' is an Arabic term for a river bed which fills with water only when it rains; 'Nahal' is the equivalent Hebrew word.

46 See D. M. Gropp, N. L. Lapp, 'Daliyeh, Wadi ed-' in *EDSS*. See also M. Leith, *Wadi Daliyeh Seal Impressions I*, Oxford (DJD XXIV: 1997).

47   See again M. Leith, *Wadi Daliyeh Seal Impressions I*, Oxford (DJD XXIV: 1997).

48   On Masada, see the overview by H. Eshel and others, 'Masada' in *EDSS*. Note also Y. Yadin and others, *Masada: Final Reports*, Jerusalem (1989–1999).

49   The former included parts of Leviticus, Deuteronomy, Ezekiel, Psalms, Ben Sira, and Jubilees; the latter incorporates various letters, military documents, name lists, and similar material.

50   A number of manuscripts believed at first to have come from Wadi Seiyal (also known as Nahal Se'elim) were, it now transpires, retrieved from Nahal Hever to the north of it. For more information, see H. M. Cotton, H. Eshel, 'Se'elim, Nahal' in *EDSS*.

51   These included Genesis, Exodus, Numbers, Deuteronomy, Isaiah, the Twelve Minor Prophets, and Psalms. See further J. T. Milik, R. de Vaux, *Les grottes de Murabba'at*, Oxford (DJD II: 1961), and E. Tov (ed.), *The Greek Minor Prophets Scroll from Nahal Hever (8HevXIIgr)*, Oxford (DJD VIII: 1990). More generally, see H. M. Cotton, H. Eshel, 'Hever, Nahal' and H. Eshel, E. Stern, 'Murabba'at' in *EDSS*.

52   The supporters of bar Kosba (or, perhaps, bar Kosiba) appear to have made a pun on his surname by restyling it 'bar Kokhba' (Aramaic for 'son of the star'), a kind of messianic title based on Numbers 24:17. After the defeat of the Second Revolt, however, others preferred an alternative pun, 'bar Koziba' ('son of the lie')! See further B. Isaac and others, 'Bar Kokhba' in *ABD*.

53   See again J. T. Milik, R. de Vaux, *Les grottes de Murabba'at*, Oxford (DJD II: 1961), and E. Tov (ed.), *The Greek Minor Prophets Scroll from Nahal Hever (8HevXIIgr)*, Oxford (DJD VIII: 1990). Note also H. Cotton, A. Yardeni, *Aramaic and Greek Texts from Nahal Hever*, Oxford (DJD XXVII: 1997).

54   See below, p. 97, however, for an important inscribed pottery fragment recovered from Khirbet Qumran in 1996. See also the Appendix for a list of important Qumran DSS.

Chapter 2

1   See further C. D. Osburn, 'The Johannine Comma' in *ABD*.

2   A prime example was James Moffat's *The New Testament: A New Translation* in 1913. His Old Testament appeared in 1924, and a revision of Moffat's complete Bible came out in 1935.

3   For examples, see R. G. Bratcher 'Translations: English Language' in B. M. Metzger, M. D. Coogan (eds.), *Oxford Companion to the Bible*, Oxford (1993). This volume is hereafter dubbed *OCB*.

4   See the Preface to the *New International Version*, London (1986), p. v.

5   See further A. G. Hunter, *Psalms*, London (1999), pp. 15–32.

6   See the *Holy Bible: New Revised Standard Version with Apocrypha*, New York

(1989), p. xiv. The translation's production is recounted in B. M. Metzger and others, *The Making of the New Revised Standard Version of the Bible*, Grand Rapids (1991).

7   The story of the REB is told in R. Coleman, *New Light and New Truth: the Making of the Revised English Bible*, Oxford/Cambridge (1989).

8   The acronym Tanakh – T(orah)aN(evi'im)aK(etuvim)h – is a traditional way of referring to the threefold Jewish Bible, comprising the Law (Torah), Prophets (Nevi'im), and Writings (Ketuvim).

9   Chapter and verse numbers, it should be noted, were first added to the Latin Bible in the early thirteenth century CE.

10   Academic study of the New Testament will feature more fully in Chapter 5.

11   See further R. J. Coggins, *Introducing the Old Testament*, Oxford (2001).

12   Relevant chapters in H. Shanks (ed.), *Ancient Israel: A Short History from Abraham to the Roman Destruction of the Temple*, London (1989), provide an introduction to some of these matters. More in-depth treatment can be found in J. A. Soggin, *An Introduction to the History of Israel and Judah*, London (1999).

13   For discussion of individual books, see J. A. Soggin, *Introduction to the Old Testament*, London (1989).

14   Daniel is the youngest of all, compiled during the 160s BCE, as details in Daniel 11 show, several centuries after Daniel was supposed to have lived.

15   For further examples, see J. A. Soggin, *Introduction to the Old Testament*, London (1989), pp. 92–5.

16   See again J. A. Soggin, *Introduction to the Old Testament*, London (1989), pp. 365–378.

17   This was tentatively suggested, e.g., in F. Davidson and others, *New Bible Commentary*, London (1954), p. 560.

18   An unconvincing reassertion of traditional dates is E. J. Young, *Introduction to the Old Testament*, London (1960).

19   In addition, various secondary versions, prepared on the basis of the Masoretic Text or Septuagint, have long been in circulation. Latin translations, e.g., were made by Christians in the first few centuries CE, the most famous being the Vulgate of Jerome (342–420 CE). As for the Jews, during the same period, they produced an Aramaic paraphrase of nearly every biblical book in the form of the Targums or Targumim (singular: Targum). For more information, see J. N. Birdsall and others, 'Versions, Ancient' in *ABD*.

20   K. Elliger, W. Rudolph, *Biblia Hebraica Stuttgartensia*, Stuttgart (1997) is a special edition of the Leningrad Codex, including in footnotes variant readings compiled by modern scholars from the LXX, Samaritan Pentateuch, and elsewhere.

21   The Letter of Aristeas can be found in J. H. Charlesworth, *Old Testament Pseudepigrapha*, II, New York (1985), pp. 7–34.

22   In light of this account, some reserve 'Septuagint' for the Greek rendering of the Pentateuch only, while others adopt 'Old Greek' for the original

Jewish translation, as opposed to later Christian copies. In what follows, 'Septuagint' is used as a general designation for the whole Greek Bible.

23 An accessible edition of the LXX is A. Rahlfs, *Septuaginta*, Stuttgart (1979). Note that a Greek Deuteronomy fragment in Manchester University's Rylands Library may be second century BCE in origin.

24 The text can be consulted in A. F. von Gall, *Der Hebräische Pentateuch der Samaritaner*, I–IV, Giessen (1914–8); reprinted Berlin (1966).

25 For more information on the MT, LXX, and Samaritan Pentateuch, see relevant entries in *ABD*.

26 The clearest example of bias can be seen in the Ten Commandments of Exodus 20 and Deuteronomy 5. The Samaritan Pentateuch has made the building of an altar on Mount Gerizim one of the commandments, asserting this site – not Jerusalem – as God's true holy place.

27 Five identifiable Greek biblical manuscripts are as follows:

Exodus:	7QLXXExodus	
Leviticus:	4QLXXLeviticus[a];	4QLXXLeviticus[b]
Numbers:	4QLXXNumbers	
Deuteronomy:	4QLXXDeuteronomy	

See further E. Ulrich, *The Dead Sea Scrolls and the Origins of the Bible*, Grand Rapids/Leiden (1999), pp. 165–183.

28 The arrangement is according to the traditional order of the Jewish Bible. Further details can be found under entries for each book in *EDSS*.

29 See below, p. 106.

30 For detailed discussion, see E. Tov, *Textual Criticism of the Hebrew Bible*, Minneapolis (1992), and E. Ulrich, *The Dead Sea Scrolls and the Origins of the Bible*, Grand Rapids/Leiden (1999).

31 See *Jewish Antiquities*, 6.68–71, and F. Polak, 'Samuel, First and Second Books of' in *EDSS*.

32 Ulrich provides further examples from Exodus, 1–2 Samuel, and Daniel in *The Dead Sea Scrolls and the Origins of the Bible*, Grand Rapids/Leiden (1999), pp. 51–78.

33 For further discussion, see E. C. Ulrich, 'The Qumran Biblical Scrolls – the Scriptures of Late Second Temple Judaism' in T. H. Lim and others (eds.), *The Dead Sea Scrolls in their Historical Context*, Edinburgh (2000), pp. 67–87. This volume is hereafter abbreviated to *DSSHC*.

34 The Nahal Hever and Murabba'at caves together contained the following biblical texts:

Genesis	2	Isaiah	1
Exodus	1	Twelve Minor Prophets	2
Numbers	3		
Deuteronomy	2		

35 Some have argued that the MT, LXX, and Samaritan originated in Babylon, Egypt, and Palestine, respectively, while others have highlighted the partisan nature of the religious groups – Jews, Christians, and Samari-

tans – responsible for preserving each. For a critique of such theories in light of recent research, see E. Ulrich, *The Dead Sea Scrolls and the Origins of the Bible*, Grand Rapids/Leiden (1999), pp. 79–98.

36 The Hebrew of Ben Sira was composed in the early second century BCE, whereas the author's grandson translated it into Greek in the 130s BCE. The latter forms part of the LXX and is here deemed 'Ecclesiasticus', whilst what remains of the Hebrew from Qumran and elsewhere can be called 'Ben Sira'. See further A. A. Di Lella, 'Wisdom of Ben-Sira' in *ABD* or, for a detailed investigation into the work's original context, J. K. Aitken, 'Biblical Interpretation as Political Manifesto: Ben Sira in his Seleucid Setting', *Journal of Jewish Studies* 51 (2000), pp. 191–208.

37 An English translation of the collection is accessible in NRSV editions with the Apocrypha/Deuterocanonicals. See also J. J. Collins, 'Apocrypha and Pseudepigrapha' in *EDSS*.

38 'Deuterocanonical' implies that the books form a secondary layer of authoritative Scripture from the church authorities' viewpoint; in this context, 'Apocrypha' can then be employed to denote works outside the Bible which are called 'Pseudepigrapha' in the discussion below.

39 To be clear, apart from the divergent order of the same Old Testament books, the only difference between modern Jewish and Protestant Bibles is the presence or absence of the New Testament.

40 The remains of a Hebrew copy of Ben Sira, it should be noted, were also found at Masada.

41 See again J. J. Collins, 'Apocrypha and Pseudepigrapha' in *EDSS*.

42 As noted earlier, experts from the nineteenth century onwards came to realize that many books in the Old Testament, Apocrypha, and New Testament were similarly pseudepigraphical.

43 Most of the Pseudepigrapha are translated in H. D. F. Sparks, *Apocryphal Old Testament*, Oxford (1984); 'apocryphal' in the title here is employed in the sense described in note 38 above. A more wide-ranging translation is J. H. Charlesworth, *Old Testament Pseudepigrapha*, I–II, New York (1983/ 1985).

44 An English rendering of the remains of both can be found in F. García Martínez, *The Dead Sea Scrolls Translated*, Leiden (1994), pp. 238–59.

45 See above, pp. 11–12.

46 Note that *CDSSE*, as well as F. García Martínez, *The Dead Sea Scrolls Translated*, Leiden (1994) and M. Wise, M. Abegg, E. Cook, *The Dead Sea Scrolls: A New Translation*, London (1996), incorporates translations of numerous Qumran DSS from this second category.

47 See M. Broshi, 'Acts of A Greek King' in *EDSS* and below, p. 96.

48 For a recent defence of this position, see B. A. Jones, 'Canon of the Old Testament' in D. N. Freedman (ed.), *Eerdmans Dictionary of the Bible*, Grand Rapids (2000). Hereafter, this dictionary is abbreviated to *EDB*.

49 See further E. Ulrich, 'Canon' in *EDSS*.

50 Such a designation appears, e.g., in 2 Maccabees 15:9 ('from the law and the prophets') and Romans 3:21 ('attested by the law and the prophets').

51   For more detail, consult J. G. Campbell, '4QMMT[d] and the Scriptural Canon' in *Journal of Jewish Studies* 51 (2000), pp. 181–190.

52   The Qumran caves yielded thirty-seven copies of the Psalms, while the surviving portions of 4QpPsalms[a–b] comment on Psalms 37, 45, and 127 in much the same way that 1QpHabakkuk treats Habakkuk 1–2.

53   The same broad point is made by E. C. Ulrich, 'The Qumran Biblical Scrolls – the Scriptures of Late Second Temple Judaism' in *DSSHC*, p. 72.

54   In addition, CD 4:13 seems to refer to an earlier form of part of the Testaments of the Twelve Patriarchs.

Chapter 3

1   See further G. C. Doudna, 'Carbon-14 Dating' in *EDSS*. For an in-depth study, consult his 'Dating the Scrolls on the Basis of Radiocarbon Analysis' in P. W. Flint, J. C. VanderKam (eds.), *The Dead Sea Scrolls After Fifty Years: A Comprehensive Assessment*, I, Leiden (1998), pp. 430–471. This volume and its companion are hereafter abbreviated to *DSSFY*, I–II.

2   For the original report, see O. R. Sellars, 'Radiocarbon Dating of the Cloth from the "Ain Feshkha Cave"', *Bulletin of the American Schools of Oriental Research* 123 (1951), pp. 24–26.

3   See G. Bonani and others, 'Radiocarbon Dating of Fourteen Dead Sea Scrolls', *Radiocarbon* 34 (1992), pp. 843–49.

4   On the important distinction between the date of original composition and subsequent copying, see above, p. 28.

5   See A. J. T. Jull and others, 'Radiocarbon Dating of Scrolls and Linen Fragments from the Judean Desert', *Radiocarbon* 37 (1995), p. 14. Most recently, Doudna, in 'Dating the Scrolls on the Basis of Radiocarbon Analysis' in *DSSFY*, I, pp. 430–471, has argued that first-century CE AMS datings are generally best discounted as 'measurement scatter' from the first-century BCE.

6   This finding will re-emerge in Chapter 7 as fatal to attempts to link 1QpHabakkuk with Jesus or early Christianity.

7   The Nash Papyrus, a second-century BCE Egyptian fragment of Deuteronomy 5–6, was the oldest known Hebrew manuscript before the DSS were found.

8   See Map 2 and above, pp. 19–21.

9   See again G. Bonani and others, 'Radiocarbon Dating of Fourteen Dead Sea Scrolls', *Radiocarbon* 34 (1992), p. 845.

10   The classic discussion of palaeography is F. M. Cross, 'The Development of the Jewish Scripts', in *The Bible and the Ancient Near East: Essays in Honour of William Foxwell Albright*, New York (1965), pp. 170–264. More accessible is his 'Paleography' in *EDSS*.

11   See R. de Vaux, *Archaeology and the Dead Sea Scrolls*, London (1973).

12   R. de Vaux, *Archaeology and the Dead Sea Scrolls*, London (1973) pp. 5, 116–7, as well as below, p. 189, note 15.

13 Josephus mentions this earthquake in *Jewish Antiquities*, 15.121. All of Josephus' works are translated in H. StJ. Thackery and others, *Josephus*, I–X, Cambridge Mass. (1926–1955).

14 See Figure 1.

15 See J. Magness, 'Pottery' in *EDSS*.

16 See again R. de Vaux, *Archaeology and the Dead Sea Scrolls*, London (1973) pp. 78–87. H. Stegemann, *The Library of Qumran*, Grand Rapids/Leiden (1998), pp. 36–44, maintains the activity was tanning.

17 See J. Patrich, 'Archaeology' in *EDSS* and, for more detail, J. Magnes, 'Qumran Archaeology: Past Perspectives and Future Prospects' in *DSSFY*, I, pp. 58–65.

18 See *Jewish War*, 2.55–65.

19 Unless otherwise stated, citations of non-biblical Qumran DSS are from *CDSSE*. Square brackets in this translation denote words constituting a reconstruction of a document's damaged parts; regular brackets supply supplementary English words to aid the modern reader.

20 See the last two chapters of H. Shanks (ed.), *Ancient Israel: A Short History from Abraham to the Roman Destruction of the Temple*, London (1989). More detail can be found in L. L. Grabbe, *Judaism from Cyrus to Hadrian*, London (1992), or J. A. Soggin, *An Introduction to the History of Israel and Judah*, London (1999).

21 See above, p. 14.

22 See Map 1.

23 See T. Rajak, 'The Hasmoneans and the Uses of Hellenism' in P. R. Davies, R. T. White (eds.), *A Tribute to Geza Vermes*, Sheffield (1990), pp. 261–280, for a fuller discussion.

24 Consult further A. A. DiLella, 'Wisdom of Ben Sira', and J. C. Vanderkam, 'Jubilees, Book of' in *ABD*.

25 See L. L. Grabbe, *Judaism from Cyrus to Hadrian*, London (1992), pp. 276–293.

26 This event is still celebrated by many Jews today at the annual winter festival of Hanukkah ('Dedication').

27 Compare 1 Kings 4:25 and Micah 4:4.

28 'Hasmonean' comes from 'Hasmon', the name of Judah's great-great-grandfather, according to Josephus in *Jewish War* 1.36.

29 See Map 4.

30 Reports of this 'Judaization' may have fuelled negative pictures of Judaism among many Gentile writers soon afterwards. The first-century BCE classical author Cicero, e.g., described Judaism as a 'barbarous superstition' in *Pro Flacco*, 67.

31 On the Jericho palace, see initially T. A. Holland, E. Netzer, 'Jericho' in *ABD*.

32 See further E. Bloch-Smith, R. Hachlili, 'Burials' in *ABD*.

33 *Jewish Antiquities*, 13.288, 298.

34 *Jewish Antiquities*, 13.372.

35 *Jewish Antiquities*, 13.380–83.

36 'Ephraim' and 'Manasseh', the half-tribes of Joseph's two sons, seem to have become by-words for rebellion among those inhabiting Qumran.
37 See the Babylonian Talmud, tractate Ta'anit 23a.
38 *Jewish War*, 1.203.
39 For further general background, see M. Goodman, *The Roman World: 44 BC–AD 180*, London (1997).
40 Josephus goes into Herod's reign in some detail in both *Jewish War*, 1 and *Jewish Antiquities*, 15–17.
41 See again Map 4.
42 See Mark 15:1.
43 Josephus has a moving, if imaginative, account of their fate in *Jewish War*, 7.252–388.
44 See above, pp. 10–12.
45 Relevant passages from both writers, too numerous to list, can be found in G. Vermes, M. Goodman, *The Essenes according to the Classical Sources*, Sheffield (1989).
46 *Jewish Antiquities*, 13.171–2.
47 On these aspects of Essene outlook according to Josephus, see *Jewish War*, 2.136, 142, 154–159.
48 Josephus mentions four individual Essenes – Judas, Menahem, Simon, John – whom he places between *circa* 100 BCE and 67 CE.
49 These headings have been borrowed from T. S. Beall, 'Essenes' in *EDSS*.
50 Previously unattested, this Aramaic word is now found in 4QAramaic Levi[b], a work released in 1991.
51 This derivation is proposed by G. Vermes, *Introduction to the Complete Dead Sea Scrolls*, London (1999), p. 123.
52 For this and other suggestions, see T. S. Beall, 'Essenes' in *EDSS*.
53 *Jewish War*, 2.137–142.
54 *Jewish War*, 2.147.
55 *Jewish War*, 2.122.
56 See *Jewish War*, 2.160–1.
57 *Jewish War*, 2.120 and *Jewish Antiquities*, 18.21.
58 *Jewish War*, 2.129–31.
59 See *Jewish War*, 2.148–149, as well as Deuteronomy 23:12–13.
60 See *Natural History*, 5.73.
61 'Below' here could signify 'underneath', with the Essene settlement then above the 'Ein-Gedi cliffs. But, since Pliny is moving north-south in his geographical description, it is more likely to mean 'south of'.
62 See also CD 2:6–10 and 1QH[a] 1:7–8.
63 Most references are either ambiguous or imply immortality of the soul; however, 4QMessianic Apocalypse, a text released in 1991, speaks of the resurrection of the dead.
64 See, e.g., Acts 11:26.
65 For further discussion of the etymology of 'Essene', see J. C. VanderKam, 'Identity and History of the Community' in *DSSFY*, II, pp. 490–499.

66   This sort of transaction is also reflected in a Qumran ostracon (inscribed pottery fragment) recovered in 1996 and discussed below, pp. 97–8.

67   See further R. Reich, 'Miqva'ot' in *EDSS*.

68   See further below, p. 83.

69   Thus, 1QS 6:18–22 assumes complete communality, whereas 1QS 7:8–9 and CD 14:12–13 presume the retention of some personal property.

70   See Philo in *Every Good Man is Free*, 12.78–79.

71   Josephus makes this assertion in his *Life*, 10–12.

72   See *Antiquities*, 15.371 and *Life*, 12.

73   See also J. C. VanderKam, 'Identity and History of the Community' in *DSSFY*, II, pp. 499–523.

74   See Acts 5:17 and *Jewish Antiquities*, 13.296–98; 18.4; 20.199. Consult further E. Hain, 'Sadducees' in *EDSS* or, alternatively, G. Stemberger, 'The Sadducees – their History and Doctrines' in W. Horbury (ed.), *The Cambridge History of Judaism*, III, Cambridge (1999), pp. 428–443. This volume is hereafter abbreviated to *CHJ* III.

75   See *Jewish War*, 1.110–112. In *Jewish Antiquities* 13.288–99, Josephus states that the first Hasmonean ruler, John Hyrcanus, changed allegiance from the Sadducees to the Pharisees; however, this is problematic, since it is not mirrored in Josephus' earlier account in *Jewish War* 1.67.

76   The text known as 4QMMT^{a-f}, released in 1991, confirms this impression. See below, pp. 79–80.

77   One such attempt was that of R. North, 'The Qumran Sadducees', *Catholic Biblical Quarterly* 17 (1995), pp. 164–88.

78   See further A. I. Baumgarten, 'Pharisees' in *EDSS*. More detailed is J. Schaper, 'The Pharisees' in *CHJ* III, pp. 402–27.

79   This is a much-disputed subject. Contrast, e.g., J. Neusner, *From Politics to Piety: the Emergence of Pharisaic Judaism*, New Jersey (1973) and E. P. Sanders, *Jewish Law from Jesus to the Mishnah*, London (1990), pp. 131–254.

80   For the Pharisees' special 'regulations', see *Jewish Antiquities*, 13.297.

81   See *Jewish Antiquities*, 17.42.

82   One advocate of close links was C. Rabin, *Qumran Studies*, Oxford (1957).

83   See above, pp. 56–7.

84   See A. Oppenheimer, 'Zealots' in *EDSS* or, alternatively, M. Smith, 'The Troublemakers', in *CHJ* III, pp. 501–68.

85   *Jewish Antiquities*, 18.1–5.

86   This position was advanced by C. Roth, *The Historical Background of the Dead Sea Scrolls*, Oxford (1958), and G. R. Driver, *The Judaean Scrolls: The Problem and a Solution*, Oxford (1965).

87   See above, p. 20.

88   The designation 'Qumran–Essene Hypothesis' is borrowed from H. Stegemann, 'The Qumran Essenes – Local Members of the Main Jewish Union in Late Second Temple Times' in J. T. Barrera, L. V. Montaner (eds.), *The Madrid Qumran Congress: Proceedings of the International Congress on the Dead Sea Scrolls, Madrid 18–21 March 1991*, I, Leiden (1992), pp. 83–166.

89   The Qumran–Essene Hypothesis' classic expression in English has been

G. Vermes, *The Dead Sea Scrolls: Qumran in Perspective*, London (first edition: 1977; second edition: 1982). For variations by Stegemann, Cross, Charlesworth, Dimant, and others, see initially A. S. van der Woude, 'Fifty Years of Qumran Research' in *DSSFY*, I, pp. 1–45.

90 Others have argued that Simon Maccabee, Jonathan's brother and successor, was the Wicked Priest, notably F. M. Cross, *The Ancient Library of Qumran*, London (first edition, 1958), pp. 135–153; (third edition, 1995), pp. 105–120. See also T. H. Lim, 'Wicked Priest' in *EDSS*.

91 See M. A. Knibb, 'Teacher of Righteousness' in *EDSS*.

92 This translation is from *CDSSE*, with line numbers added for convenience.

93 See J. Murphy-O'Connor, 'La genèse littéraire de la *Règle de la Communauté*', *Revue Biblique* 76 (1969), pp. 528–549; 'An Essene Missionary Document? CD II,14-VI,1', *Revue Biblique* 77 (1970), pp. 201–229; 'The Essenes and their History', *Revue Bibliqe* 81 (1974), pp. 215–244; 'The Damascus Document Revisited', *Revue Biblique* 92 (1985), pp. 223–246.

94 See P. R. Davies, *The Damascus Covenant: An Interpretation of the 'Damascus Document'*, Sheffield (1982); *Behind the Essenes: History & Ideology in the Dead Sea Scrolls*, Atlanta (1987); *Sects & Scrolls: Essays on Qumran & Related Topics*, Atlanta (1996).

95 Indeed, unlike CD 1:3–13, the accounts in CD 2:14–4:12 and 6:1–11 focus solely on the sixth century BCE. For further discussion, see J. G. Campbell, 'Essene–Qumran Origins in the Exile: A Scriptural Basis?', *Journal of Jewish Studies* 46 (1995), pp. 143–156.

96 F. García Martínez, A. S. van der Woude 'A "Groningen" Hypothesis of Qumran Origins and Early History', *Revue de Qumrân* (1990), pp. 521–542. See also F. García Martínez, J. Trebolle Barrera, *The People of the Dead Sea Scrolls*, Leiden (1995).

97 On 'apocalyptic', see below, p. 124.

98 See especially P. R. Davies, 'How Not to Do Archaeology: the Story of Qumran', *Biblical Archaeologist* 51 (1988), pp. 203–207, as well as P. R. Davies, 'Hasidim in the Maccabean Period', *Journal of Jewish Studies* 28 (1977), pp. 127–140.

99 This section draws on J. G. Campbell, 'Hebrew and Its Study at Qumran' in W. Horbury (ed.), *Hebrew Study from Ezra to Ben-Yehuda*, Edinburgh (1999), pp. 38–52.

100 See above, pp. 16–19.

101 See D. Dimant, 'Apocrypha and Pseudepigrapha at Qumran', *Dead Sea Discoveries* 1 (1994), pp. 150–159.

102 See above, pp. 10–12.

103 For bibliographical details, see below, p. 191, note 42.

104 See below, p. 191, note 43.

105 For detailed studies on some of this new literature, see G. J. Brooke (ed.), *New Qumran Texts and Studies*, Leiden (1994), and M. Bernstein and others (eds.), *Legal Texts and Legal Issues*, Leiden (1997).

106 See especially P. R. Davies, *Behind the Essenes: History & Ideology in the Dead Sea Scrolls*, Atlanta (1987).

107 See above, pp. 43–5.

Chapter 4

1 This section draws on J. G. Campbell, 'The Qumran Sectarian Writings' in *CHJ* III, pp. 798–821.

2 See also A. S. van der Woude, 'Fifty Years of Qumran Research' in *DSSFY*, I, pp. 6–27.

3 See *CDSSE*, although Vermes employs a different scheme in *An Introduction to the Complete Dead Sea Scrolls*, London (1999). For other delineations, note D. Dimant, 'Qumran: Written Material' in *EDSS*, and J. C. VanderKam, *An Introduction to Early Judaism*, Grand Rapids/Cambridge (2001), pp. 154–158.

4 Vermes' four 'apocalyptic' documents are: 4QpApocalypse of Weeks (entitled 'Apocalyptic Chronology' in *CDSSE*); 4QHistorical Text A ('Acts of a Greek King' in *CDSSE*); Mysteries (1QMysteries, 4QMysteries[a–c]); and 4QMessianic Apocalypse. The first and last have been placed within 'Scriptural Interpretation', while the remaining two are under 'New Pseudepigrapha'.

5 See further J. Baumgarten and others, *Qumran Cave 4, XXV: Halakhic Texts*, Oxford (DJD XXXV: 1999), pp. 1–24.

6 On the vital distinction between composition date and subsequent copying, see above, p. 28.

7 This rendering is the author's own, based on the Hebrew in G. García Martínez, E. J. C. Tigchelaar, *The Dead Sea Scrolls Study Edition*, Vol. II, Leiden (1998), p. 803.

8 See E. Qimron, J. Strugnell, *Qumran Cave 4, V: Miqsat Ma'ase ha-Torah*, Oxford (DJD X: 1994), p. 00.

9 See further C. Hempel, *The Damascus Texts*, Sheffield (2000).

10 The tiny 5QD and 6QD appeared in M. Baillet and others, *Les petites grottes de Qumrân*, Oxford (DJDJ III: 1962).

11 These 'hidden things' feature elsewhere too, as in 1QS 5:9–11 and 4QFestival Prayers[b] fragment 2.

12 See further T. H. Lim, 'Liar' in *EDSS*.

13 It is worth noting here in passing the fragmentary 4QCommunal Ceremony, 4QFour Lots, and 4QHarvesting, all released in 1991.

14 The phrase 'sons of the dawn' (Hebrew, *bene ha-shahar*) probably occurs in CD 13:14, although before 1991 it was read as 'sons of the pit' (*bene ha-shahat*).

15 Other cryptic works include 4QPhases of the Moon, 4QCalendrical Document E[c], and 4QHoroscope.

16 For details, see P. Alexander, S. Pfann (eds.), *Qumran Cave 4, XXVI: Cryptic Texts and Miscellanea, Part 1*, Oxford (DJD: XXXVI: 2000). 'SE' here stands for *Serekh ha-'Edah*, 'Rule of the Congregation'.

17 The poorly preserved 4QPolemical Fragment may reflect a similar scenario.

18 See below, p. 210, note 26.

19 Other studies refer to them as Tohorot A–C.

20 Legal Texts A–C are often termed Halakhot A–C.

21 Less dramatically, Legal Texts A–B cover subjects – niece marriage and the Sabbath – appearing in the Damascus Document and 4QWays of Righteousness.

22 See further G. J. Brooke (ed.), *Temple Scroll Studies*, Sheffield (1989), and S. W. Crawford, *The Temple Scroll and Related Texts*, Sheffield (2001).

23 The translation of 11QT^a 56:12–18 is the author's own, mirroring the NRSV as far as possible.

24 Compare, e.g., 11QT^a 45:11–12 and CD 12:1–2 on avoiding sexual intercourse in Jerusalem.

25 The reverse side of 4QS^e preserves the similar but damaged 4QHymnic Fragment.

26 This could be the Teacher of Righteousness, but certainty is impossible.

27 See the composite text in J. H. Charlesworth, C. A. Newsom (eds.), *Angelic Liturgy: Songs of the Sabbath Sacrifice*, Tübingen/Louisville (1999).

28 See above, pp. 19–20.

29 These were named 'Plea for Deliverance', 'Apostrophe to Zion', and 'Hymn to the Creator' in J. A. Sanders, *The Psalms Scrolls from Qumran Cave 11 (11QPs^a)*, Oxford (DJDJ IV: 1965).

30 See further J. C. VanderKam, *Calendars in the Dead Sea Scrolls*, London (1998), and J. R. Davila, *Liturgical Works*, Grand Rapids (2000).

31 See D. Barthélemy, J. T. Milik, *Qumran Cave 1*, Oxford (DJD I; 1955), and M. Baillet, *Qumran Grotte 4, III (4Q482–520)*, Oxford (DJD VII: 1982).

32 'Luminaries' is taken from Genesis 1:14 ('lights' in NRSV).

33 See J. T. Milik, 'Milkî-ṣedeq et Milikî-reša' dans les anciens écrits juifs et chrétiens', *Journal of Jewish Studies* 23 (1972), pp. 130–135, and E. Schuller, C. Newsom (eds.), *Qumran Cave 4, IV: Poetical and Liturgical Texts, Part 1*, Oxford (DJD XI: 1998).

34 Four fragmentary items may likewise reflect the Qumran group: 4QWorks of God, 4QCommunal Confession, 4QPersonal Prayer, and 4QIncantation. 4QExorcism, however, shows no sign of being sectarian.

35 See above, p. 51.

36 Little remains of the Hebrew of 4QHoroscope, but 4QPhysiognomy seems to be an Aramaic equivalent, penned in cryptic script.

37 See further D. J. Harrington, *Wisdom Texts from Qumran*, London (1996).

38 Also rather fragmentary are: 4QComposition concerning Divine Providence, 4QWays of Righteousness, 4QInstruction-like Work, and 4QAdmonitory Parable.

39 See M. J. Bernstein, 'Interpretation of Scriptures' in *EDSS*.

40 See above, pp. 56–7.

41 Dimant deems the two manuscripts separate compositions; see her 'Ages of Creation' in *EDSS*.

42 See A. Steudel, *Der Midrasch zur Eschatologie aus der Qumrangemeinde (4QMidrEschat^{a–b})*, Leiden (1994).

43   See further U. Glessmer, 'Targumim' in *EDSS*.
44   Two further damaged texts in this genre are: 4QConsolations, and 4QParaphrase of Genesis-Exodus. The former may be sectarian but the latter is probably not.
45   See relevant entries in *EDSS* for detailed discussion.
46   For 4QHistorical Text A, also linked to Daniel, see above, p. 42. As for 4QApocryphon of Daniel, see below, pp. 167–8.
47   Three very fragmentary texts are: 4QTwo Ways, 4QList of Netinim, and 4QList of False Prophets. It is just possible that the Hasmonean ruler, John Hyrcanus, features negatively in the latter.
48   Milik, e.g., argued it was placed there in *circa* 100 CE in M. Baillet and others, *Les petites grottes de Qumrân*, Oxford (DJDJ III: 1962).
49   For the former view, note S. Goranson, 'Sectarianism, Geography, and the Copper Scroll', *Journal of Jewish Studies* 43 (1992), pp. 282–287. For the latter, see A. Wolters, 'History and the Copper Scroll' in M. Wise and others (eds.), *Methods of Investigation of the Dead Sea Scrolls and the Khirbet Qumran Site: Present Realities and Future Prospects*, New York (1994), pp. 285–298.
50   F. M. Cross, E. Eshel, 'Ostraca from Khirbet Qumrân', *Israel Exploration Journal* 47 (1997), pp. 17–28.
51   See, respectively, A. Yardeni, 'A Draft of a Deed on an Ostracon from Khirbet Qumrân', *Israel Exploration Journal* 47 (1997), pp. 233–237, and S. J. Pfann, P. Alexander (eds.), *Qumran Cave 4, XXXVI: Cryptic Texts and Miscellanea, Part 1*, Oxford (DJD 36: 2000), pp. 497–507.
52   Thus, we do not find the pro-Hasmonean 1 Maccabees or the hellenized Wisdom of Solomon.
53   See F. García Martínez, 'The History of the Qumran Community in the Light of Recently Available Texts' in F. H. Cryer, T. L. Thompson (eds.), *Qumran Between the Old and New Testaments*, Sheffield (1998), pp. 194–216.
54   See H. Stegemann, 'The Qumran Essenes – Local Members of the Main Jewish Union in Late Second Temple Times' in J. T. Barrera, L. V. Montaner (eds.), *The Madrid Qumran Congress: Proceedings of the International Congress on the Dead Sea Scrolls, Madrid, 18–21 March 1991*, I, Leiden (1992), pp. 83–166, as well as his *The Library of Qumran*, Grand Rapids/Leiden (1998). Both entail a substantial reworking of his *Die Entstehung der Qumrangemeinde*, Bonn (1971).
55   See G. Boccaccini, *Beyond the Essene Hypothesis: the Parting of the Ways between Qumran and Enochic Judaism*, Grand Rapids/Cambridge (1998).
56   On 1QS 3:13–4:14, see immediately below, pp. 108–9.
57   See F. M. Cross, *The Ancient Library of Qumran*, Sheffield (1995), p. 191; G. Vermes, *An Introduction to the Complete Dead Sea Scrolls*, London (1999), p. 96.
58   See further E. C. Ulrich, 'The Qumran Biblical Scrolls – the Scriptures of Late Second Temple Judaism' in *DSSHC*, p. 81.
59   For 4QM^{a-g}, see J. H. Charlesworth and others, *Damascus Document, War Scroll, and Related Documents*, Tübingen/Louisville (1995).

60   See *Jewish War*, 2.161.

61   Many of the studies in *DSSHC* discuss aspects of this question, especially that by E. P. Sanders, 'The Dead Sea Sect and Other Jews: Commonalities, Overlaps and Differences', pp. 7–43.

62   See further J. C. VanderKam, 'Identity and History of the Community' in *DSSFY*, II, pp. 524–531.

63   '390' comes from Ezekiel 4:5, while 'twenty' probably represents half a generation.

64   Stegemann has long proposed that the Teacher of Righteousness was the High Priest deposed by Jonathan Maccabee in 152 BCE, although he has not been followed by many scholars. See his chapter detailed above, note 54.

65   Other elements in 1QpHabakkuk's description of the Wicked Priest tally with Jonathan Maccabee's career: he built up Jerusalem and was victorious in battle, only to be captured and killed by a foreigner. See M. Knibb, *The Qumran Community*, Cambridge (1987), pp. 221–46.

66   See above, p. 52.

67   See especially J. Murphy-O'Connor, 'The Essenes and their History', *Revue Biblique* 81 (1974), pp. 215–244.

68   See A. S. van der Woude, 'Fifty Years of Qumran Research' in *DSSFY*, I, 36–39.

69   See further S. D. Fraade, 'Hagu, Book of' in *EDSS*.

70   For a useful overview, albeit sceptical as to the practicality of such a calendar, see S. Stern, 'Qumran Calendars: Theory and Practice' in *DSSHC*, pp. 179–186.

71   The arrangement is that of A. Jaubert, as set out by J. C. VanderKam, *Calendars in the Dead Sea Scrolls*, London (1998), p. 55.

72   See above, p. 34.

73   On the question of women, see further E. Schuller, 'Women in the Dead Sea Scrolls' in *DSSFY*, II, pp. 117–144.

74   See above, p. 100, as well as J. A. Fitzmyer, 'Marriage and Divorce' in *EDSS*.

75   If most of those utilizing Khirbet Qumran were males who were required to be sexually abstinent, at least during their time there, this yearly activity may account for the limited number of female and child skeletons recovered from the margins of the Qumran cemetery. See G. Vermes, *An Introduction to the Complete Dead Sea Scrolls*, London (1999), pp. 112–113.

76   See further H. K. Harrington, 'Biblical Law at Qumran' and S. Metso, 'Constitutional Rules at Qumran' in *DSSFY*, I, pp. 160–185 and 186–210.

77   See below, p. 140.

78   See above, p. 62.

79   For detailed discussion, see M. A. Knibb, 'Eschatology and Messianism in the Dead Sea Scrolls' in *DSSFY*, II, pp. 379–402.

80   Both often appear together, but the former in particular sometimes features alone (e.g. 4QpPsalms[a] 3:15 and CD 6:11).

81   A similar combination is found in the Testament of the Twelve Patriarchs. See M. de Jonge, 'Patriarchs, Testaments of the Twelve' in *ABD*.

82   The odd references to the 'Messiah of Aaron and Israel' in the Damascus Document (CD 12:23; 14:19; 19:10–11; and 20:1) most likely denote both the 'Messiah of Aaron and (the Messiah of) Israel'.

83   See further M. A. Knibb, 'Interpreter of the Law' in *EDSS*.

84   The sect may have held the Teacher of Righteousness himself to have been this prophet, as proposed by G. Vermes, *An Introduction to the Complete Dead Sea Scrolls*, London (1999), p. 166.

Chapter 5

1   For a detailed recent survey, see L. L. Grabbe, *Judaic Religion in Second Temple Period*, London/New York (2000).

2   For a literary overview, see M. Stone (ed.), *Jewish Writings of the Second Temple Period: Apocrypha, Pseudepigrapha, Qumran Sectarian Writings, Philo, Josephus*, Assen/Philadelphia (1984).

3   See above, pp. 133–4.

4   *Jewish Antiquities*, 18.259–260.

5   Not only did his brother, Alexander, serve as an important magistrate or 'alabarch', but his nephew, Julius Tiberius Alexander, became prefect of Egypt (66–70 CE) after a stint as procurator of Judaea (46–48 CE).

6   See C. T. R. Hayward, 'Therapuetae' in *EDSS*.

7   See further R. Williamson, *Jews in the Hellenistic World: Philo*, Cambridge (1989).

8   Henceforth, he was called Flavius Josephus, adopting the Flavian emperors' family name.

9   We have already referred to the first three works. The *Life* is a short justification of Josephus' role in the First Revolt, while *Against Apion* defends Judaism against charges levelled by a certain Apion and others.

10   For an in-depth study, see T. Rajak, *Josephus: the Historian and his Society*, London (1983).

11   Thus, note L. L. Grabbe, *Judaism from Cyrus to Hadrian*, London (1994), pp. 13–16.

12   Thus, see S. J. Tanzer, 'Judaisms of the First-century CE' in *OCB*, or, more fully, J. Neusner and others, *Judaisms and their Messiahs at the Turn of the Christian Era*, Cambridge (1987).

13   However, that scribes formed another distinct community is unlikely. 'Scribe' was probably a loose designation for various literary functionaries, often priests, who worked administratively in the Temple and elsewhere (e.g., Mark 2:15). See A. J. Saldarini, 'Scribes' in *ABD*.

14   See especially J. M. G. Barclay, *Jews in the Mediterranean Diaspora*, Edinburgh (1996).

15   See D. Winston, 'Solomon, Wisdom of' in *ABD*.

16 I am grateful to Prof. George Brooke of Manchester University for suggesting 'Venn diagram' imagery at this point.

17 See M. A. Knibb, 'Joseph, Apocryphon of' in *EDSS*.

18 The same assumption is found in older scholarship, such as the detailed G. F. Moore, *Judaism in the First Three Centuries of the Christian Era*, I–III, Cambridge Mass. (1927–30), or the more popular I. Epstein, *Judaism*, London (1959).

19 On the Sadducees and Pharisees, see above, pp. 67–9.

20 See L. L. Grabbe, *Judaism from Cyrus to Hadrian*, London (1994), pp. 465–526, for baptismal sects, 'Herodians', and others.

21 Based on several factors (e.g. grain production, size of inhabited areas, Josephus' figures), scholarly estimations of the Jewish population in our period vary; see M. Broshi, 'Estimating the Population of Ancient Jerusalem', *Biblical Archaeological Review* 4 (1978), pp. 10–15. Overall, a figure of several million worldwide by late Second Temple times seems reasonable.

22 On Jewish women, in particular, see relevant chapters in D. F. Sawyer, *Women and Religion in the First Christian Centuries*, London (1996).

23 See E. P. Sanders, *Judaism: Practice and Belief 63 BCE-66 CE*, London (1992).

24 There were some exceptions, of course, as already observed in relation to Philo.

25 Biblical instructions for the spring and summer festivals of Passover and Weeks, as well as the autumn convocations of Tabernacles and the Day of Atonement, are found in Exodus 23, Leviticus 16 and 23, and Deuteronomy 16.

26 See especially Matthew 17:24 and Philo, *On the Embassy to Gaius*, 156.

27 We saw that this is reflected in 4QOrdinances; see above, p. 94.

28 This humiliating decree was never officially revoked.

29 See above, p. 54.

30 See, e.g., 1 Maccabees 12:6; *Jewish Antiquities*, 14.165–179; and Mark 14:53–55.

31 See *Jewish Antiquities*, 13.256.

32 For other sanctuaries, see B. Porten, 'Elephantine Papyri' and R. T. Anderson, 'Samaritans' in *ABD*.

33 For more detail, see L. Levine, 'Synagogue' in *OCB*.

34 See above, p. 87.

35 See R. E. Friedman, 'Tabernacle' and C. Meyers, 'Temple, Jerusalem' in *ABD*, as well as above, pp. 83–4, on the Temple Scroll.

36 See further E. P. Sanders, *Jewish Law from Jesus to the Mishnah*, London (1990).

37 New Testament scholars of a previous generation were especially prone to this, as, e.g., in some entries in G. Kittel, G. Friedrich (eds.), *Theological Dictionary of the New Testament*, I–X, Grand Rapids (1964–1976).

38 For a selection of Graeco-Roman views on Jews and Judaism, see relevant sections in M. Whittaker, *Jews and Christians: Graeco-Roman Views*, Cambridge (1984).

39 Cassius Dio, *Roman History*, 37.16.2.

40 For the Sabbath and the prohibition against images, see Exodus 20:4–5, 8–11 and Deuteronomy 5:8, 12–15; the command to circumcise is found in Genesis 17:12. For food laws, see Leviticus 11 and Deuteronomy 14, while some purity regulations appear in Leviticus 15.

41 See *Jewish War*, 2.169–74.

42 *Jewish Antiquities*, 18.15, 17.

43 See *Jewish Antiquities*, 18.16.

44 See G. W. E. Nickelsburg, 'Eschatology (Early Jewish)' in *ABD*.

45 For an overview, see J. G. Campbell, 'Messianic Hope in Second Temple Judaism', in F. Bowie (ed.), *The Coming Deliverer*, Cardiff (1997), pp. 77–101.

46 Note especially the so-called Animal Vision in 1 Enoch 91:11–17 and 93:1–10.

47 See P. D. Hanson and others, 'Apocalypses and Apocalypticism' in *ABD*.

48 Note the short overview by J. J. Collins, 'The Nature of Messianism in the Light of the Dead Sea Scrolls' in *DSSHC*, pp. 199–217.

49 See above, p. 109.

50 For a historical survey, see M. de Yonge, 'Messiah' in *ABD*.

51 On the transition to the Rabbinic period, see L. H. Schiffman, *From Text to Tradition: A History of Second Temple and Rabbinic Judaism*, New Jersey (1991).

52 For details, see relevant sections of H. Shanks (ed.), *Christianity and Rabbinic Judaism*, London (1993).

53 Hence, the NRSV is unwise to use 'Rabbi' instead of 'sir' in Mark 9:5 and 11:21.

54 This story is narrated in several Rabbinic sources, including the Babylonian Talmud in tractate Gittin 59b. Babylon, it should be noted, took over as the centre of Jewish learning from the fourth century CE, explaining why the Babylonian Talmud (*circa* 550 CE), rather than the Palestinian (*circa* 450 CE), gained the upper hand.

55 On such parallels, consult L. H. Schiffman, 'The Qumran Scrolls and Rabbinic Judaism' in *DSSFY*, II, pp. 552–571. See also below, pp. 155–7, on the laws of 4QMMT[a–f].

56 Initially, see further S. Himelstein, 'Synagogue' in R. J. Zwi Werblowsky, G. Wigoder (eds.), *Oxford Dictionary of the Jewish Religion*, Oxford (1997).

57 For introductions to Rabbinic works, see G. Stemberger, *Introduction to the Talmud and Midrash*, Edinburgh (1996).

58 This citation is from H. Danby, *The Mishnah*, Oxford (1933), pp. 446–7, where 'b.' denotes Hebrew *ben*, 'son of'.

59 Rabbinic literature often refers to a given legal decision as a *halakhah* (plural: *halakhot*), a Hebrew noun derived from a verb 'to walk' (i.e. 'to behave'). Consequently, the whole Rabbinic legal corpus can be referred to collectively as the Halakhah.

60 On the 'Dual Torah', see J. Neusner, *Torah through the Ages*, London (1990).

61 See above, pp. 68 and 105.

62 A portion of text engaging in such activity is often referred to as an *aggadah*, a Hebrew noun derived from a verb 'to narrate'. The entire aggadic corpus can be called the Aggadah.

63 Further examples can be found in E. Schürer, G. Vermes and others, *The History of the Jewish People in the Age of Jesus Christ*, II, Edinburgh (1983), pp. 346–355.

64 See further D. Mendels, 'Baruch, Book of 2 (Syriac)' and M. E. Stone, 'Esdras, Second Book of' *ABD*.

65 The precise course of the Second Revolt is problematic. See L. L. Grabbe, *Judaism from Cyrus to Hadrian*, London (1994), pp. 569–584.

66 On the eighth-century CE reform movement known as Karaism, e.g., and its likely roots in earlier traditions, see initially D. J. Lasker, 'Karaites' in R. J. Zwi Werblowsky, G. Wigoder (eds.), *Oxford Dictionary of the Jewish Religion*, Oxford (1997).

67 Still, Temple laws were preserved and elaborated in tractates like Zevahim ('sacrifices') in both the Mishnah and Babylonian Talmud.

68 See, e.g., the Babylonian Talmud, tractate Menahot 29b.

69 In the first instance, see further 'Mysticism' and 'Philosophy' in R. J. Zwi Werblowsky, G. Wigoder (eds.), *Oxford Dictionary of the Jewish Religion*, Oxford (1997).

70 On Orthodox, Conservative, and Reform Judaism, consult N. de Lange, *An Introduction to Judaism*, Cambridge (2000).

71 For fuller analyses, see J. Neusner, *Judaism in Modern Times: an Introduction and Reader*, Oxford (1995), and J. Sacks, *One People? Tradition, Modernity and Jewish Unity*, London (1993).

72 See above, pp. 37–8.

73 See above, pp. 126–8.

74 See further J. R. Baskin, 'Women in Contemporary Judaism' in J. Neusner, A. J. Avery-Peck (eds.), *The Blackwell Reader in Judaism*, Oxford (2001), pp. 316–332.

75 On Judaism in modern Britain, see J. G. Campbell, 'The Jewish Community in Britain', in S. Gilley, W. J. Sheils (eds.), *A History of Religion in Britain: Practice and Belief from Pre-Roman Times to the Present*, Oxford (1994), pp. 427–48.

Chapter 6

1 For a survey of New Testament scholarship with this title, see J. K. Riches, *A Century of New Testament Study*, Cambridge (1993).

2 For a recent overview, see B. D. Ehrman, *The New Testament: A Historical Introduction to the Early Christian Writings*, Oxford (2000).

3 Individual books of the New Testament are discussed in detail by W. G. Kümmel, *Introduction to the New Testament*, London (1975).

4 Luke and Acts were almost certainly composed by the same person, and

there is a scholarly consensus that the anonymous author worked around 85 CE. For further discussion, see L. T. Johnson, 'Luke-Acts, Book of' in *ABD*.

5 For an unsatisfactory attempt to re-establish traditional datings for the Gospels, see J. Wenham, *Redating Matthew, Mark and Luke*, London (1991).

6 On this theme, see J. Reumann, *Variety and Unity in New Testament Thought*, Oxford (1991).

7 It is widely held that 2 Peter, presented pseudonymously as the last will and testament of the Apostle Peter, was penned at the start of the second century CE. See further J. N. D. Kelly, *2 Peter and Jude*, London (1969).

8 Most books now in the New Testament were almost certainly in wide use among Christians from the late second century CE onwards, although the oldest surviving list recording them all dates to 367 CE. A collection of later gospels and letters excluded from the New Testament, including the Gospel of Thomas and usually referred to as the New Testament Apocrypha, can be found in English translation in J. K. Elliot, *The Apocryphal New Testament*, Oxford (1993).

9 See further S. Davies, 'Thomas, Gospel of' in *EDB*.

10 José O'Callaghan argued that the fragmentary 7Q3–18 were remnants of Mark, Acts, Romans, 1 Timothy, James, and 2 Peter in 'Papiros neotestamentarios en la cueva 7 de Qumran?', *Biblica* 53 (1972), pp. 91–100; he has been followed by C. P. Thiede, most recently in *The Dead Sea Scrolls and the Jewish Origins of Christianity*, London (2000). A more sober judgement would describe 7Q3–18 as unidentified scraps, some possibly constituting remains of Greek scriptural texts.

11 See further O. Betz, R. Riesner, *Jesus, Qumran and the Vatican*, London (1994), pp. 114–124.

12 For an overview focusing on recent reconstructions, see M. A. Powell, *The Jesus Debate*, London (1998).

13 A. Schweitzer, *The Quest of the Historical Jesus*, London (1910), was an example of the former, while the latter is represented by R. Bultmann, *Theology of the New Testament*, I–II, London (1952, 1955).

14 Thus, see G. Vermes, *Jesus the Jew*, London (1973) and *The Religion of Jesus the Jew*, London (1993), as well as E. P. Sanders, *Jesus and Judaism*, London (1985) and *The Historical Figure of Jesus*, London (1993).

15 This reconstruction requires us to discount the placing of Jesus' birth at the time of a Roman census, as claimed in Luke 2:1–7, since Quirinius' census must have taken place in 6 CE when Judaea became an imperial province.

16 See T. Prendergast, 'Trial of Jesus' in *ABD*.

17 See *Jewish War*, 2.258–60, *Jewish Antiquities*, 20.97–8, and Acts 5:36.

18 Most North American scholars participating in the so-called Jesus Seminar reject both, as in J. D. Crossan, *The Historical Jesus*, San Francisco (1991). Similarly, some traditionally-minded Christian historians arguably under-

play one or both elements, as in N. T. Wright, *Jesus and the Victory of God*, London (1996).

19 A useful comparison is H.-W. Kuhn, 'Jesus' in *EDSS* or, more fully, C. A. Evans, 'Jesus and the Dead Sea Scrolls' in *DSSFY*, II, pp. 573–598.

20 See Suetonius, *The Twelve Caesars*, 2.94.

21 *Life*, 9

22 See R. L. Webb, 'John the Baptist' in *EDSS*.

23 See *Jewish War*, 2.120.

24 There are, however, resumés of John the Baptist and Jesus in *Jewish Antiquities*, 18.62–4 and 116–9, respectively. While the former is probably genuine, it is generally agreed that the latter was either composed or expanded by a later Christian copyist. According to G. Vermes, 'The Jesus Notice of Josephus Re-examined', *Journal of Jewish Studies* 38 (1987), pp. 1–10, Josephus' original words were:

> 'At about this time lived Jesus ... He accomplished astonishing deeds ... He won over many Jews ... He was [called] Christ. When Pilate, upon the indictment brought by the principle men among us, condemned him to the cross, those who loved him from the very first did not cease to be attached to him ... And the tribe of the Christians, so called after him, has to this day not disappeared'.

25 See above, pp. 49–50 and 102–5, for names such as Antiochus IV, Demetrius III, Salome Alexandra, and Aemilius Scaurus, as well as the Teacher of Righteousness, the Wicked Priest, and the Seekers of Smooth Things.

26 Unfortunately, whether 1QSa 2:11–12 reads 'When God engenders (the Priest) Messiah', drawing on Psalm 2:7, remains unclear; compare the conflicting judgements in *CDSSE*, p. 159, and L. H. Schiffman, 'Rule of the Congregation' in *EDSS*. See also above, pp. 82–3.

27 We observed in Chapter 2 that Greek became the common language of the churches outside Palestine and that the LXX translation of the scriptures was already available for Christian usage.

28 On 11QMelchizedek, see above, pp. 93–4.

29 See above, p. 123.

30 See above, p. 109.

31 See Hebrews 1:5 (citing Psalm 2:7 and 2 Samuel 7:14) and 4:14–16.

32 For further details, see B. Pixner and others, 'Mount Zion: The Gate of the Essenes Re-excavated', *Zeitschrift des Deutshen-Palaestina-Vereins* 105 (1989), pp. 85–95, as well as R. Riesner, 'Jesus, the Primitive Community and the Essene Quarter of Jerusalem', in J. H. Charlesworth (ed.), *Jesus and the Dead Sea Scrolls*, New York (1993), pp. 198–234.

33 See *Jewish War*, 5.145, and *Jewish Antiquities*, 15.373–79.

34 See, e.g., M. Black (ed.), *Peake's Commentary on the Bible*, Walton-on-Thames (1962; reprinted 1982), p. 870.

35 An older work of this type is N. Perrin, *Jesus and the Language of the Kingdom*, Philadelphia (1976), and a newer example is N. T. Wright, *Jesus and the Victory of God*, London (1996).

36 This heading has been borrowed from M. Casey, *From Jewish Prophet to Gentile God: the Origins and Development of New Testament Christology*, Cambridge (1991), whose ideas have had considerable influence on what follows.

37 For discussion of Paul, see first E. P. Sanders, *Paul: A Very Short Introduction*, Oxford (2001), or J. Ziesler, *Pauline Christianity*, Oxford (1990). More detailed is J. D. G. Dunn, *Paul the Apostle*, Edinburgh (1998).

38 From the period of Paul and afterwards, therefore, come sayings in the Gospels and Acts, such as Mark 16:15 and Acts 1:8, in which Jesus is portrayed commanding a Gentile mission.

39 Josephus testifies to the existence of such Gentile sympathizers (*Against Apion*, 2.123; *Jewish War*, 7.45; *Jewish Antiquities*, 14.110), as do passages in Acts (e.g. Acts 13:26 and 17:4).

40 On Philippians 2:6–11, see M. Casey, *From Jewish Prophet to Gentile God: the Origins and Development of New Testament Christology*, Cambridge (1991), pp. 112–115.

41 More broadly, see J. A. Fitzmyer, 'Paul and the Dead Sea Scrolls' in *DSSFY*, II, pp. 599–621.

42 The beginnings of this are in Paul himself (e.g. 1 Corinthians 10:1–11 and 2 Corinthians 3:7–11).

43 See further B. D. Ehrman, *The New Testament: A Historical Introduction to the Early Christian Writings*, Oxford (OUP, 2000), pp. 375–391, discussing the Epistle of Barnabas (penned around 130 CE), as well as the views of Justin Martyr (*circa* 100–165 CE), Melito of Sardis (died *circa* 190 CE), and Tertullian (*circa* 160–225 CE).

44 On the euphemistic 'Blessing of the Minim ('heretics')', see E. Schürer, G. Vermes, *The History of the Jewish People in the Age of Jesus Christ*, II, Edinburgh (1979), pp. 455–463.

45 See further F. S. Jones, 'Ebionites' and 'Jewish Christians' in *EDB*.

46 On the Johannine corpus, see B. Lindars and others, *The Johannine Literature*, Sheffield (2001).

47 See initially 'Ignatius, St.' in F. L. Cross, E. A. Livingstone (eds.), *The Oxford Dictionary of the Christian Church*, Oxford (1997).

48 For further discussion, see M. Casey, *From Jewish Prophet to Gentile God: the Origins and Development of New Testament Christology*, Cambridge (1991); J. D. G. Dunn, *The Parting of the Ways*, London (1991); and J. T. Sanders, *Schismatics, Sectarians, Dissidents, Deviants: The First 100 Years of Jewish–Christian Relations*, London (1993).

49 For a different reconstruction, however, see W. Horbury, *Jewish Messianism and the Cult of Christ*, London (1998).

50 For more details on the contents of such creeds and definitions, see in the first instance relevant entries in F. L. Cross, E. A. Livingstone (eds.), *The Oxford Dictionary of the Christian Church*, Oxford (1997).

51 These periods are covered in A. Hastings (ed.), *A World History of Christianity*, London (1999).

52 A. N. Wilson, *God's Funeral*, London (1999), provides an interesting account of nineteenth-century crises of Christian faith.
53 For surveys, see relevant sections of H. Küng, *Christianity*, London (1995), or A. Hastings (ed.), *A World History of Christianity*, London (1999).
54 For a recent sample of differing viewpoints, see R. Gill (ed.), *Readings in Modern Theology: Britain and America*, London (1995).
55 To pursue this theme, see the joint Jewish–Christian study by R. Rubinstein, J. K. Roth, *Approaches to Auschwitz*, London (1987).
56 See *inter alia* C. Rowland, *Christian Origins*, London (1985).
57 For further discussion, see R. P. Carroll, *Wolf in the Sheepfold: the Bible as Problematic for Theology*, London (1997).

Chapter 7

1 See above, pp. 73–5 and 99.
2 See his 'The New Halakhic Letter (4QMMT) and the Origins of the Dead Sea Sect', *Biblical Archaeologist* 53 (1990), pp. 64–73, and 'The Sadducean Origins of the Dead Sea Scroll Sect', in H. Shanks (ed.), *Understanding the Dead Sea Scrolls*, London (1992), pp. 35–49.
3 On this linguistic connection, see above, p. 68.
4 This translation is from H. Danby, *The Mishnah*, Oxford (1933), p. 784.
5 This rendering is the author's own, based on the Hebrew text in G. García Martínez, E. J. C. Tigchelaar, *The Dead Sea Scrolls Study Edition*, Vol. II, Leiden (1998), p. 793.
6 See J. M. Baumgarten, 'The Pharisaic–Sadducean Controversies about Purity and the Qumran Texts', *Journal of Jewish Studies* 31 (1980), pp. 157–170.
7 See above, pp. 68–70. It is noteworthy that 4QMMT[a–f] states elsewhere that 'we separated from the multitude of the people'. The Hebrew for 'we separated' (*parashnu*) comes from the verb *parash*, from which the name Pharisee is probably to be derived.
8 See above, p. 114.
9 L. H. Schiffman, *Reclaiming the Dead Sea Scrolls: The History of Judaism, the Background of Christianity, and the Lost Library of Qumran*, Philadelphia (1994).
10 See especially L. H. Schiffman, *Reclaiming the Dead Sea Scrolls: The History of Judaism, the Background of Christianity, and the Lost Library of Qumran*, Philadelphia (1994), pp. 83–112.
11 See L. H. Schiffman, *Reclaiming the Dead Sea Scrolls: The History of Judaism, the Background of Christianity, and the Lost Library of Qumran*, Philadelphia (1994), pp. xiii, xxiii–xxiv.
12 M. Wise, M. Abegg, A. Cook, *The Dead Sea Scrolls: A New Translation*, New York (1996).
13 See above, pp. 66–7.
14 Their reconstruction has some similarities with the earlier work of both A.

Dupont-Sommer, *The Essene Writings from Qumran*, Oxford (1961), and J. Carmignac in J. Carmignac and others (eds.), *Les Textes de Qumran Traduits et Annotés*, Volumes II, Paris (1963), pp. 48–55.

15 *Jewish War*, 1.111–114.

16 See above, p. 103.

17 See N. Golb, 'The Problem of Origin and Identification of the Dead Sea Scrolls', *Proceedings Of the American Philosophical Society* 124 (1980), pp. 1–24, and 'Who Hid the Dead Sea Scrolls?' *Biblical Archaeologist* 28 (1987), pp. 68–82.

18 K.-H. Rengstorff, *Hirbet Qumran and the Problem of the Dead Sea Caves*, Leiden (1963), first suggested this, as Golb acknowledges in *Who Wrote the Dead Sea Scrolls?*, London (1995), p. 157.

19 N. Golb, *Who Wrote the Dead Sea Scrolls?*, London (1995).

20 N. Golb, *Who Wrote the Dead Sea Scrolls?*, London (1995), pp. 256–258.

21 See above, p. 87.

22 See above, p. 97.

23 See above, p. 98.

24 For more detail, see M. Broshi, 'Qumran: Archaeology' in *EDSS*.

25 See again N. Golb, *Who Wrote the Dead Sea Scrolls?*, London (1995), pp. 3–14.

26 See R. de Vaux, *Archaeology and the Dead Sea Scrolls*, Oxford (1973), p. vii.

27 For P. Donceel-Voûte, see her ' "Coenaculum" – La salle à l'étage du *locus* 30 à Khirbet Qumrân sur la mer morte', *Res Orientales* 4 (1993), pp. 61–84.

28 See Figure 1.

29 Partially related theories have been offered by Y. Hirschfeld, 'Early Roman Manor Houses in Judaea and the Site of Khirbet Qumran', *Journal of Near Eastern Studies* 57 (1998), pp. 161–189, and by J.-B. Humbert, 'L'Espace sacré à Qumran', *Revue Biblique* 101–2 (1994), pp. 161–214.

30 See R. Reich, 'A Note on the Function of Room 30 (the "scriptorium") at Khirbet Qumran', *Journal of Jewish Studies* 46 (1995), pp. 157–60.

31 See A. Crown, L. Cansdale, 'Qumran: Was It an Essene Settlement?', *Biblical Archaeology Review* 20 (1994), pp. 24–36, 73–78.

32 M. Baigent, R. Leigh, *The Dead Sea Scrolls Deception*, London (1991).

33 Indeed, the German edition was entitled *Verschlussache Jesus*, 'Classified Information on Jesus'.

34 See further J. Murphy-O'connor, 'Ecole Biblique et Archéologique Française' in *EDSS*.

35 See above, p. 135.

36 See a selection of his studies in J. A. Fitzmyer, *The Dead Sea Scrolls and Christian Origins*, Grand Rapids (2000).

37 Eisenman's main works include *Maccabees, Zadokites, Christians and Qumran*, Leiden (1993), and *James the Just in the Habakkuk Pesher*, Leiden (1986).

38 See above, pp. 106–7.

39 See above, p. 104.

40 *Jewish Antiquities*, 20.200.

41 For this heartless action, it ought to be added, Josephus goes on to inform us that more fair-minded Jews had Ananus deposed.

42 R. H. Eisenman, M. Wise, *The Dead Sea Scrolls Uncovered*, London (1993).

43 R. H. Eisenman, M. Wise, *The Dead Sea Scrolls Uncovered*, London (1993), p. 29.

44 See, e.g., the article entitled 'Scrolls Question Messianic Theory' in *The Times*, 9 November 1991, p. 10.

45 See R. H. Eisenman, M. Wise, *The Dead Sea Scrolls Uncovered*, London (1992), pp. 12–13, where palaeographical work and carbon dating are dismissed in three short paragraphs.

46 See above, p. 47.

47 Thus, see J. A. Fitzmyer, 'The Contribution of Qumran Aramaic to the Study of the New Testament', *New Testament Studies* 20 (1974), pp. 382–401.

48 Among the former, note 'The Date of Composition of the Temple Scroll', in G. J. Brooke (ed.), *Temple Scroll Studies*, Sheffield (1989), pp. 99–120. For the latter, see B. Thiering, *Jesus the Man: A New Interpretation from the Dead Sea Scrolls*, London (1992); this appeared in North America as *Jesus and the Riddle of the Dead Sea Scrolls: Unlocking the Secrets of His Life Story*, San Francisco (1992).

49 See above, p. 120.

50 See above, pp. 106–7.

51 See above, pp. 46–7.

52 See above, p. 91.

53 Nevertheless, Thiering has gone on to produce *The Book that Jesus Wrote*, London (1998).

54 See E. Wilson, 'A Reporter at Large', *New Yorker*, 14 May 1955, and *The Scrolls from the Dead Sea*, New York (1955); the latter was expanded as *The Dead Sea Scrolls 1947–1969*, London (1969).

55 For Dupont-Sommer, see his *The Essene Writings from Qumran*, Oxford (1961).

56 See O. Betz, R. Riesner, *Jesus, Qumran and the Vatican*, London (1994), pp. 83–98, and H. Shanks, *The Mystery and Meaning of the Dead Sea Scrolls*, London (1998), p. 183.

57 See further R. de Vaux and others, 'Letter concerning certain Broadcast Statements of Mr J. Allegro', *The Times*, 16 March 1956, p. 11.

58 J. M. Allegro, *The Sacred Mushroom and the Cross*, London (1970).

59 This report featured in the *New York Times*, 25 December 1910, p. 1, under the headline 'Jewish Manuscript Antedating Gospels'.

60 S. Schechter, *Documents of Jewish Sectaries: Fragments of a Zadokite Work*, Cambridge (1910).

61 See, e.g., G. Bornkamm, *Jesus von Nazareth*, Stuttgart (1956). This German work, translated into English as *Jesus of Nazareth* as late as 1960, reflects the common assumptions of much late nineteenth- and early twentieth-century scholarship. It maintains that, while Jesus clearly grew up within

the Jewish world of his day, spiritually he stood outside its narrow legalistic confines which represented a deterioration of the pure religion of Old Testament times.

62 See *The Independent*, 1 September 1992, p. 5. It ought to be added that this example has been more than outweighed by many other accurate articles in *The Independent* over the years. See, e.g., the report of renewed excavations in the Qumran region, 'Dead Sea Scroll search reopens', on 19 December 1995, p. 11.

63 See above, p. 149.

Index